The Integration of Social Work Practice

The Integration of Social Work Practice

Ruth J. Parsons
University of Denver

James D. Jorgensen
University of Denver

Santos H. Hernández
Our Lady of the Lake University

Brooks/Cole Publishing Company
Pacific Grove, California
1994

 **ITP**™ The trademark ITP is used under license.

A CLAIREMONT BOOK

Brooks/Cole Publishing Company
A Division of Wadsworth, Inc

Printed in the United States of America
10 9 8 7 6 5 4 3 2 1

Library of Congress Cataloging-in-Publication Data

Parsons, Ruth J., [date]
    The integration of social work practice
      p.   cm.
    Includes bibliographical references and index.
    ISBN 0-534-22284-6
    1. Social service.   2. Social work education.   I. Jorgensen,
James D.   II. Hernández, Santos H., [date] .
    HV40.P26   1994
    361.3'2—dc20   93-37937
                                                           CIP

Sponsoring Editor: *Claire Verduin*
Editorial Associate: *Gay C. Bond*
Production Editor: *Laurel Jackson*
Manuscript Editor: *Robin L. Witkin*
Permissions Editor: *Roxane Buck Ezcurra*
Interior and Cover Design: *Publishing Principals Inc.*
Art Coordinator: *Lisa Torri*
Interior Illustration: *Graphic Arts*
Indexer: *James Minkin*
Typesetting: *Bookends Typesetting*
Cover Printing: *Color Dot Graphics, Inc.*
Printing and Binding: *Arcata Graphics/Fairfield*

Chapter Four is a revised and expanded version of the material that originally appeared in Parsons,
R. J. "Empowerment: Purpose and practice principle in social work," *Social Work with Groups,* 1991,
14(2), 7–21. Copyright © 1991 by The Haworth Press, Inc.

This book is dedicated to our students who have tested and critiqued the ideas presented here and have helped this book through its development.

Contents

Chapter 10
The Broker Role 225

Preface

This text provides a framework for developing and organizing advanced generalist curricula for courses in social work practice, either at the graduate or undergraduate level.

Most students who enter social work education are interested in doing therapeutic work with individuals and families. Often, they are unfamiliar with other client systems and roles and view social work problems as therapeutic problems. Either at the undergraduate level or in graduate foundation courses, students are introduced to a broader, generalist approach. This approach suggests that social work is practiced not only with individuals and families but across systems, between and within organizations, in communities, at the social policy level, and in a variety of social work roles. Students often are overwhelmed by the array of alternatives for social work intervention and are given little guidance for deciding where to intervene in actual practice. In addition, because generalist approaches allow practitioners to view clients and problems from a variety of theory bases, students tend to drift back to familiar theories or to what initially attracted them to social work—or they simply assume that the agency will decide what they should do and where they should intervene. Because of this inherent open-endedness, instructors in foundational curricula often wonder how they can help students synthesize the generalist base of social work into a framework for practice. This book is an attempt to present social work practice as integrated across systems within a specific framework. The framework provides guidance for deciding where and how to intervene with clients from a generalist base.

In this text, social work practice is conceived as intervention across multi-level client systems, from micro to macro and through the six roles social work professionals assume: conferee, enabler, broker, advocate, mediator, and guardian. These roles are applicable across multilevel client systems, from victim-based rehabilitation to educating and enabling, developing needed service delivery systems, and creating and mobilizing social welfare policies.

This book incorporates a problem-solving approach within each social work role and as an organizing framework for the text. It extends the generalist perspective into what may be relevant for an advanced generalist curriculum. In this book, we develop the principles of social problem focus and consider the political and economic environment of the populations that present the social problems. The interactionist perspectives of deviance

and labeling are used to help the reader understand and assess the presenting problems. We emphasize competency-based assessment and present empowerment as the overriding principle in generalist practice.

We also stress using principles of habilitation and education when
deciding what to do about clients' problems. Role-taking decisions are
presented in an organizational and political context, and social work roles
are extended and applied to social problems in a way not currently found
in the literature on social work practice. Further, we articulate a schema
for evaluating generalist practice and, through case studies, show how practitioners can apply it.

This text differs from other texts with generalist foundations. It is not
a substitute for a basic practice skills book; rather, it provides a philosophical
perspective and conceptual foundation for more comprehensive integration
of the generalist base. This practice perspective is most appropriate for work
with disempowered populations because the concepts of labeling and devaluation are used to understand clients' empowerment and disempowerment.

We consider integrated practice a unique perspective that extends beyond
most generalist approaches. Incorporating the Gestalt of the person-in-
environment paradigm, we see clients in problem situations as fundamentally healthy, adaptive individuals striving for mastery in the face of environmental demands, stresses, and normal life tasks.

This framework suggests that practitioners must be able to select among
and apply a broad range of interventive techniques across micro and macro
systems, depending on the specific problem. Clients' problems are fundamentally located in broader social contexts, which are themselves legitimate
targets for intervention. Therefore, the focus of this perspective is on social
problems rather than on methods; Integrated practice builds on the premise
that practitioners must have a breadth of social work skills within their repertoire and must "go where the problem takes them."[1]

Integrated practice goes beyond perceptions of generalist practice as
merely a multimethod approach; it is both a perspective of and an approach
to practice. As such, it incorporates how practitioners view practice and how
they actually practice. Using systems thinking as a foundation, advocates of
integrated practice see interventions as points on a continuum from micro
to macro rather than as choices between dichotomous extremes. This theoretical framework offers a humanistic perspective to practice. It extends the
concepts of micro- and macro-generalist, as developed by Anderson[2] into
a specific conceptual framework from which to view problems and to choose
and implement intervention strategies. Using a conceptual screen for viewing social problems and for selecting strategies narrows the array of concepts

---

[1]See, for example, G. G. Wood and R. Middleman, *The Structural Approach to Direct Practice
in Social Work* (New York: Columbia University Press, 1989).

[2]J. Anderson, *Social Work Methods and Processes* (Belmont, CA: Wadsworth, 1981).

within generalist practice to a more usable framework. This narrowing thus serves as an anchor and philosophy for generalist practice.

CONTENTS OF THE FRAMEWORK

Principles of Social Work Practice

Social Problems as Deviance and Labeling. The focus of problem assessment and intervention is social problems. Using labeling and deviance theories to understand social problems, advocates of integrated practice reject theoretical screens that direct intervention exclusively either to the "victims" or to the problem's political or structural aspects. Through positive visibility, competency screening, and normalization, practitioners who use labeling and deviance theories guide intervention toward preventing disempowerment. In this text, social problem perspectives, particularly deviance and labeling, are illustrated through case application.

Prevention and Education as Priority Functions. Prevention is a viable, necessary function in social work practice, and communication and education are critical to all levels of prevention. The prevention process does not require the practitioner to identify the causes of problems; but it can be directed toward known contributing factors. Prevention takes place with identified clients as well as nonidentified consumers. Education is used to empower client systems to prevent and cope with the social problems that affect them.

Assessment for Competency. Clients are seen as striving for competence in mastering their lives and as having the capacity for learning, understanding, and solving problems. Their coping skills can be increased, but ultimately they have the right to risk and to fail. Clients are considered important resources in understanding their own problems and as collaborators in planning solutions.

The Principle of Habilitation. Habilitation implies promoting growth or providing a means of problem solving. By contrast, rehabilitation implies rebuilding or restoring. Behavior is viewed on a normative continuum, and the practitioner expects risk and responsibility from the client.

Normalized View of Behavior. A normalized view of behavior suggests that behavior must be viewed in terms of a person's intentions, motives, and reasons. Seen in its environmental context, behavior becomes understandable in specific circumstances; it is purposive and may be intended to convey a message; and it is viewed in a culturally derived code of conventions.

Empowerment. Empowerment—the process of reducing powerlessness in client systems—is critical both in planning and in implementing interventions. The goals of empowerment-oriented interventions are that clients learn more about the problems confronting them and that they create and carry out solutions that teach them how to deal with future problems. In this text, empowerment is illustrated through case studies.

The Functional Roles of Social Work

Social work intervention is carried out through the assumption of social work roles: conferee, enabler, mediator, broker, advocate, and guardian. These roles are applicable to all client systems and contain a general set of skills that are related to and embellished by the various methodologies available in social work practice. The selection of specific strategies from available methodologies is guided by the above-mentioned principles. In this book, we use case studies to illustrate social work role taking in general, as well as each of the roles practitioners can assume.

ORGANIZATION OF THE BOOK

The book is organized into three parts. As an introduction to the book as a whole, Chapter 1 presents both the overall perspective and the components of the integrated-practice framework as applied to the social problem of high school dropouts. Part One provides the basic concepts of the integrated-practice perspective and elaborates those concepts used to view and assess social problem situations. Chapter 2 introduces the assessment concepts through a look at social problems as a focus for practice intervention. In this chapter, the social problem perspectives prevalent in social work literature are also discussed. Social problem intervention is presented through multisystem levels, preventions, communication, and diffusion of innovation and change. Chapter 3 provides the interactionist view of social problems through a discussion of deviance, labeling, and devaluation of client groups as part of assessing social work problems. Competency-based screening and normalization are presented as necessary antidotes to labeling and devaluation.

Part Two is an overview of concepts that relate to deciding, along with clients and agencies, what to do about social problem situations. Chapter 4 includes a discussion of empowerment as a goal and process principle in integrated practice. In this chapter, sources of powerlessness are defined, empowerment is explicated, and components of empowerment-based practice are identified. Chapter 5 offers an examination of role-taking decisions in the organizational and political context, social change strategies and the social worker's orientations, and the demands of the practice situation. Chapter 6 contains a schema and illustration for evaluating integrated practice, with an emphasis on approaches that are consistent with the principles and values of integrated practice—namely, action research and goal attainment scaling. In this chapter, application of practice evaluation principles is demonstrated through the school dropout problem introduced in Chapter 1.

Part Three deals with implementation of social work goals and objectives through a detailed discussion of social work functions defined as the six professional roles—conferee, enabler, advocate, broker, mediator and guardian—in Chapters 7 through 12.

ACKNOWLEDGMENTS

We wish to acknowledge and thank our students in the integrated-practice curriculum who have read, critiqued, and added to our ideas and offered their own contributions. We acknowledge Joan Harwick, Peter Judd, Pam Metz, and Howard Raiten, colleagues who have taught alongside us and helped formulate concepts in this perspective. We would also like to acknowledge Pam Landon, who stimulated our thinking about the integration of social work practice and who was instrumental in creating curricula for integrated practice. Kay Vail's contribution to the thinking and realization of integrated practice is also appreciated. We recognize Marsha Gould for her contributions to the principle of habilitation versus rehabilitation in practice. Two students, Robin Pederson and Marsha Porter, contributed to the school dropout case used in Chapter 1, as well as to other parts of the book.

We also wish to acknowledge those who reviewed earlier versions of the manuscript for this book, including Joseph D. Anderson, Norfolk State University; Leonard N. Brown, Rutgers University; Frank W. Clark, University of Montana; M. Lynn Jacobsson, California State University, Fresno; James Mahalik, Boston College; David C. Pritchard, San Diego State University; and Jack M. Richman, University of North Carolina.

Two grants supported our research. The University Research Award for 1988–1989 at California State University at Fresno and the Affirmative Action Faculty Development Award of 1989–1990 funded literature searches and graduate assistants for work on the manuscript.

We thank Janet Officer for her typing assistance through many revisions of this manuscript. Finally, we acknowledge the editors and staff at Brooks/Cole for their encouragement and assistance with the development of this manuscript.

Ruth J. Parsons
James D. Jorgensen
Santos H. Hernández

◆

Integrated Practice:
A Framework for Problem Solving

Chapter 1, "Integrated Practice: A Framework for Problem Solving," provides an overall framework for organizing the integrated social work perspective. The chapter begins with a description of the components of this framework: purpose, sanction to practice, values, and knowledge. This is followed by a discussion of the way social workers use various types of knowledge, such as knowledge for organizing the practice, knowledge for communicating and building relationships, knowledge for analyzing and understanding problems, knowledge for deciding what actions to take and evaluating what has been accomplished, and knowledge for implementing the actions and ending the work. Role taking across client systems is depicted in a grid format. Chapter 1 also introduces the subjects of subsequent chapters, placing each in the context of the integrated-practice framework. The social problem of high school dropouts is used to illustrate the integrated-practice model.

CONTEXT AND RATIONALE

As we approach the end of the 20th century, we enter a postindustrial era characterized as technologically advanced and information based (Naisbitt, 1982; Naisbitt & Aburdene, 1990; Bell, 1973; Kennedy, 1993). Technological advancement increases the potential of growing alienation and decreasing connectedness between people and their communities. The April 1992 riots in Los Angeles, and the increased frequency of protest demonstrations and other organized action by members of disempowered groups are evidence of growing alienation. Centralized decision making has weakened the "mediating" structures between individuals and society, such as geographic communities, local organizations, family, and peer groups. People are left with feelings of fear, anxiety, alienation, and disconnectedness from their environmental systems, as Nisbet suggested (1953).

Social work has been defined as the transaction between people and their environments (see Karls & Wandrei, 1992). As that transaction gap widens, social work practice is similarly diverted into isolated domains of specialists' skills. Social service delivery in the 1980s and 1990s has been characterized by the specialization and privatization of public problems and issues (Abramovitz, 1986; Kahn & Kamerman, 1989). Third-party payment for services has supported and emphasized both an intrapersonal screen for viewing human problems and psychotherapeutic intervention strategies that are focused exclusively on individual functioning. Integrated social work practice is a framework based on the historical definition of social work as an activity that has a dual focus on the "person" and the "environmental" ends of the transaction. This framework helps bridge the widening gap between people and their environments. As a generalist perspective, integrated practice provides a useful framework from which social work can take the lead in defining social problems and mobilizing resources toward their resolution. Practice is defined from a broader perspective than the specialist mode that has characterized the latter 20th century. Isolation and alienation are addressed by strengthening ''mediating'' structures to empower people to engage in problem solving in their own behalf. This framework assumes that individuals' isolated problems are often symptoms of social problems that are embedded across multiple layers of social systems from individuals, families, and groups to organizations, communities, societies, and countries. A strength perspective is embedded in this framework.

Practitioners, as generalist social workers, must grasp a broad domain in which social problems and solutions require the investments of many institutions and professions, only a small portion of which may be social workers. Generalists guide and engineer the problem definition and the means of solution and, along with clients, lead the development and management of community resources for mutual problem solving. Generalists are creative problem solvers in a specific practice arena (Heus & Pincus, 1986), integrating numerous methods in their interventions. They are prepared to design and lead interventions into social problems, but they are not in-depth specialists within limited components of social problems. Social work roles are taken across a continuum of points of intervention (Hernández et al., 1985). Social workers are educators and mobilizers of resources. Their practice is guided by principles of normalization, competency assessment and promotion, habilitation, and empowerment. Integrated practice assumes a dual focus on assisting clients to mobilize resources to solve their own problems and on facilitating change in environmental systems to create a more hospitable environment. Organized around the problem-solving process, differential role taking across client systems includes teaching problem-solving skills, networking, team building, mutual aid, and self-help. These concepts are developed to form a conceptual framework for the integration of generalist practice.

COMPONENTS OF INTEGRATED PRACTICE

A research neonatal physician in an inner-city hospital ward for failure-to-thrive infants once remarked to the social worker on the ward, ''You social workers amaze me. I don't see how, in the face of myriad problems in families and communities, you decide what to do.'' Deciding what to do involves a complex process of combining many concepts selected through the construction of reality formed within the professional social work rubric. Social work is practiced through a professional component base, which includes a professional purpose, values, a sanction to practice, a guiding code of

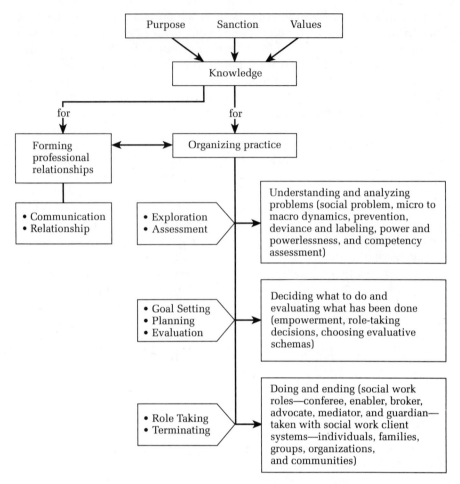

Figure 1.1 An integrated practice perspective of social work

ethics, and a knowledge base. Figure 1.1 depicts the conceptual schema for components of integrated practice. These concepts, which help the social worker decide what to do, will be discussed in relation to a social problem: high school dropout rates. This problem was addressed by two of the authors' students in their master's field practicum.

CASE STUDY: *Lewis High School* ◆

Lewis High School is an inner-city high school located in a city of about 500,000 people. The school has 2,000 students. Along with other schools in the district, Lewis is under scrutiny because of its dropout rate. Thirty-six percent of students who enter the ninth grade drop out before graduation. The other ten high schools in the city have an average dropout rate of 25%. Minority parents have been particularly vocal in their criticism of Lewis High because the Hispanic and African American students' dropout rates were 42% and 37% respectively. Because of the high numbers of ethnic minority dropouts, the problem threatened to divide the school community, as parents blamed teachers and teachers blamed administrators and parents.

_____ ♦

Figure 1.1 shows that social work's purpose, value base, sanction, and knowledge form the basis for decision making.

Purpose

What is the purpose of social work in the school dropout problem? The purpose of the integrated social work practice is to bring together and facilitate interaction between clients and the environment, find a balance between the needs and the resources of client groups, and promote both individual growth and the optimum functioning of environmental systems. From this dual focus on individuals and the environment, social work responds to this problem by promoting change in both the dropout and potential dropout students and their environments; that is, the family, the school, and the community.

Sanction to Practice

Where do social workers get the authority and sanction to intervene in this problem? Authorization to practice social work comes from the *society* that passes the laws and formulates the policies that provide help and intervention for the client systems; from the social work *profession* that guides the values, knowledge, and methods for intervention; from the *agency* that structures the intervention; and from the *client* who gives permission and agrees to the helping arrangements. Professional values and ethics often provide social workers with the sanction to intervene with systems beyond the identified client in order to facilitate client and environmental functioning. The social work practitioners in this case helped the school system identify a common problem shared by parents, teachers, and community residents.

Values

How are social workers guided in their thinking about problems and interventions? Are social workers' personal values, religious values, and philosophies the driving force in conceptualizing social work? Indeed not;

workers are guided by a specific set of professional values. In fact, this value base has been called social work's most binding and consistent thread. The primary values of the profession include:

♦ The inherent dignity of the individual

♦ The individual's right to growth and self-actualization

♦ The individual's responsibility to contribute to the well-being of society

♦ The rights of the individual to self-determination and participation to the fullest extent possible in decisions that determine his or her course of life

♦ Commitment to social justice in society

♦ Respect for confidentiality with client systems

♦ Respect for individual and group differences

These values are incorporated into the profession's code of ethics developed by the National Association of Social Workers. The code of ethics guides the professional practitioner in value premises of practice and professional conduct. The integrated-practice perspective is based on this value base, which recognizes the rights to dignity and self-determination and the need for all people to work toward a better environment. These values guide student practitioners with basic premises concerning the dropout problem.

Knowledge

Beyond the sanction, value base, and professional purpose, the ultimate question—the one that confronted the neonatal physician—is how does the social worker know what to do? What tells us how to proceed? There is a vast amount of knowledge for social work practice, and it is used at various points in the helping process. Knowledge comes from empirical research and from practice wisdom. The knowledge used in this practice framework (see Figure 1.1) is divided into five major parts: organizing, communicating, understanding, deciding what actions to take, and doing and ending the work. How these various levels of knowledge are used is discussed in terms of the high school dropout problem.

Knowledge for Relating and Communicating

One kind of knowledge that helps social workers know what to do is knowledge about communication and forming relationships.

Social work practice is carried out through professional relationships and built through effective communication across cultural, ethnic, gender, socioeconomic, and lifestyle boundaries. The knowledge necessary for forming effective relationships includes theories of communication, awareness of differences in communication styles, and how relationships differ with various clients between the social worker, the agency, the client populations, and the community. In the school dropout problem, the social workers needed to develop professional relationships with many "clients," such as the students, families, teachers, staff, administrators, and members of the community. The ability to communicate with a variety of clients from different cultures, genders, and social classes was critical.

Relationship.   A social work relationship is a professional relationship with the following characteristics: (1) it is purposeful, (2) it is time limited, and (3) it is client centered (Perlman, 1979). The relationship also takes on other characteristics that are specific to the principles inherent in the integrated-practice framework.

For example, the agency-based practice creates power differences between the client and the social worker. However, the principle of empowerment in integrated practice suggests relationships that are mutual, coequal problem-solving partnerships in which the client is expected to learn new skills for coping, to take risks, and to take responsibility, along with the social worker, for change outcomes.

Communication.   Communication is the basis of building relationships. In social work practice, many barriers must be crossed to build useful helping relationships. These barriers include the diversity represented in client populations, the worker, and the agency.

As diversity increases, communication barriers grow as well. To attend to these barriers, social workers must acquire knowledge in at least three domains: (1) knowledge of various cultures and groups to understand perceptions, behaviors, and values; (2) knowledge and awareness of their own background to decrease any ethnocentric perceptions; and (3) knowledge of the culture of social services agencies to mediate between the cultural differences between the agency and the client. Attention to these areas can help build effective professional relationships that will facilitate the work. Knowledge for communication is an ongoing process. Social workers must continuously improve their communication skills. In Lewis High School, the social workers need to be aware of their own backgrounds, the cultural values and communication patterns of the students and their families, and the agency or organization (that is, the high school itself).

Through the communication process and professional relationships, social workers engage their clients in a problem-solving process. The first step is to understand the problems presented.

Knowledge for Organizing Our Work

Integrated practice is organized around a phased problem-solving method: Exploration, Assessment, Goal setting, Planning, Evaluating, Role taking, and Terminating. This organizing schema helps practitioners know how to begin, where to go next, and how to finish their work on school dropouts. Each of these phases is discussed in the following paragraphs.

Knowledge for Understanding and Analyzing Problems: Exploring and Assessing

Exploration and assessment are depicted in Figure 1.1 as the beginning steps in problem solving. Although they contain different tasks, they are intricately linked and tend to function as one phase. During *exploration*, the social worker gathers data on the presenting problem. Exploration includes determining the history of the problem, who is affected by it, who would define or own it as a problem, what resolution attempts have been made, and with what results. In *assessment*, workers use theoretical concepts to understand the presenting problems. Social workers vary greatly in their use of theoretical concepts, and the choice of concepts partially determines how they think about solutions and interventions. Integrated practice employs the following concepts for assessment and analyses of problems:

♦ Social problems represented by the presenting problem

♦ The problem's embeddedness from micro to macro systems and linkages between these systems

♦ Individual and environmental interacting forces (client's psychosocial functioning and environmental factors)

♦ Prevention intervention possibilities

♦ Negative effects of the labeling and deviance process and the perceived powerlessness of the client group

♦ Oppression and discrimination issues including ethnicity, race, sexual orientation, gender, class, and age

♦ Normalization and positive visibility

♦ Competency-based assessment including strengths and vulnerabilities

These concepts help social workers form an assessment of client problems and the social problems represented by the clients.

CASE STUDY: *Lewis High School* ♦——————————

Failure to complete high school in today's world leaves youths unemployable except in marginal jobs and vulnerable to permanent unemployment. The youth who drop out of schools threaten our economic future as a nation (Kennedy, 1988). They confront the social values inherent in high technology and ultimately, the greatest value of all, economic survival. Many young dropouts see no particular relationship between their education and their future. At the point of leaving school, the typical youth exhibited poor attitudes toward the school, was likely to be failing, was behind in academic progress, and had a low grade-point average. Such alienation from the school may result in alienation from society.

Social Problem as a Target.   In the integrated-practice perspective, the target of social work intervention is the social problem, rather than the exclusive rehabilitation of the victims or survivors. The traditional purpose of social work has been to promote the interaction between individuals and their environment for the betterment of both (Bartlett, 1970), implying that the location of the problem is not of concern. The intervention may focus on many aspects of a social problem that is embedded across several social systems. Even though a problem is presented by a specific client, it may also be defined as being located in the interaction between the individual and the environment or within the environment, rather than simply within the individual. The location of the problem and the focus of intervention are not always the same. Using systems concepts as a theory base, social work practice is framed as boundary work (Hearn, 1970). Intervention in macro systems (the broader society and communities), meso systems (neighborhoods, organizations, and groups), or micro systems (individuals and families) can affect results at other levels. Multisystem-level intervention is needed for a social problem in order to link systems across these boundaries and synthesize the energy directed toward resolution or reduction of the problem. Understanding the school dropout problem from this concept guides workers to question the ownership of the problem by students, teachers and other school staff, families, and the community and provides multiple points of intervention.

CASE STUDY: *Lewis High School* ♦────────────

A *social systems approach* to social problems examines a problem in terms of the various systems that impact that problem and its solutions. Social workers identified the critical systems that affect school dropouts as *education* and *family*. They noted that historically the *educational system* has been the focus of much of the blame for the school dropout problem. While the school is a part of the problem, dropping out is also a result of dysfunction in many systems, including the family. The workers stressed that over the years the educational system has been forced to take on roles beyond its original mandate, such as social controller, disciplinarian, life skills teacher, social services provider, often without proper funding—an impossible task for any one social institution. In spite of the difficulty schools have in dealing with the dropout problem, the workers urged the school board to formulate an official policy so that administrators, teachers, and staff would have guidelines for dealing with the problem. They identified ten areas in which the school can impact the dropout ratio:

1. Adequate reporting, recording, and follow up on truancy
2. Consistent enforcement of school attendance regulations
3. Relevance of curriculum
4. Appropriate school placement
5. Appropriate retention and promotion policies
6. More attention to school transitions
7. Suspension and expulsion policies
8. Quality of teaching
9. Teacher absenteeism rates
10. School environment

Another system involved in the problem is the *family*. While a common misconception exists that families of dropouts are apathetic regarding their children's school progress, the problem is as much a matter of the parents' degree of control and influence. With many youth the influence of peers and street gangs and the reality of racial tensions in the school far outweigh their parents' attempts (often a single parent) to keep them in school.

A Needs Assessment. The social workers used a needs assessment to gather information for the study. A mailed survey instrument was sent to each identified youth who had dropped out over the last four years and followed up with an interview schedule. The return rate of the survey instrument was 48%. The workers interviewed nearly one-fourth of those who completed the survey or their parents. In addition, a survey instrument was sent to a selected sample of teachers, school administrators, school counselors, school social workers, and school psychologists. Finally, they examined census data from the census tracts that corresponded with the Lewis High School catchment area.

Then social workers gave the school board and the principal a copy of the needs assessment. In summary, the findings were that, compared with those who stay in school, youth who leave school before graduating:

1. Are more likely to have experienced high levels of truancy
2. Are more likely to have had behavior problems in school
3. Have higher rates of suspension and expulsion
4. Are more likely to come from single-parent families
5. Are more likely to come from families who are receiving public assistance
6. Are more likely to belong to gangs
7. Are not likely (20%) to reenter school of their own volition

8. Are more likely to be members of a minority, ethnic, or racial group
9. Are more likely to have lower grade-point averages
10. Are more likely to have attended special education classes
11. Have lower self-esteem
12. Are less likely to be involved in school extracurricular activities

The needs assessment also reflected that school personnel were generally frustrated with the school system's seeming inability to relate to this problem. They felt that the school's resources were inadequate and that the following services should be initiated or strengthened.

♦ Counseling (group and individual)
♦ Health care and birth control information
♦ Alternative curriculum and/or schools
♦ Outreach to parents of at-risk children
♦ Combined employment-school programs
♦ Private-sector involvement with at-risk youth
♦ A long-term master plan to reduce dropout rates
♦ Increased tutoring capability
♦ Enforcement of school attendance laws
♦ After-school programs

Although the high school dropout problem was clearly defined by most of the community, the various segments did not agree on one definition. Some defined the problem as inherent in the school itself, others placed the problem in the dropout behavior, and still others saw it as a family problem.

What action is required in a multiple definition of the problem? What resources should be used? In other words, how should the problem be constructed? How does the problem construction determine the proposed solutions? Value clashes and differences over possible problems and solutions combine to create both an economic problem and a political problem. The school could not compromise quality of education. In the conventional wisdom, a teacher's time could best be used on "motivated" students. How much of their time should be spent "babysitting" or managing behavioral problems of students who didn't wish to attend school? Should their time be used to motivate parents to motivate their children?

On the other hand, ignoring the problem was not feasible. Unlike those who dropped out of school in the past, modern-day youth will not necessarily be absorbed by a factory assembly line. They may not be able to find a job and participate in the legitimate economic system. They may be forced to resort to such illegitimate employment as drug dealing and thus become the victims of other costly social problems. Relative to those who complete high school, dropouts are destined to earn less money, suffer more unemployment, have more health problems, and be more dissatisfied with their personal lives. One year's dropout population costs the nation $240 billion in future taxes and earning (Kennedy, 1988).

♦

Prevention. Viewing social work practice in this broad context opens up the option of prevention as a viable practice arena. Since pinpointing the cause of social problems is often politically and theoretically baffling, the potential of prevention as an intervention is often dismissed. However, it is not necessary to know the exact cause in order to create prevention intervention. Identification and intervention with contributing factors are possible, even though these factors may not be identifiable as a cause.

As Bloom (1979) suggested, a new paradigm for prevention in mental health abandons the search for cause and pays closer attention to precipitating factors. Assuming that we human beings are variously vulnerable to stressful life events and may respond differently to the same event, prevention programs can be organized around facilitating mastery or reducing the incidence of particular stressful life events. Preventive services can be linked with events such as entering school, parenting, divorce, and widowhood. Bloom argued that competence building may be the single, most persuasive preventive strategy for dealing with individual and social issues in most communities. The availability and accessibility of community resources are essential to building a sense of power, self-esteem, and competence within individuals. Identifying critical life events that may affect potential student dropouts and their families may be a key to decreasing the incidence of school dropouts. Prevention, which will be discussed later in this book, is a viable option for social problem intervention.

CASE STUDY: *Lewis High School* ♦

Many students today have suffered from poor prenatal and postnatal care and nutritional problems. These deficiencies set the stage for low learning thresholds, which will not be raised significantly by remediation and are certainly beyond the control of the two school social workers at Lewis High or even the Lewis High Mental Health Team. What is quite apparent, however, is the relationship between prenatal care, child health services, and nutritional policy today and the high school dropout rate in the year 2010. The lack of health care and nutrition today sows the seeds of poor school performance and school dropouts tomorrow. The needs assessment also identified other contributing factors. A profile of the student dropout helps identify a population for prevention intervention.

These are social policy and primary prevention issues, and while they are within the domain of the social work profession, they extend beyond to other disciplines as well.

───◆

Deviance and Labeling Perspective of Social Problems.   Many social work clients are members of social groups that have been collectively disempowered and devalued. These groups include the lower socioeconomic class (Findlay, 1978), ethnic minorities who have color visibility in the dominant society (Lum, 1992), and women (Longres, 1990). Other status differences may be based on religion, age, sexual preference, or physical and mental disability. These differences tend to exponentially exacerbate the devaluation and oppression of the members of the group (Staples, 1987). Although devaluation and lack of access to opportunities based on group status are perpetuated by the members of the groups themselves, rights and access are still systematically denied by the more powerful, dominant culture through laws, policies, practices, and attitudes.

The deviance and labeling perspective of social problems (Rubington & Weinberg, 1981) suggests that social problems are defined as reactions to an alleged violation of rules, norms, or expectations. This perspective focuses on the conditions under which behaviors, situations, or groups of people come to be defined as problematic or deviant. Labeled deviance is often accompanied by devaluation and the persons carrying the label are discriminated against. Power and the lack thereof is a reciprocal process. The lack of power in client groups is an important factor in assessing the client's problems, strengths, and capacity to change.

Politically conservative views of social problems and solutions during the 1980s influenced social work practice to move toward social pathology as an explanation and psychotherapeutic methods as interventions. Described as "specialization by solution" (Heus & Pincus, 1986, p. 15), this tendency has guided social workers to work only with the victims of social problems in ways that may increase individual blame for the problem. The victims are often those targeted by society as "deviants." They may be drinkers in the social problem of alcoholism, the abused in the social problem of child abuse, or the depressed or angry women and minorities in the social conditions of sexism and racism. Victims are often the most accessible, least powerful, and most easily labeled participants in social problems, and society more readily sanctions social workers to work with victims than other participants who may in fact benefit from social problems. For example, drug dealers benefit from youths' drug addictions; slumlords benefit from lack of adequate housing for poor people. It is more politically acceptable to diagnose and treat victims of social problems as needing psychotherapy rather than suggest that the cause and solution lie in the environmental structure.

Integrated practice views oppression as a function of deviance and labeling and therefore assumes the need to counter negative devaluation of specific client groups by emphasizing positive visibility, normalization, competency screening, and empowerment-based interventions. From this view, the problem is identified as belonging not only to the student dropouts themselves, but also to the entire educational community.

Competency as a Screen. As an antidote to negative labeling, devaluation, and powerlessness, social workers view the so-called victims (or as some prefer, ''survivors'') of social problems as fundamentally competent persons who are participants in a problem interaction; that is, a condition that is broader and more encompassing than their behavioral reactions. Clients are seen as having the capacity for learning, understanding, and solving problems and for increasing their coping skills. They have a right to risk and fail, and they have the expertise and resources to solve their problems.

CASE STUDY: *Lewis High School* ◆ ─────────────────

Youth who drop out of school are negatively labeled and stigmatized by society. Such stigmatization may lead to discrimination in employment and training opportunities. The school and the community may see these youth as incompetent and unmotivated. However, the strengths, coping skills, and capacities of the dropout students and their families are a critical factor, as are the strengths, capacities, and motivations of the school and community. In effect, the message of the program was that an individual's strengths, if mobilized, far outweigh his or her liabilities. The interventions were geared toward "doing with" rather than "doing to" or "doing for" students. This distinction is important. It's the difference between seeing oneself as an object or a partner. The students were more than recipients of a service. They were participants and deciders who were assumed to be adept, not inept. In the process of helping them help themselves, their strengths were tapped and developed, and the school's strengths were accentuated as well.

─── ◆

Normalization. A view of behavior from a normative environmental context instead of a normal/abnormal dichotomy attempts to decrease labeled deviancy. Traditional views of dysfunctional behavior attribute linear cause to either the individual or the environment. A normalized approach suggests that behavior cannot be viewed objectively, but must be seen in terms of a person's intentions, motives, and reasons.

Thus, behavior is examined in its political-socioeconomic context. This perspective has serious implications for social work, considering the large number of clients who are women and minorities, populations known to be economically and socially discriminated against. The political-socioeconomic context of client problems becomes a major factor in assessment. A normalized view looks at these three factors and understands the response of dropping out as normative, albeit destructive.

CASE STUDY: *Lewis High School* ◆

In working with the students, the social workers made every effort to avoid negative labeling and employ neutral or positive labels such as "student" or "participant." The programs were "normalized" in that they were relevant to the culture of the clients and their families. Tutors were reframed as "mentors"; another normalizing term in that everyone can relate to someone who has at one time filled that role. The dropout problem was defined and understood in its environmental context, code of conventions, and culture, not in terms of individual dysfunction.

The workers showed sensitivity to and understanding of the school and its environment. They attempted to shape it as a user-friendly, helping environment in contrast with the alien, inhospitable environments many schools have become. The school was helped to shape services relevant to the problem at hand, creating more normalized service delivery.

◆

In summary, knowledge for understanding and assessing client problems includes focusing on social problems embedded across systems, the interactions between personal and environmental factors, the power differentials of clients in the labeling and deviance perspective, competency-based assessment, and the client's needs and resources. This assessment schema is illustrated in Chapter 7 on the conferee role. The next section on knowing what to do moves into deciding what actions to take after an initial assessment is formulated.

Knowledge for Deciding What Action to Take and Knowing When It Is Done: Goal Setting, Planning, and Evaluating

Beyond assessing and understanding the dropout problem, another level of knowledge is needed when considering what to do about the school dropout rate. What will help? This may be one of the most critical areas in the conceptual framework, and it will be influenced by how we understand the problem. Knowing what to do and when it is done includes consideration of change and change strategies, empowerment, habilitation, role taking, and evaluative methods. Once data gathering and assessment are completed, the social workers must formulate goals and develop plans for reaching those goals. The following steps are included in this process:

1. Promoting client strengths through empowerment in the process and as an outcome
2. Setting agreed-on goals
3. Identifying systems to be involved in the change effort
4. Arriving at an agreement with the client systems about the desired outcomes
5. Developing of specific strategies and roles to be taken, and by whom
6. Determining how outcomes will be evaluated and measured

Empowerment. Empowerment is the major principle in the framework that guides work with the client systems. Definition of this principle and its components comes from the work of Barbara Solomon (1976). According to Solomon, empowerment is a "process whereby the social worker engages in a set of activities with the client or client system that aims to reduce the powerlessness that has been created by negative valuations based on membership in a stigmatized group" (p. 19).

Solomon (1976) further described powerlessness as the inability to manage emotions, skill, knowledge, or material resources so that effective performance in valued social roles leads to personal gratification. Therefore, an individual's powerlessness can be viewed as his or her inability to obtain and use resources to achieve personal goals, and powerlessness in groups and communities can be seen as the inability to use resources to achieve collective goals. Empowerment then is "the process of development of an effective support system for those who have been blocked from achieving individual or collective goals" (Solomon, 1976, p. 19).

Power in the Helping Process. The element of power is central to a helping process that enables clients to solve their own problems. If clients lack power, then social workers must enable them to achieve it in relationship to themselves and to oppressive systems. To some extent, self-esteem depends on the inclusion of a sense of power within the self-concept. That is, mentally healthy people must be able to perceive themselves as at least minimally powerful and capable of influencing their environment to their benefit (Ryan, 1971). Competence, power, and self-esteem are inextricably linked; their loss may constitute a powerful stressor.

The social worker must be a power broker and educator who provides supports that help clients access the benefits and prerequisites accorded to the mainstream of society. In empowerment-based intervention, the client must have retained the capacity to solve problems after the worker departs. An evaluation of empowerment asks, ''Did the client system retain increased capacity for solving problems when the social worker was no longer present?'' ''Was expertise given to the client?'' The belief that clients have the capacity for problem solving is based on the use of self-fulfilling prophecy as a positive expectation. Workers must decrease the client's learned helplessness. Educating clients is critical to empowerment (Solomon, 1976). The practitioner needs to understand the dynamics of the social problem as a whole and the problem-solving process. He or she then shares this knowledge with clients, including individuals, families, groups, organizations, and communities. Education is an antidote for learned helplessness and a basis for influencing and mobilizing change. In the school dropout problem, increasing the capacity of students, families, the school, and the community to solve interactive problems is a significant consideration in planning how to intervene.

CASE STUDY: *Lewis High School* ◆─────────────────

To every extent possible, the social workers helped the youth and their parents exercise control of their lives. Through the collective self-help processes, they began to help others, an important milestone in helping themselves. Educating the students, parents, and the school community about the problem was an important step in empowerment. The creation of an advisory committee helped involve all parts of the community. The committee included three teachers, two parents, two students, a janitor, a secretary, a teacher's aid, and a food-service worker. By learning more about the problem, the committee members increased their levels of empowerment for problem solving.

───◆

Habilitation.   Habilitation is a principle in integrated practice that implies a focus on strength and the promotion of growth. Although a social worker cannot deny impairment or dysfunction as a result of experiencing a social problem, habilitation focuses on strength, assuming that clients are fundamentally competent and have a right to risk. While integrated practice includes one-on-one work with individuals, the differences between habilitation and traditional pathology-oriented perspectives for intervention with individuals are significant. Habilitation is compatible with a strengths perspective (Saleebey, 1992). Table 1.1 presents some differences between habilitation and more traditional specialist-based views of practices. The major differences occur in the social worker's view of the client

Table 1.1 Comparison of Habilitation and Rehabilitation Principles

Major Differences	Habilitation Principles	Rehabilitation Principles
View of the client	• Problems exist between the person and the environment. • Client is a victim of social problem. • Social worker expects fundamental competence and learning of coping skills.	• Problem exists within the person. • Client is a devalued deviant with a dysfunctional condition.
View of the client's behavior	• Behavior is on a normative continuum. • Behavior is viewed in an environmental context. • Current events cause current behavior. • Behavior is troubling to society.	• Specialist expects helplessness. • Behavior is dichotomous: abnormal or normal. • Behavior is attributed to need, deficiency, or pathology. • Current behavior is rooted in the past. • Behavior is a problem for the client.
Relationship between social worker and client	• Coequal problem solvers, each has unique expertise. • Treatment expertise is not needed, but education and mobilization are. • Risk and responsibility are expected from the client. • Client is expected to learn new coping skills and resources.	• Client is dysfunctional; specialist is the healer. • Expert therapist; client is a recipient of service. • Fosters dependency of client. • Client is expected to be dysfunctional due to pathology.
Intervention	• Intervention is independent of etiology. • Education and acquisition of new skill required.	• Cause is necessary to determine the cure. • Treatment and cure are implied.

and his or her behavior, the relationship between the client and the social worker, and the intervention assumptions.

CASE STUDY: *Lewis High School* ♦———————————

Intervention in the Lewis High School dropout problem used the principles of habilitation. The social workers defined the problem in the transaction between individuals and environments. They studied the behavior of the identified clients—the youth who dropped out—in its environmental context rather than as deficits in the dropouts themselves. Students who dropped out, their families, the school, and the community were all seen as coequal problem solvers. The social workers did not see themselves as having all the answers or as being the sole interveners. Intervention was multilevel, not directed at a single cause, and education was a key characteristic.

———————————————————————————————♦

Social Work Roles and Role Taking.   Decisions about role taking are made in the political arena of practice, in terms of the agency's purpose and function, the practice demands presented by the client, and the social worker's orientations toward change and conflict. Role taking can be conceptualized on a continuum of social work roles from least to greatest context (Wood & Middleman, 1989); that is, from conferee and enabler on one end of the continuum to guardian on the other (Hernández et al., 1985). There are six professional roles: conferee, enabler, broker, advocate, mediator, and guardian. Roles may also be viewed from a principle of least to greatest disruptions (Specht, 1969). The change strategies used in role taking include educative and power-based strategies (Bennis, Benne, & Chin, 1969). Integrated practice is a multimethod approach, so social work roles are assumed across client systems of individuals, families, groups, organizations, and communities, with both "victims" of social problems and "nonvictims." Table 1.2 presents a schematic view of the intervention continuum in integrated practice. The intervention focuses on both small and large systems and on specific purposes ranging from education and sensitization to rearrangement of structures and policies for prevention purposes.

CASE STUDY: *Lewis High School* ♦———————————

The principal at Lewis High appointed two senior social workers on the mental health team to spearhead a study of the dropout problem and work with a team to devise a plan. This process culminated in a meeting between the board of

Table 1.2 Integrated Practice Intervention Continuum

Small Systems ——————————————————————— Large Systems			
Continuum			
Client			
Individuals or groups of victims	Groups of victims	Victims and nonvictims	Victims and nonvictims or nonvictims only
Purpose			
Habilitation, education and rearrangement, sensitization, alleviation, and prevention of social problems	Enablement of victims to create support	Creation of and access to needed services	Structure

Source: Parsons et al., 1988.

education, the principal, and the social workers responsible for developing the plan.

Intervention was planned across systems. Those agencies that were already involved with students were mobilized into a consortium or network, bringing to life the systems adage that the whole is greater than the sum of its parts. The network became an action system that enhanced the services of all the agencies and amplified agency communication.

Another community resource, the volunteer mentors and tutors, helped expand the learning process while providing important social support. Various social systems linkages were made between the problem "carriers" and their community.

For the most part, this program operated in a cooperative mode with a great deal of joint action, information sharing, and consensual decision making. When conflict arose, the social workers mediated and joined the contestants in cooperative action.

The social workers moved back and forth judiciously among the six professional roles, based on the practice demands presented by the problem. They understood that each role facilitated the other roles, and that all roles were necessary for a comprehensive intervention.

This approach attempted to involve as many people as possible in studying and analyzing the problem, planning for remediation, and conducting the interventions. In short, the community, the school board, the school staff and faculty, the parents, and the students were reeducated and then mobilized to become their own problem solvers.

Based on the findings of the needs assessment, the mental health team, the principal, and the board met to formulate goals. They agreed on the following goals:

1. To increase the graduation rate of at-risk students at Lewis High School
2. To aggressively identify and reach out to students who are at risk
3. To identify each at-risk student's barriers and difficulties to school achievement and success
4. To involve parents of at-risk children in ensuring school attendance and involvement
5. To programmatically employ a multisystems approach in intervening with potential dropouts

Planning.   Given the findings of the needs assessment and the goals mentioned above, the workers developed an intervention program that would emanate from the school system but focus on the students and their families. Intervention would occur on an individual basis.

The workers' next step was to convene the mental health team to formulate a plan. In order to extend themselves into the Lewis High School community, the team formed three ad hoc task forces. These task forces conducted a series of public forums within the school, one sponsored by the PTA, another by the student association, and several in connection with staff meetings. The meetings were held to update each constituency on the problem and to elicit ideas for achieving the goals. Anyone was allowed to speak to the problem and written ideas were also collected.

The workers recognized that it would be easy to become identified as the "experts" on the problem. To counter this, they used these hearings to involve the entire community, including the student body. They wanted to expand the action system involved in the problem-solving process.

Incorporating the ideas from the community forums and from the community needs assessment, the mental health team finalized the plan and agreed to the following programmatic services:

1. *A community volunteer (mentor) program*—This program would recruit volunteers from the community, train them, and match them with at-risk students.

2. *An interorganizational network of agencies*—This consortium of agencies would be formulated from among those agencies known or believed to be involved with the problem at some level. The consortium would share resources and the available pool of expertise.

3. *A brokerage model of service delivery*—The team would serve as case managers for each volunteer "match," linking them with needed services.

4. *An informal monthly activity for all participants*—This would be a social gathering of some sort focused on having fun.

5. *A self-help network*—This network would have a dual focus: one self-help group would consist of parents of at-risk children or children who had already dropped out of school, and the other would be comprised of at-risk students.

6. *A tutoring program*—This service called for after-school tutoring sessions. Tutoring would be provided by volunteers, teachers, and the existing peer-tutoring program.

─── ◆

Evaluation. When plans for decreasing the dropout rate are implemented, we have to be able to answer the question "How will we know the interventions work?" Because goals in this practice framework may be broadly defined, evaluation of intervention may be elusive at times. Broad goals, as well as more narrowly defined objectives, are evaluated in order to assess the efficiency and effectiveness of a practice framework. Chapter 6 contains suggested evaluative strategies useful for this framework. Approaches for evaluating integrated practice need to be flexible across systems, as empowering as possible, and have a high degree of client input. Action research and goal-attainment scaling are presented as appropriate strategies for evaluation.

Knowledge for Doing, Implementing, and Ending

When goal setting and planning are formulated, and a design for evaluation is in place, the social worker carries out the plan through the continued assumption of the six roles. These roles are necessary interventive functions across the five client systems, depending on the chosen point or points of intervention (Hernández et al., 1985); see Table 1.3.

Conferee Role. The *conferee* role, derived from the idea of "conference," focuses on actions that are taken when the social worker is the primary source of assistance to the consumer or client. This role encompasses defining the problem, deliberating about alternative courses of action, and planning for carrying out activities. It may encompass using therapeutic intervention or raising the client's sensitivity to and awareness of various problems and issues (Solomon, 1976).

CASE STUDY: *Lewis High School* ◆─────────────────────────

As is so often the case in practice, workers find themselves in the conferee role at the beginning of an intervention. The workers at Lewis High began in this role when they conferred with the principal. He saw the workers as the "experts." The school board also placed the workers in this role when the board directed

Table 1.3 Helper Role-Taking Activities Across Client Systems

Role	Individual	Family	Small Group	Organization	Community
			Client Systems		
Conferee	Counseling assisted problem solving	Family therapy Problem solving	Group problem solving	Supervision Consultation	Consultation Problem solving
Enabler	Modeling teaching skills	Family education modeling	Education Training	Organization development Training	Social planning Community education
Broker	Casework Information referral	Information and referral casework	Promotion of self-help	Networking	Needs advocacy
Mediator	Decision making	Family conflict Divorce Custody resolution	Intragroup or inter-group mediation	Third-party peace making	Community conflict resolution
Advocate	Case advocacy	Case advocacy	Education Mobilization of group	Grant writing	Cause advocacy Bargaining
Guardian	Individual protective services	Family protective services	Coerced group participation	Controlling	Initiating legal action

Source: From S. H. Hernández, J. D. Jorgensen, P. Judd, M. Gould, and R. J. Parsons, "Integrated practice and advanced generalist curriculum to prepare social problem specialists." *Journal of Social Work Education,* 1985, 21(3), 28–35. Copyright © 1985 by the Council for Social Work Education. Reprinted with permission of CSWE.

them to come up with a plan to reduce dropouts and report back. The workers assumed the role until they began to involve others in problem-solving activities.

Being considered the "sole source" of problem-solving potential can be flattering and enticing, but to remain in this position may disempower the client. The workers quickly shifted to the enabler role as soon as it seemed appropriate. For instance, when the workers met with the school board and presented the ten areas in which they felt the school could have an impact, they asked the board to begin to own the problem. By involving the board and the principal in formulating goals, the social workers' choice of collaborative problem solving created an empowerment process for all participants.

Working with student dropouts and their mentors also required the workers to temporarily assume the conferee role. Sharing information that they (the students) didn't have was necessary in introducing students to the program; however, the workers quickly moved to enable them rather than continuing as the sole source of assistance.

◆

Enabler Role. The enabler role is assumed when the social worker structures, arranges, and manipulates events and interacts with the client system and the environment to facilitate system functioning. This role includes the teacher-trainer role and the mobilization of the energy within the system to move and act on its own behalf.

Of all six roles, enabling is perhaps the most empowering, for it means exactly that—to empower. The case study shows several examples of how the workers enabled or initiated an empowerment process for both the action system and the "carriers" or "victims" of the problem.

CASE STUDY: *Lewis High School* ◆

As noted, the principal and the board were involved in goal setting. As the planning process began, the team used public forums to involve the whole school community. Through these forums, people were recruited for further involvement, such as serving on a project advisory committee. In the planning process, it is quite easy to avoid citizen involvement because it is time consuming and often invites conflict. However, if citizens aren't involved and the planning is done solely by professionals with technical expertise, the community is ultimately disempowered. The workers at Lewis High wisely kept the project in the hands of as many people as possible.

The social workers realized that reducing the dropout problem could not be done by counseling alone. Many systems had to be involved. These systems— the school, the family, agencies, and volunteers—were all potential resources to the extent that they were "manipulated." Thus the training and assigning of volunteers was actually mobilization of an important human resource to combat the problem. Initiation of self-help groups for dropouts and their parents also "enabled" people to act on a problem that had previously disabled and immobilized them.

♦

Broker Role.   In the role of broker, the worker's objective is to link clients with goods and services and to coordinate and control the quality of those goods and services. Brokerage includes case management and interagency collaboration. Of necessity, brokerage requires some enabling; it transcends enabling in that it links the client to resources and services that might not otherwise be used.

CASE STUDY: *Lewis High School* ♦────────────────

The case-management process of facilitating an array of services for the client was evident as students were referred to agencies and agency services began to flow. The forming of a consortium of agencies (an action system) and the ongoing management and ultimate expansion of the network are clear examples of the workers acting as brokers.

♦

Advocate Role.   In the *advocate* role, the social worker secures services and resources on behalf of consumers either in the face of identified resistance or when these goods and resources do not exist. This role includes policy development and advocacy for policy change. Case advocacy is done for one client, one case; cause advocacy is on behalf of a larger problem.

CASE STUDY: *Lewis High School and Regency Middle School* ♦────────────

In this problem, the workers were forced to engage in both case advocacy and cause advocacy. Case advocacy was called for when the school principal, in what the workers considered arbitrary and capricious behavior, expelled five students in the project without any semblance of due process or review. On a case-by-case basis, the workers, with the sanction of the youths and their parents, interceded and induced the principal to back down from a hardened position that couldn't be defended.

Cause advocacy was occasioned during the middle of the school year. At Regency Middle School, a feeder school for Lewis High, a major issue developed over the high expulsion rate of sixth graders. The workers were aware of studies showing that children expelled in middle school are prime candidates to become high school dropouts. They alerted the board to this possibility and were subsequently invited to meet with the Regency Middle School principal and school social worker. Together, they drew up plans to establish profiles of the students being expelled and involved these students and their parents in behavioral contracts with the school. The workers reported back to the school board and recommended that action be taken to address expulsion policy at all middle schools as one means of primary prevention. At the end of the academic year, the board was struggling over the direction such a policy would take. It was obviously a difficult political issue with differing sentiment within the community.

———————————————————————————————————◆

Guardian Role. The guardian role is taken when the worker exercises social control or takes protective action when the client's competence does not equal the demands on the client. Although resisted by social workers, guardian is a common role.

CASE STUDY: *Lewis High School* ◆————————————

Three of the student mentor matches were discontinued when the social workers learned that mentors had made sexual advances to the students. These incidents presented a serious threat to the program and a dilemma for the students. The workers needed to exercise social control by protecting these students.

The workers learned of one incident when a victim (a male student) refused to meet with his mentor. He would give no specific reason, simply stating he had tired of the relationship. A meeting with the youth's mother revealed that he had been moody but refused to discuss his feelings. The worker asked the student why he wanted to withdraw from the program, emphasizing that he had every right to do so. At this point, the student revealed he had been "improperly touched." He informed the worker that he wasn't the only one to whom this had happened, implicating two other boys and their mentors.

On investigation, the workers learned that one of the boys had been invited to a mentor's home to watch a pornographic film. The boy had left when offered beer and had then decided not to continue the relationship. The third youth related an incident of his mentor's getting "too friendly." He asked to be transferred to another mentor.

The three boys were interviewed separately and informed of the worker's legal obligation to report sexual abuse. The boys were both surprised and relieved.

The social workers contacted the Department of Social Services, and the students' allegations were substantiated. The three mentors were ultimately charged with sexual abuse in criminal court. At the end of the first year of the project, they had not yet gone to trial.

While these incidents cast some negative publicity on the school dropout program, the student's identities were protected and the mental health team made every effort to use the incidents to educate the public on the problem of sexual abuse.

─── ♦

Mediator Role.   The social worker assumes the *mediator* role when two or more parties are in conflict, but mutual interests exist. Activities include education about conflict and facilitation of negotiation bargaining and interests-based problem solving. The practice demand for this role occurs when the social worker must reconcile opposite or disparate points of view and engage the disputants in unified action.

CASE STUDY: *Lewis High School* ♦ ─────────────────────

Mediation was carried out on two separate occasions during the year of the program. A conflict developed between the school PTA and the school administration when the PTA verbally attacked the school for "undermining" their role in working on the dropout problem. This attack threatened to disrupt the program because the PTA had a vocal, albeit small, membership.

The social workers met with the principal, the school board president, and the president and vice-president of the PTA and offered to help iron out the difficulty. Through a process of mutual perception checking, the social workers determined that the PTA was concerned in particular about the role of parent self-help groups. They felt that the PTA should be the chief sponsor of such groups lest it become irrelevant to the life of the school. The social workers explained the nature of self-help and formulated an agreement that the school would ask parents in the self-help groups to join PTA. The PTA was invited to appear at the next self-help group's meeting to explain their efforts in dropout prevention. Eventually, the PTA gave financial support to the group and were also able to enroll eight new PTA members from the group.

Mediation also became necessary when a neighborhood group objected to students' using a vacant lot across the street from Lewis High as a smoking zone. Since the school had been declared "smoke free," there was little choice but to use the vacant lot for "open smoking" or accept the reality of concealed smoking in rest rooms, neither of which was inviting to the school administration.

The matter was ultimately mediated by one of the social workers when she convened a delegation of the neighborhood group, the principal, and the student body president. An agreement was struck that the lot would be maintained daily by students who smoked. They would police the area for cigarette butts. The school also agreed to incorporate a series of stop-smoking campaigns, which were sponsored by a local hospital, into their student assemblies.

Obviously, some blurring of these roles occurs. The conferee and enabler roles are often blurred, as are the broker and advocate; the mediator and advocate roles are often taken simultaneously, one in order to achieve the other.

Choosing Strategies for Carrying Out Roles. The broad territory of knowledge and skill necessary in role taking may appear too encompassing. Social workers do not have to know everything in order to work from this perspective. Instead, they should use a narrowing focus to select strategies used within the roles along the continuum of intervention. Strategy selection is guided by the principles used to understand problems and decide what to do (habilitation, empowerment, education, normalization, etc). Some strategies fit better with this practice perspective than others. As a principle, empowerment guides which strategies are useful in choosing what to do. Solomon (1976) suggested that roles should be carefully selected for their empowerment potential. She emphasized the educational nature of empowerment-based social work and suggested that roles should be taken from an educational perspective. Strategies that can be taught and transferred to clients are the obvious choice.

An organizing strategy in all roles is problem solving. A problem-solving process provides a basis for deciding how to intervene. It includes exploration, assessment, goal formulation, planning, evaluation, and implementation. The specific strategies that follow this model are selected for intervention because of their problem-solving nature; these strategies are also easy to teach to clients and others. Self-help, mutual aid, education, and skill-development groups are considered significant strategies because of their educational nature. In the mediator role, the social worker focuses on educating client systems about alternative means for negotiating and resolving conflictual problems. In organizational and community intervention, those models that educate are team-building, conflict resolution, networking, self-help strategies, and process consultation methods of organizational development. Role-taking strategies share a commonality of education and empowerment.

CASE STUDY: *Lewis High School* ◆————————————

This case study of the social problem of school dropout behavior in an urban high school has been used to depict how social workers can intervene in social problem dynamics while also serving those who suffer from the problem. Using the six professional roles (conferee, enabler, broker, advocate, mediator, and guardian) with the five client systems (individuals, families, groups, organizations, and the community), the workers were able to reduce the number of student dropouts in one academic year.

The workers developed a network of those agencies that were already serving kids who dropped out and brokered their services to students through case management. In addition, they developed a program of volunteer mentors whose mission was to provide at-risk students with one-to-one support in completing their education. The social workers set up a self-help network of both parents and students that ultimately became a source of empowerment for both groups. They also developed a tutoring program. The workers mobilized the school system itself, including staff, teachers, the principal, and the board of education with the ultimate goal of self-assessment and change.

In accomplishing these tasks, the workers employed client empowerment, assumption of client competency, normalization of the environment, maximum utilization of the community, prevention, the normative reeducative approach to change, and engaged in the political process through social policy examination and reformulation.

————————————————————————————————————◆

SUMMARY

This practice approach is relevant to emerging social work practice tasks. In a postindustrial era, this model asserts that social workers need to be educators about broad social problems and mobilizers of a wide diversity of resources for problem solving. Intervention occurs across a continuum of all five client systems, using a variety of social work roles to resolve and reduce social problems.

Problem assessment includes studying behavior through a combination of social problem perspectives, particularly deviancy and labeling, the political-socioeconomic aspects of the social problem and client population, normalization, and assumption of the client's fundamental competency. Intervention is based on habilitation and growth promotion rather than on dysfunctionality and pathology. Empowerment and education are the guiding principles used to select intervention strategies.

Current practice models in the social work literature provide the bases of this approach. Integrated practice, however, uses education and the teaching of problem solving as a generic guide for the selection of intervention strategies.

This chapter has presented an overview of the integrated-practice perspective, including its professional components, knowledge for understanding and analyzing problems, knowledge for knowing what to do and when it is done, and knowledge for doing and ending the process. These concepts and their uses will be elaborated on in subsequent chapters of this book.

STUDY QUESTIONS

1. What are the components of a social work practice framework and how were they identified in the case study of high school dropouts?
2. What are the types of knowledge used in social work interventions and how were they used in the school dropout problem?
3. What were examples of empowerment principles in the school dropout problem?
4. Identify the components of assessment suggested by this framework for social work practice and discuss how they were used in the school dropout study.
5. What are the strengths and limitations of this framework for work with oppressed populations or at-risk populations?
6. Are all social work roles relevant to all client systems or are some roles more applicable to specific client systems?
7. Identify the major differences between habilitation and rehabilitation principles. How were they applied to the school dropout problem?

REFERENCES

Abramovitz, M. (1986). The privitazation of the welfare state: A review. *Social Work*, *31*(4), pp. 257–262.

Anderson, J. (1981). *Social work methods and processes*. Belmont, CA: Wadsworth.

Bartlett, H. (1970). *The Common base of social work practice*. New York: National Association of Social Workers.

Bell, D. (1973). *The coming of a post-industrial society: A venture in social forecasting*. New York: Basic Books.

Bennis, W. G., Benne, K. D., & Chin, R. (1969). *The planning of change* (2nd ed.). New York: Holt, Rinehart & Winston.

Berger, P. L., & Luckman, T. (1966). *The social construction of reality.* New York: Doubleday.

Berger, P. L., & Neuhaus, R. (1977). *To empower people.* Washington, DC: American Enterprise Institute for Public Policy Research.

Bloom, B. (1979). Prevention of mental disorders: Recent advances in theory and practice. *Community Mental Health Journal 15,* pp. 179–191.

Brill, N. (1978). *Working with people* (2nd ed.). White Plains, NY: Longman.

Compton, B., & Galaway, B. (1989). *Social work processes* (4th ed.). Pacific Grove, CA: Brooks/Cole.

Findlay, P. C. (1978). Critical theory and social work practice. *Catalyst 3,* p. 55.

Germain, C. B., & Gitterman, A. (1980). *The life model of social work practice.* New York: Columbia University Press.

Glazer, S. (1989 April). Dropouts: An F for education? *Editorial Research Reports.* Washington, DC: Congressional Quarterly, pp. 211–226.

Hearn, G. W. (1970, April 9). Social work as boundary work. Paper presented to the Third Annual Institute on Services to Families and Children, School of Social Work, University of Iowa, Iowa City.

Hernández, S. H., Jorgensen, J. D., Judd, P., Gould, M. S., & Parsons, R. J. (1985). Integrated practice: Preparing the social problem specialist through an advanced generalist curriculum. *Journal for Social Work Education 21,* pp. 28–35.

Heus, M., & Pincus, A. (1986). *The creative generalist.* Barneveld, WI: Micamar.

Kahn, A. J., & Kamerman, S. B. (Eds.). (1989). *Privatization of the welfare state.* Princeton, NJ: Princeton University Press.

Karls, J. M., & Wandrei, K. E. (1992). PIE: New language for social work. *Social Work* 37(1), pp. 80–87.

Kennedy, E. M. (1988 Sept.). When students drop out, we all lose. *Vocational Education Journal,* pp. 34–35.

Kennedy, P. (1993). *Preparing for the twenty-first century.* New York: Random House.

Kominski, R. (1990). Estimating the national high school dropout rate. *Demography* 27.

Longres, J. F. (1990). *Human behavior in the social environment.* Itasca, IL: F. E. Peacock.

Lum, D. (1992). *Social work practice and people of color.* Pacific Grove, CA: Brooks/Cole.

McKnight, J. (1977). Professionalized service and disabling help. In I. Illich (Ed.), *Disabling professions,* pp. 69–91. London: M. Boyars.

Naisbitt, J. (1982). *Megatrends.* New York: Warner Books.

Naisbitt, J., & Aburdene, P. (1990). *Megatrends 200.* New York: Avon Books.

Nisbet, R. (1953). *Community and power.* New York: Oxford University Press.

Parsons, R. J., Hernández, S. H., and Jorgensen, J. D. (1988). Integrated practice: A framework for problem solving. *Social Work,* 35(5), pp. 417–421.

Perlman, H. H. (1979). *Relationships: The heart of helping.* Chicago: University of Chicago Press.

Pincus, A., & Minahan, A. (1973). *Social work practice: Model and method.* Itasca, IL: F. E. Peacock.

Rubington, E., & Weinberg, M. (1981). *The study of social problems* (3rd ed.). New York: Oxford University Press.

Ryan, W. (1971). *Blaming the victim.* New York: Random House.

Saleebey, D. (Ed.). (1992). *The strengths perspective in social work practice.* New York: Longman.

Solomon, B. (1976). *Black empowerment: Social work in oppressed communities.* New York: Columbia University Press.

Specht, H. (1969). Disruptive tactics. *Social Work* 14(2), pp. 5–15.

Staples, L. (1987). *Powerful ideas about empowerment.* Boston: (Unpublished Manuscript).

Wood, G. G., & Middleman, R. (1989). *The structural approach to direct practice in social work.* New York: Columbia University Press.

Concepts for Understanding and Analyzing Problems: Exploration and Assessment

Part One

The first part of this book provides the concepts that make up the exploration and assessment phases of the integrated-practice framework. This section contains knowledge for understanding and analyzing social work problems.

Chapter 2, "Social Problems: Analysis and Intervention," presents a comprehensive discussion of social problems, including the definition of a social problem, political ideologies and theoretical perspectives for viewing social problems, applications of these perspectives, an assessment framework for viewing social problems, and guidelines for social problem–focused intervention through multilevel systems. Because social problems are the focus of the integrated-practice perspective, an understanding of the social problem as a concept provides a critical context for integrated practice.

Chapter 3, "Deviance and Labeling," presents the perspective of deviance and labeling for viewing the devalued status of client groups and develops a 14-step downward spiral of labeling, devaluation, and disempowerment that can occur with the victims of long-standing social problems. The spiral depicts how stigmatized problem carriers become alienated and disenfranchised from mainstream society. Normalization and competency-based screening are antidotes for the devaluation of these victims. These chapters establish the knowledge base for viewing social problems as a context for social work practice. With Part One as a foundation, Part Two deals with the context of deciding what to do.

Social Problems: Analysis and Intervention

I n a few years, the 21st century will arrive. People who were born in 1900 have witnessed the Industrial Revolution and its demise, the atomic age, the space age, and now the information age. They have observed two world wars, the Holocaust, and countless regional conflicts. They have seen societies collapse in some parts of the world. The social problems that have arisen at the end of the 20th century show no signs of receding. Certainly, they cannot be wished away. Looking back, we can perhaps be excused for approaching the next century with a sense of foreboding.

While looking backward may cause some apprehension, it need not prevent us from facing the social problems that lie ahead. A retrospective view can help us gain a sense of history, and through an understanding of history we can probe the genesis of many of our problems and begin to invent a future.

Because social problems will likely dominate our immediate future, this book is concerned with preparing social workers to intervene in the dynamics of these problems. We wish to promote a model of social work practice in which intervention with the victims is only one part of a larger interventive strategy.

Some readers may take issue with this position, contending with some justification that social problems are too large and too complex to be solved by social work or any other profession for that matter. Others might respond that social work has always addressed social problems. The issue, they say, isn't how simple or complex social problems are, but rather that social workers simply cannot be all things to all people.

This is true. We are not chemists, pharmacists, engineers, or physicists. We are professional social workers and that's the issue. The "social" in social work confronts us with how we want to define the social nature of our concerns. Do we want to confine our area of concern to the victims of social problems or expand the parameters to the generators of social problems as well? In short, how social should social work be?

If our conclusion is that social work is not about the business of engaging the origins of social problems, the next question should be "What are we about?" If social work's concern is not social problems, then whose concern is it? Social psychologists? Sociologists? Environmentalists? Lawyers? The clergy? The military? There seems to be no lack of takers.

Our proposition is that social workers should define as well as solve social problems. This proposition is based on three major tenets: (1) our history and our roots are firmly entrenched in defining and acting on social problems, (2) our unique "social" perspective provides us with an overview of social problems that other professions do not possess, and (3) our code of ethics call on us to "improve social conditions and to promote social justice" (National Association of Social Workers, 1980).

We will not retrace the actions of our founders in engaging social problems, but the roots are well established. From Edith Abbot, chief of the

Children's Bureau, to Grace Abbott, who called for unified state and local governmental response to public welfare (Abbott, 1930); to Florence Kelley, who exposed working conditions of women and children and became the pioneer in consumer advocacy (Smith & Zeitz, 1970); to Nobel Peace Prize recipient Jane Addams, founder of Hull House; to Dorothea Dix, and her efforts on behalf of the deaf and the mentally ill; to Mary Richmond, who spoke about rectifying social need in her landmark *Social Diagnosis* (Richmond, 1917); to Frances Perkins, Franklin Roosevelt's appointee to his cabinet and the first woman to sit there; to Harry Hopkins, director of the New Deal's Temporary Emergency Relief Administration; to Bertha Reynolds, trade union activist and social work educator dedicated to eradicating the root causes of war; to Wilbur Cohen, President Lyndon Johnson's appointee as under-secretary of Health Education and Welfare—we can call the roll of leaders who have addressed political and economic injustice.

We can look back with pride at our origins as muckrakers and social reformers, but somewhere along the way our erstwhile definers of social problems gave way to modern-day "treaters" of social problem victims. The power that went with highlighting social problems was forfeited and somehow transferred to disciplines that lack the unique perspective of social work.

We need only consult a daily newspaper to recognize that problems of magnitude are being defined unilaterally and simplistically. We can be appalled at fundamentalist ministers who declare in the name of the "moral majority" that AIDS is God's punishment for the sins of homosexuality or we can be angered at the Central Intelligence Agency's clumsy attempts to undermine unfriendly regimes, but we must recognize that the power to define social problems is in the public domain and is a matter of competing in the world of ideas. Others will define problems for us, if we choose not to define them ourselves.

We may well have arrived at a time in our development when the old definitions of problems are in decline. If so, the time is opportune for the modern-day social worker to move back into the limelight. By training and inclination, today's practitioner is steeped in the knowledge of the interplay among social systems and their environment. The systems principle—"The whole is greater than the sum of the parts"—has special meaning for the present-day social worker who practices at the vortex of intermeshing social problems. Who has a better vantage point of the origins of social problems and their impact on humans? Who better understands the relationship between social conditions and the promulgation and maintenance of social problems? While we cannot claim any instant panaceas, we view the world from the unique perspective of the devalued people we represent.

THE SCOPE OF SOCIAL PROBLEMS

Attempting to draw boundaries around social problems is a daunting experience. We are unable to neatly excise the problem of homelessness from that of poverty, alcoholism, or chronic mental illness, nor can domestic violence be viewed outside the context of other violence. Social problems are inextricably linked. This linkage extends beyond the problems themselves to the increasing global connections among nations (Kennedy, 1993). For example, population explosion in one part of the world has implications for the food-growing capacity of the entire world. Practices that increase global warming in the United States will have repercussions elsewhere on the planet.

Given this relationship, certainly no single profession commands the resources to solve major social problems. Social work isn't unique in this respect. Historically, impacts on major problems have been achieved through the commitment of the energy and expertise of many disciplines, acting in concert with the support of a large part of the population. Some problems (witchcraft, for example) have been "solved" by citizens' deciding over time that the problem was not really a problem after all. Yet the importance of other problems wanes when the "definers" take their final journey to the cemetery. Of course, they are ultimately replaced by new definers with new definitions.

Can We Do Anything About Social Problems?

Construction of a reality about the cause-and-effect relationships that explain social problems ultimately establishes parameters for modifying them. Weick describes this aptly:

> The massive scale on which social problems are conceived often precludes innovative action because the limits of bounded rationality are exceeded and arousal is raised to dysfunctionally high levels. People often define social problems in ways that overwhelm their ability to do anything about them. [1984, p. 40]

When the public feels overwhelmed by the complexity and ambiguity of social problems, they are more susceptible to accepting simple, even simplistic, definitions. Problems are thus attributed to a single cause, creating the illusion that the problem is at last manageable and therefore is amenable to less complex interventions (Baker & Anderson, 1987, p. 55). While such problems may appear to be solvable, single-cause interventions often result in unintended consequences. The worst consequence may be that while remaining beyond solution, the problem becomes even more intractable.

Violent crime is one example. The problem is initially defined in terms of violent criminals. According to the common wisdom, there are so many violent criminals because too many have been released from jail or prison. It is further assumed that a longer incarceration would result in less violent behavior. Thus, the solution to the problem is to jail violent criminals for longer periods. To achieve this solution, judges must impose longer sentences, and parole boards must delay granting parole. The result is yet another social problem; prison overcrowding. The solution to prison overcrowding is to build or expand prisons. And this is accomplished by taxing citizens to build more cell space. This money must be derived from a finite source, which, in the zero-sum nature of the budgeting game, means someone must surrender some of their financial resources to build these correctional facilities. Once built, the cells will be filled, but will that solve the problem of violent crime or prison overcrowding? Probably not. The newly created monster will likely become an expensive downpayment on more violence in the future.

Many social problems are defined as "emergencies." While such definitions may spur public interest and response, they also imply that problems can be addressed through emergency measures rather than through a serious examination of social policy, which might produce more comprehensive and long-range solutions (Lipsky & Smith, 1989).

What we see in the violent criminal scenario is a common theme in attempts at social problem solving: "If what is being done doesn't control the problem, do more of it." Thus, the industry sanctioned to manage the problem is regularly expanded to manage it in even greater magnitude. This is not social problem solving or even social problem management. The ever-expanding problem finally outgrows its managers until management becomes a matter of processing people who are the "carriers" of the problem.

Our challenge, it seems, is to avoid the extremes of becoming overwhelmed and immobilized by complex definitions of social problems and of being seduced into doing the wrong things by simple single-cause formulations. Can we find this middle ground?

Who Is to Blame?

Characteristically, social problems have been interpreted within the dichotomy of two competing explanations: the person-blame approach and the systems-blame approach (Eitzen, 1983). The person-blame orientation holds individuals responsible for their plight. Crime is thus attributed to "bad" people. School failure is blamed on unmotivated students and apathetic parents. On the other hand, systems-blame advocates see people as victims of insensitive social institutions. Crime flows from a racist criminal justice system and school failure is an expected by-product of inadequate curriculum and unmotivated or culturally insensitive teachers. The ongoing debate between these two schools of thought has become polarized and largely unproductive. Public education is unlikely to be enhanced if the discussion continues at this level.

Social problem solving is first and foremost a political process conducted in the public arena. It demands that the problem be placed on the public agenda for debate and discussion, with the ultimate goal being a more informed level of public awareness and interest. Public education requires some forethought. As noted earlier, the kind of reality construction used to explain a problem also describes its ultimate solution.

Defining Social Problems

What is a social problem? Rubington and Weinberg define it as:

> An alleged situation that is incompatible with the values of a significant number of people who agree that action is needed to alter the situation. Such a definition is useful in that it can be dissected and examined. [1989, p. 4]

"An Alleged Situation."   Saying there is a problem doesn't mean there necessarily is one, but if the public believes a problem exists, their belief system will likely override evidence to the contrary.

In the 1950s, Senator Joseph McCarthy convinced a large segment of the general public that Communists were infiltrating the government. Although this was not the case, the allegation outweighed the public's ability to see beyond their fear and hatred.

"Incompatible with Values."   Inherent in a social problem is value conflict. Some part of the population feels that their values are being sacrificed or trampled on. This is particularly true with regard to abortion. The value of "life" held by the "right-to-life" advocates is in direct conflict with the value of "choice" held by the "pro-choice" proponents.

"Significant Number of People."   This phrase doesn't signify a majority by any means. A "significant" number may be a minority because, as we know, some people are more significant than others. On the abortion issue, for example, polls indicate that the pro-life faction represents a minority of the population, yet they have enough power in many communities to define the issue on their own terms. Gun control, another volatile issue, has been defined and controlled by another minority, the National Rifle Association, even though polls show that a vast majority of the population would prefer more stringent control of weapons.

"Action Is Needed." When a social problem is identified, there is agreement that action is required but not what that action should be. Antiabortionists would have a constitutional amendment outlawing abortion while pro-choicers would promote public education, family planning, and birth control. Neither side would find common cause with the other's position.

Our working definition of a social problem is as follows:

> An adverse social condition that is commonly recognized as having developed to a point of seriousness, such that collective action must be taken to minimize its impact on society and to prevent and/or control its growth.

As noted earlier, social problem definitions are political in nature. "Economic, political and social institutions determine the allocation of scarce economic resources and goods; through these allocative patterns, social problems are defined and emerge" (Gordon, 1977, p. xiii). According to Ross and Staines (1972), unmet human need is perceived as a social problem to the degree that there is substantial divergence between reality and an ever-demanding ideal. The solution to social problems, in their view, involves a sequence of defining problems, transforming them into public issues, and subjecting them to competing political analyses with a resulting conflict that ultimately results in political outcomes.

POLITICAL IDEOLOGIES AND SOCIAL PROBLEM DEFINITION

Ideological perspectives about the political system and how change comes about are important in that they influence how social problems are defined by the power structure, how we as professionals choose to be involved in that definition, and the nature of interventions in which we will engage.

Three principal analytic and normative ideologies are most typically applied to understanding the political economy of social problems in the United States: the radical, liberal, and conservative views of society. Each interprets the sources of problems differently, tends to suggest varying solutions, and draws different implications for the direction of social interventions.

Radical

Radical ideology suggests that social problems are inevitable and will always be present in a classist, sexist, racist system that sets up inequality and injustice through class differences that are further magnified in a capitalistic system. Solutions can come about only as a result of completely changing or restructuring the social, political, and economic systems. This perspective drives the thinking in the critical perspective of social problems, which will be discussed later. From this perspective, people are seen as victims and treated by those in power as "exploited objects" rather than as partners; therefore, they have to fight to gain power and access to social resources. Social work approaches involve environmentally active change, initiating class advocacy and social and political action (Billups, 1984).

The liberal and conservative analyses of social problems begin with the same underlying view of society; that is, the market produces an income distribution in which some earn too little to live, and therefore, some way should be found to assist the poorest. Each of these perspectives insists that problems develop from minor imperfections in the basic social mechanisms, principally from inadequate information or shortsightedness among individuals. But the two ideologies differ on what should be done about such problems.

Liberal

In the liberal view, the state reflects individual wishes through group representatives. The government is justified in acting because it incorporates the preferences of all individuals and seeks to advance the interests of all citizens. From this perspective, individuals and groups are seen as healthy "citizens," "participants," or "members" who are potentially vulnerable to becoming "lesser partners." Social work approaches include prevention, education, and increased opportunity structures (Billups, 1984). There are three principal kinds of government action that society both prefers and requires. First, the government should redistribute income. Second, the government should act when private-market mechanisms cannot effectively satisfy consumer preferences. Third, the government should act to provide certain goods that the market mechanism is incapable of providing, like national defense. Such ideological views of the political economy support several problem perspectives like social pathology, social disorganization, value conflict, and deviancy and labeling, all of which will be discussed later.

Conservative

The conservative ideology views the political system as basically functional and best left alone. It proposes instead to change individuals and their behavior. Problems are seen as failures in individuals, not in the system; therefore, problems are owned by individuals, not by the system. This ideology opts to keep government's role limited in the search for solutions and stresses change in individuals and subgroups instead (Dluhy, 1981). Social pathology perspectives and some views of deviant behavior have their roots in this ideology. Individuals and groups are seen as "clients," "patients," "maladjusted," or "deviants." The predominant social work approach involves clinical and direct service approaches aimed at helping people adjust to their social environment. The differences represented among these three perspectives impact the nature and direction of social policy and programs in this country. As York (1982, p. 50) points out, "differences in perceptions of social problems among groups suggest that the definition and analysis of social concerns may be as much 'political' as 'rational.'"

Political ideologies reflect philosophical views of the causes of social problems and influence attempts at intervention. These orientations to understanding problems will be described.

PHILOSOPHICAL PERSPECTIVES OF SOCIAL PROBLEMS

Rubington and Weinberg (1989) have traced the development of social problems through six different sociological perspectives: social pathology, social disorganization, value conflict, deviant behavior, labeling, and the critical perspective. These perspectives are derived from the political ideologies discussed earlier and are discussed here in terms of their implications for explaining social problems and social work interventions.

Social Pathology

Social problems were not recognized as such until the late eighteenth century (Green, 1975). Until then, social conditions were considered beyond human intervention and were explained away in the name of God. Social pathology, although now considered a simple approach to understanding social problem phenomena was in retrospect a conceptual breakthrough.

By its very name, *social pathology* infers a disease model. Emanating from conservative political ideology, social pathology views organisms as healthy by nature and thus "good." A disease process begins when the organism fails to adapt to its surroundings or when parts (i.e., individuals) of the organism interfere with or fail to adjust to the organism. Social pathologists tend to spread the problem among both the "bad" institutions and the "bad" people. Problems are defined in moralistic terms, and social problems are thus easily recognized as deviations from moral expectations.

Since disease can spread, it is important to restore the organism to health by socializing people to the proper value system, appropriate attitudes, and acceptable behaviors.

Social pathology certainly had its impact on early social work practice. As one of its goals, the Settlement House movement taught people how to behave within the constraints of middle class morals, in part to curb the spread of undesirable behaviors (Weinberg, Rubington, & Hammersmith, 1981). The good intentions behind the early penitentiaries, which paved the way to the hell of our modern prisons, was not to punish inmates but to prevent them from infecting or being infected by other inmates with the contamination of criminality.

There appears to be some resurgence of the social pathology ideation at this stage of our development, although currently social pathologists are less inclined to blame individuals for creating the sick society. Instead, a sick society is blamed for producing sick individuals. The sick society concept, coming from a more radical political ideology, provided the impetus for many alternative communal settlements that sprung up during the 1960s. Founded on the premise that communes could somehow shut out the larger diseased society, these experiments were short lived, perhaps demonstrating more than anything else the problems of life in a closed system (Vonnegut, 1975).

One severe limitation of this construction of reality is that its moral orientation causes it to be very arbitrary and absolute in defining what is "right" in a culturally pluralistic society. Modern-day social pathologists, speaking as leaders of emerging social movements, may use the terms *public education* or *moral education* (Edelman & Goldstein, 1981) in presenting their goals, but they are ultimately faced with a serious question: "Which public is to be educated, and whose morals are to be taught?"

Politically, defining social problems as pathological more likely places the responsibility for resolution into the realm of the health and mental health industries (Weinberg, Rubington, & Hammersmith, p. 16). Defining victims of social problems as "patients" who are "sick," while perhaps humane and well intentioned, detracts from their personal responsibility for their behavior and restrains their empowerment.

Yet we should not dismiss social pathology out of hand. There appears to be an emerging realization of the need for some societal consensus regarding moral standards. Bloom (1987), in his discussion of "nihilism, American style," decries "philosophic indifference to good and evil" and pleads for the responsibility of the university community in matters of moral education. Relativism can be a problematic concept when society finds itself in need of a sense of community and social control. The "social conscience," which has sometimes been attributed to social work, can provide an important element to a society in search of moral standards.

Social Disorganization

As waves of immigrants were incorporated into the "melting pot" of our country, it became apparent that some groups melted quicker than others while some seemed not to melt at all. Absorbing people from all over the globe into the fabric of a single nation was difficult, but another movement was taking place within the country. Rural inhabitants were moving to the city and staying, even though they lacked the knowledge and skills needed to live in an urban environment. The problems generated by this chaos could no longer be accounted for by social pathology. The new explanation was *social disorganization* (Rubington & Weinberg, 1989).

Social problems were interpreted as manifestations of the lack of fit between the old culture and the demands of the new environment. When old behaviors no longer worked, the rules that had governed social situations gave way as well. The societal machine that had hummed so smoothly now teetered on the edge of a breakdown. Too much change in too short a period had created social environments that were alienating and disorganizing.

Coming from a more liberal political ideology, social disorganization has a ring of authenticity in explaining many social problems, even today. The flow of immigrants to the United States has never really ceased and has even increased recently (Kennedy, 1993, p. 312). Migration from rural to urban America is only now slowing. Some people still fail to melt into the mainstream. We have attempted to reorient ourselves to this problem by modifying our language; substituting *mosaic* for melting pot, while affirming the reality and the value of "cultural pluralism."

When social disorganization is considered the driving force behind social problems, its reverse—social organization—becomes the key to intervention. *Social planning, change agent, systems analysis,* and *central planning* are just some of the terms that have been added to the lexicon of social work practice as a result of this perspective. When the system gets out of line, it is "fixed" by integrating the parts, limiting growth, enacting necessary social controls, and enforcing them. In short, the system is engineered until equilibrium is restored.

This machine orientation to society is consistent with the high-technology drive of this country. In the information age, all problems seem to be quantifiable and can be "crunched" as numbers are apparently meant to be. Answers can be found in the computer printout. Management information systems will provide us with the required feedback loops. Even world peace can be realized through something called the "Strategic Defense Initiative." Not too long ago, one computer company advertised its products as "not just data; reality."

Solving social problems through social engineering has proved a mixed blessing. At the very least, it has resulted in a number of unintended consequences. In the 1960s urban renewal came to be known as "negro removal,'' contributing to the already serious low-income need for housing. Limiting growth, where it was tried, did in fact achieve that goal, only to drive up real estate prices well beyond the reach of many people. Deinstitutionalization of the mentally ill contributed to a new horror show, the homeless mentally ill, while decriminalization of drunkenness, in the absence of substitute programs, simply left the sufferers to "detoxify" on the streets, where they joined the mentally ill as fair game for predators. Free from asylum, they both dropped to the bottom of the survival chain.

On the positive side, social engineering has brought a sense of rationality and accountability into many human service delivery systems and has forced closer scrutiny of service gaps and overlaps through community needs assessments. Planning technologies have given us a sounder basis for social welfare decision making and hold promise for the future as long as we can recognize the difference between data and reality. We must make certain that these technologies are combined with a sense of values and purpose.

Value Conflict

As the phenomenon of conflict increasingly became a subject for scrutiny, a new social reality called value conflict began to emerge as an explanation for social problems (Rubington & Weinberg, 1989).

In this more normalized view of social conflict, problems could be explained rather simply in terms of one group's values rubbing another group's values the wrong way. In seeking their ultimate expression, competing values clash, creating arenas of conflict. Within these arenas, the competing views create a highly polarized environment in which one group emerges as more dominant and dominating while the weaker group feels oppressed and victimized.

Adherence to the value-conflict interpretation of social problems is likely to lead toward revolutionary rather than resolutionary forms of redress. Change becomes less a process of finding answers to problems than a condition of ongoing struggle, where the oppressed group asserts its rights in the face of resistance from the oppressing group. Conflict is normal; thus, it is expected and even promoted as a means of achieving reform. This approach requires no elaborate theories to explain social problems, and the proposed reforms are fairly simple although not painless. Problems are ameliorated as the subservient group acts to preserve or promote its social interests until social arrangements are altered. In this context, problem resolution is an ongoing contest and social action is the primary weapon.

Confrontation and other high-contest forms of intervention are congruent with social work practice as long as they do not include physical violence and are guided by the principle of least contest; that is, the application of no more conflict than is deemed necessary to achieve the professional goals (Specht, 1969). Social action, social reform, and various social movements have had a long-standing, legitimate place in the curriculum of schools of social work, although their emphasis has waxed and waned. Tactics such as strikes and boycotts and the skills of negotiation, bargaining, and mediation are standard fare in most community organization classes. Saul Alinsky, one of the most ardent social actionists, skeptical as he was of professional social work, would be warmed to see that he has a host of admirers among social work students.

Value conflict and the attendant social conflict coming from both radical and liberal political ideologies have created a practice demand for some relatively new skills: conflict resolution and conflict management. The attendant role, that of mediator, forces the practitioner to scrutinize the limits of this role. Conflict resolution, having as its goal the termination of conflict, must deal with two important considerations: whether a conflict should necessarily be terminated, and whether conflict resolution has become a value in its own right (Bloom, 1987). The danger of resolving conflict simply to alleviate tension is that the mediator is tempted to ignore the degree of right and wrong in the opposing positions. Instead, it is much easier to validate both positions, proceed, and, through compromise, leave both contestants feeling dissatisfied and possibly sold out.

An example of this is the social issue of abortion. To the right-to-life movement, abortion is murder, which is even more reprehensible in that it has been sanctioned by the Supreme Court. In the eyes of this movement, it is a serious social problem that should be criminalized. To the pro-choice advocates, abortion is an issue of the degree of control a woman has over her body. Abortion is seen as a medical procedure that has been practiced since the beginning of humankind and will continue to be practiced with or without the sanction of law. This conflict is unlikely to be resolved through mediation because of the strong right-wrong connotations. More important, it is unlikely that mediation would be useful in the long run. The depth of feeling involved is unlikely to be surrendered. Resolution will likely be the result of public education, the resoluteness of law, advances in medicine, and the passage of time.

Deviant Behavior

This theory of social problems takes unresolved value conflict to its next logical step—*deviant behavior* (Rubington & Weinberg, 1989). As previously noted, the least-powerful group, whose values are being stepped on and who feels oppressed, eventually reaches a point when its members no longer feel bonded to the society in which they live. Their social bonds are so weakened that their integration is marginal at best. Their behavior may take on aspects of withdrawal or conformity or asocial and antisocial activity.

In the deviance school of thought, coming from a radical and liberal ideology, people who cannot identify with the larger society are left to find their identifications elsewhere, usually with other deviants who share their contempt for the predominant culture. A subculture or counterculture is thus created, which may seek out illegitimate opportunity (Cloward & Ohlin, 1965) and thus become an enemy of the people. To the extent that its members are highly visible and deviate markedly from the norms of the majority, they may become targeted for rehabilitation or reeducation.

This is where social work professionals enter the picture. Social work has been very much at home in the realm of rehabilitation. Whether in the form of casework, counseling, individual or group psychotherapy, or various self-help groups, rehabilitation has historically been our stock-in-trade. It is perhaps the one area in which we have the most societal sanction.

As a means of intervening in social problems, however, rehabilitation presents some serious impediments. Besides operating on a case-by-case approach, which is expensive and inefficient, rehabilitation is based on an assumption that devalued people can be motivated to invest themselves in the society from which they feel alienated. It also assumes that the society wants the deviant back in its fold. Both are questionable assumptions. People who have become deviants are faced with some strong driving and restraining forces that maintain this status. Rehabilitation programs, which often fail to deal with alienation and disempowerment, may in fact contribute to more alienation. This ultimately leads to public disillusionment with and withdrawal of support from such programs.

Labeling

Just as deviance is an extension of value conflict, the *labeling* view of social problem construction is an extension of deviance (Rubington & Weinberg, 1989). As observers, we find it difficult to resist the urge to classify what we experience. Our language permits us to classify rocks, animals, and plants and, as a consequence, create the disciplines of geology, zoology, and botany. In the same manner, the social sciences of sociology, anthropology, and psychology have developed. Deviant behavior ultimately resulted in a refinement of psychology, resulting in the creation of abnormal psychology and its attendant classifications.

But the labeling process is not in the naming alone. The ultimate impact rests with the new reality the label creates for the labeled and the extent to which it provides an identity. If the label solidifies an identity, it provides behavioral guidelines and possibly a new role. If successful, the labeling process can cause the person to ''become'' the referent, so to speak.

For the person who has stolen, negative labeling can facilitate a bridge to "being a thief."

This can have both positive and negative consequences. When a negative label becomes the person's description, it can freeze identity in that direction. Thus the underclass status associated with the racial epithet "nigger," carries with it the requirement of subservience unless one is relabeled "bad nigger," in which case the label connotes defiance or even violence. In either case, one who incorporates this label unto him/herself is a member of a caste and for all practical purposes is also an outcast.

A case can be made for positive labeling in the word *alcoholic.* "I am an alcoholic," the self-imposed label for members of Alcoholics Anonymous, takes advantage of the expectations of temporary sobriety, social support, and recovery that exist within members of AA.

If negative labeling can devalue people, positive labeling can value them, and therein lies its attractiveness for social work. Labeling, whether positive or negative, is a by-product of human interaction. Since social work practice is also interactional (Shulman, 1991), the antidote to negative labeling can be found in neutral or positive labeling. Redefining social situations in ways that value diversity emphasizes normalization of behavior, promotes competency rather than pathology, creates least-restrictive environments, and in some cases suggests purposeful nonintervention. All of these changes hold promise for linking people to their environments.

As with all of the orientations we have discussed, labeling carries some limitations. It joins the others in failing to adequately explain many social problems and does not account for the many people who are negatively labeled and then go on to avoid deviance.

Critical Perspective

At first examination, the critical perspective might appear to be an extension of the value-conflict explanation of social problems. In some respects, this is the case; however, this perspective, rooted as it is by the writings of Karl Marx, examines value conflicts within the larger context of class conflict (Rubington & Weinberg, pp. 235–241), as well as conflicts of gender, sexual orientation, race, and ethnicity. In particular, this perspective is a critique and criticism of the capitalist economic system. It purports that capitalism, in terms of its exploitation of the lower class, is inherently problematic and destructive.

In the critical perspective, clearly associated with the radical political ideology, capitalism acting as a servant of the upper class exploits the poor, creating poverty that in turn feeds other social problems such as crime and physical and mental illness. Moving society away from capitalism calls for radical measures, possibly even revolution, to achieve a classless society.

This perspective has always had a niche in social work. Most recently, it has been best articulated as the "radical perspective." This perspective views the social welfare system as a servant of the capitalist economic system in "regulating the poor" (Piven & Cloward, 1971). Galper defined radical social work as:

> Social work that has not compromised its own commitment to human welfare. It is social work that takes very seriously the dilemma of a people-serving profession in a people-denying society and tries to resolve that dilemma by finding ways for the profession to be of real service rather than by accommodating itself to conventional arrangements. [1975, p. 189]

The critical perspective has been criticized as being a political ideology rather than a theory. Its major flaw is that it can neither be proved nor disproved (Rubington & Weinberg, 1989).

The critical perspective presents social work with serious political obstacles in its efforts to intervene in social problems. Social work is a liberal institution, which is not given to radical departures from the existing political and economic system, and it is further constrained by its commitment to gradual reform of that system.

Since much or most of social work directly or indirectly depends on what local, state, and federal levels of government decide to do, the political and economic reality is that its boundaries are somewhere between the conservative and liberal points on the political continuum.

A conservative-to-moderate national political view prevails, which generally resists moving away from the status quo, sanctioning those changes that benefit the capitalist system. For example, conservatives would "privatize" social services, thereby removing government from the business of social work to whatever degree possible.

Marxism's decline in the world may also have undermined the critical perspective to some extent. Since Marxist governments have been unable to resolve the social problems that they have considered capitalist in origin, the credibility of their proposals has been damaged.

In short, there are very few job descriptions for social workers who would intervene from a purely radical or critical social work perspective. However, system-based causes cannot be ignored simply because the message of the critical perspective happens to be unpopular.

APPLICATION OF PERSPECTIVES

How would the six perspectives view a specific problem? In Chapter 1 we explored the problem of high school dropouts, examining how two social workers intervened in a high school community to impact the problem.

Let us discuss here how the reality of this problem would be constructed through the six perspectives.

Social Pathology

In this view, the school dropout would be the primary focus of attention, although the schools might be considered "sick" institutions. The dropouts or potential dropouts would receive counseling and enter treatment programs. They would be urged to stay in school at any cost. Special programs would be designed to give special attention in alternative classrooms. By keeping these kids in schools, proponents of this view would hope that they would avoid being "contaminated" by gangs or becoming unemployable.

Social Disorganization

The schools themselves would be the target of change in the social disorganization view. Having been designed for the industrial age, the school would be seen as obsolete in the rapidly developing information age. Educators, curriculum, student architecture, and school boundaries would all be fair game for study, with the findings providing a basis for a "master plan" for education. This master plan would include a dropout prevention program.

Value Conflict

The question here is "Who controls the schools and for what purpose?" School dropouts are seen as the natural consequence of an administration that devalues and discriminates against youth who do not identify with its goals or go along with its methods. Reducing dropout behavior would focus on teachers: hiring more culturally sensitive teachers, removing biased teachers, and training teachers to become more aware of the needs of the populations where dropouts are more prevalent.

Deviant Behavior

This perspective would classify the behavior of dropping out of school as a deviation from the norm. Intervention would occur in much the same way as the social pathology view. Students would be put into counseling. In addition, peer and public pressure would be used to encourage at-risk students to stay in school. Self-help efforts would be directed toward parents of dropouts to control their children's absences and motivate them to remain in school.

Labeling

Labeling would explain dropping out of school as a natural consequence of the students' having come to the conclusion that they are "different" in being unable to handle the school environment and having identified with negative labels (i.e., "slow learner," "behavior problem," "resistive," "hard to reach," etc.), that had been applied to them. Dropping out would be a behavior geared to avoid the unpleasantness of being identified daily in these terms. Programs to return the youth to schools might include experimental classrooms where positive labels could be substituted for negative ones.

Critical Perspective

Schools would be viewed as a servant of the larger capitalist system. Schools serve the system by preparing a labor force. Some students are channeled toward college, others toward trades with little concern for the students' aspirations. Under these conditions, many students leave because they feel oppressed. The solution is for the schools to be dismantled and returned to service under greater citizen control.

Summary of Perspectives

Whatever assets, liabilities, and practice implications are inherent in these six perspectives, each has its own unique reality. In terms of interpreting problem dynamics, a social worker would not dismiss any of them, even though value conflict, deviance and labeling, and the critical perspective seem to fit the interactional mode of social work practice better than social pathology and social disorganization and thus hold more potential for empowerment as an intervention.

Social pathology seems to have a declining place in social problem–oriented practice in view of its inclination to medicalize, psychiatrize, and "treat" the people who bear the burden of societal problems. While it may not blame victims, it does little or nothing to empower them either.

Social disorganization is also delimiting. While it offers insights into how society breaks down, it provides little input to those who are victimized, leaving societal reorganization to the "experts." Although social workers can be considered experts, our values demand that we proceed with caution in social engineering and that we must have consumer involvement in the change effort.

The value-conflict orientation reveals to social workers the reality of an interactionist perspective. One important reservation, however, is that not every problem yields to social action. Confrontation and public demonstrations require high levels of energy. Targets of social action develop methods of insulating themselves from high contest situations. The 1960s taught us that social conflict could create change, but it also taught us that social conflict does not necessarily stabilize change as we can see by the recent erosion of civil rights gains.

Deviancy and labeling are the two perspectives that seem to promise greater likelihood of promoting consumer empowerment. These approaches help us better comprehend how certain populations are placed at risk by society and how they can take steps to reorient and reorganize themselves into a more potent, valued segment of that society. Such steps are necessary if gains and achievements are to be institutionalized.

The critical perspective brings a badly needed political and economic critique to the problem definition process. It forces the investigator to consider problem carriers as unwitting, and sometimes unwilling, pawns in the political process and in so doing points the way for ultimate political reforms. However, the limited political power of the social work profession and society's skepticism of radical perspectives leave the critical perspective somewhat weakened as a useful frame of reference for intervention.

Regardless of which perspectives are used to explain social problems, social work practice focused on social problems has to consider the nature of the problems.

SOCIAL PROBLEM ASSESSMENT

In 1961 the Ford Foundation funded a National Association of Social Workers (NASW) project to define more clearly social work's contribution to solving social problems. The project was partly intended to promote the concept of prevention while establishing an improved understanding of how to intervene in social problems. Drs. Herman Stein and Irving Sarnoff developed a model for social problem analysis in connection with this project; the model is reproduced here in its final form. It requires some elaboration but is an excellent guide for problem assessment. Let us examine how it works in practice.

Model for Social Problem Analysis

The Problem
◆ Definition of the problem
  - Definition of the terms
  - Who "suffers" from the problem and with what consequences?
  - Who defines it as a problem? Why?
  - Who does not define it as a problem? Why?
◆ Etiology of the problem (as problem is defined)—sources
  - Inherent in social structure
  - Inherent in individual personality
  - In existing organizations designed to cope with the problem
  - In transitory social phenomenon
  - Other

Values
◆ Societal norms and values
  - Supporting existence of the problem
  - Opposing existence of the problem
  - Neutral to the problem

Current Operations—"The Actual"
◆ Social work operations related to the problem
  - Implicit definitions of the problem
  - Implicit value perspectives
  - Congruence with societal norms
  - Congruence with posited social work values
◆ Nonsocial work operations related to the problem
  - Implicit definitions of the problem
  - Implicit value perspectives
  - Congruence with societal norms
  - Congruence with social work norms
◆ Consequences of continuation of present program
  - For the extension or diminution of the social problem
  - For social work programs related to it
  - For nonsocial work programs related to it

Objectives—"The Ideal"
◆ The value position for social work advanced—the social change objective

---

Model for Social Problem Analysis (continued)

◆ Implications
  – Relationship to existing societal norms
  – Implications for change of societal norms
  – Relationship to existing norms of the social work profession and organizational framework
  – Implications for change of social work norms
◆ Total view of program approaches consonant with analysis of etiology and value position advanced
◆ The sector appropriate to social work
  – Existing definition of scope and function
  – Revised definition of scope and function
◆ The sector appropriate to nonsocial work operations
  – Identify nonsocial work groups in relation to program objectives
  – Relationship of social work to each of these

Relationship Between the Actual and the Ideal
◆ Specification of the gap between the actual and the ideal
◆ Sources of resistance to closing the gap
  – In social work
  – Outside social work
◆ Sources of support for closing the gap
  – In social work
  – Outside social work
◆ Action priorities for social work
  – In direct operation
  – Intrasocial work change in norms and organizational framework
  – In relation to nonsocial work groups and forces
◆ The needs in theory and research
  – For specifying etiology
  – For testing programs

Source: Cohen, 1964, pp. xi–xiii.

The Problem

This model for social problem analysis begins with an attempt to define the problem and determine its causes.

Definition of the Problem

One of the greatest impediments to problem solving is the difficulty we experience in problem definition. To be able to define a problem accurately is an important step in finding a solution.

The first step in this process is to glean the facts and weave them into a problem statement. This should be done as nonjudgmentally as possible. Thus, it is important to report the results or output of the problem on the total community: sufferers, victims, and nonsufferers as well. While giving an account of the pain and suffering of those bearing the burden of the problem is necessary, one should keep in mind that financial and any other significant impacts in the community at large bear heavily on its acceptance of a problem as such. It is possible to frame a problem in such a manner as to spread the ownership of it. Ownership and power to define a condition as a problem are central issues in problem definition.

The AIDS epidemic provides an example. Initially, AIDS was a problem of commonly devalued populations, first Africans and Haitians, then intravenous drug users (mostly African American), then gays. As long as the disease was defined in these terms, it was not felt to be a major problem. Later, when it affected babies born to drug users and heterosexuals, the problem was considered more severe. Ownership of the AIDS problem increased greatly when it was seen as a threat to the blood supply. When the financial cost of the eventual exponential growth of the disease was projected, the problem became a concern to almost everyone.

Etiology of the Problem

Once we have elicited facts about the problem, we move to its cause. Social problems are usually attributed to multiple causes. The safest course of action is to begin by identifying known causes. If causes are not known, then the problem should be so framed. If there are assumed causes, that too should be stated. Too often problem solving fails because the would-be solvers intervene ''in the dark,'' so to speak.

The drug problem is a perfect example. What are the roots of drug abuse? The initial view was that drugs were used by weak, immoral people; thus the problem was in the individual user. In the 1960s, the drug problem was considered a phenomenon of the counterculture, something that would pass. As the problem defied solution, it was said to be the result of a drug-dependent society or a function of hard-rock music. During political campaigns, the definitions took on political overtones and soft, ineffective, underfunded law enforcement became the attributed cause. Some found the cause in the drug-dependent economies of Central and South America. Perspectives of social problems suggest different philosophies of etiology that are driven by political ideology. Etiology is elusive and often deters preventive intervention because of its shifting nature.

Values

Anyone who has been involved in an assault on a social problem has probably witnessed that the problem usually strikes back, sometimes in unusual ways. Solving a problem usually requires that social arrangements must change as well. Change is resisted, however, because someone usually benefits from conditions remaining as they are. Social problems are enmeshed in conflicting societal norms and values.

A youthful child-protective worker serving a rural agricultural county found to her surprise that her efforts at protecting children from child abuse were unwanted by many members of the local clergy. They were uncooperative and rebuffed her attempts to work with abusing families. Some of the Protestant fundamentalist ministers viewed child rearing as a ''family concern.'' Several Catholic priests considered the problem to be a private concern between the parents and the church. Both saw the presence of a public child-protection worker as a threat to their values. The worker was able to penetrate this resistance only by requesting intervention of church officials at a higher level. As a result, local clergy were able to reconcile the value of public social services with the community's religious values.

In problem analysis, community values must be considered because they provide the context for the problem's definition. Areas of opposition should be anticipated and, if possible, identified.

Current Operations

This part of social problem analysis involves taking stock of current social work and non–social work efforts and determining what results have been achieved. A possible outcome might be a forecast of whether the problem will be reduced or exacerbated in the light of sustained efforts.

Examining non–social work operations as well helps the practitioner understand that intervention into social problems requires the involvement of networks of agencies that are related to the population at risk. Interorganizational coordination is one of the basic skills the worker must develop. It will be discussed in Chapter 10 as a part of the broker role.

Domestic violence is a problem that has been impacted by interorganizational efforts. Early attempts to curb battering were largely led by grassroots organizations that focused their efforts on the police and their methods of dealing with domestic disturbance calls. As the police began to arrest more batterers, reverberations spread throughout the entire system of agencies managing the problem. Eventually police, jails, shelters, district attorneys, probation officers, judges, hospitals, mental health centers, crisis centers, self-help organizations, and other related agencies were forced to interact and plan together. The result in many communities has been improved practice regarding domestic violence and a reduction in rearrests.

Objectives

Knowing the state of current operations sets the stage for setting change objectives. The interorganizational network or action system working on the problem should determine the objectives. Objectives consist of a description of outcomes that project how the problem is expected to look after the intervention. They establish a parameter for the scope of the intervention; namely, how extensive an effort should be made. Objectives do not reveal how something will be accomplished, only what outcome is intended.

Within the network of agencies, individual social work organizations are faced with making certain their objectives are congruent with total objectives.

Relationship Between the Actual and the Ideal

In this part of social problem analysis, a determination is made as to what resources are needed to close the gap between the current state of the problem and the state that would occur if the practice objectives were achieved.

Finally, action plans are formulated that establish who (which agency) will do what (specific action) by when (specific date) and how (strategies, methods, and tactics). Action planning is the preliminary step to intervention.

SOCIAL PROBLEM INTERVENTION

Social problem intervention includes multilevel systems assessment, communication across systems from microsystems to macrosystems, and promotion and prevention.

Guidelines for Social Problem–Focused Practice

Workers who focus on social problems must be prepared to operate from different guidelines. This may create some initial discomfort because the

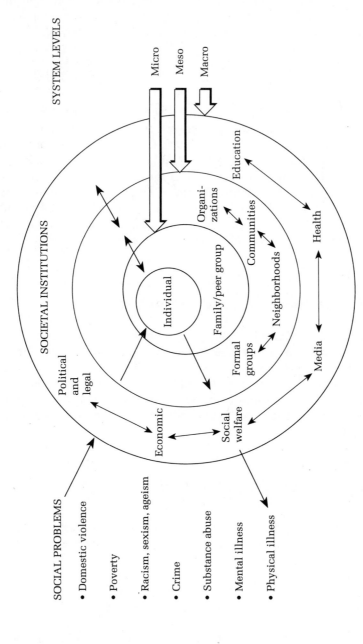

Figure 2.1 Social problems embedded across social systems

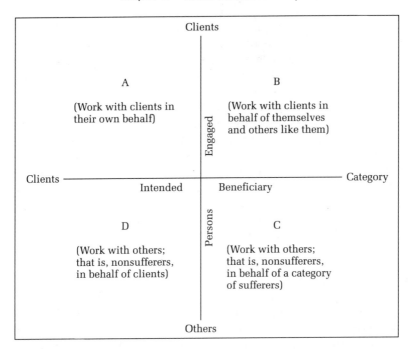

Figure 2.2 Quadrant model of intervention participants and beneficiaries. *Source:* From *The Structural Approach to Direct Practice in Social Work* by G. Wood-Goldberg and R. Middleman. Copyright © 1989 by Columbia University press, New York. Reprinted with permission.

area of concern is broader and community demands will be more stringent. Social problems are not located in one system. They are embedded among all levels, from microsystems to macrosystems, as presented schematically in Figure 2.1.

Interactions across various system levels both create and respond to social problems. Microsystems such as individuals, families, and groups interact with one another and with mesosystems such as communities, neighborhoods, and organizations. Mesosystems interact with the larger macrosystems and societal institutions such as the legal system, economic system, media, and social welfare systems around the conditions that have been defined as social problems. Because microsystems tend to be less powerful in these interactional processes, they are often the so-called victims and are labeled as the problem itself. While social problems incorporate personal factors of the victims, they also involve qualities of the environment, including political and economic factors, and the interaction between those factors. Change needs to be directed at all three levels.

Wood-Goldberg and Middleman (1989), in their structural approach to practice, developed a quadrant model that helps conceptualize the potential targets of social problem intervention (see Figure 2.2). The vertical axis represents who is engaged in problem resolution, ranging from clients to nonclients. The horizontal axis represents the intended beneficiary of the intervention, one client or a category of clients who experience similar problems. The two axes form four quadrants for possible intervention across microsystems and macrosystems.

Depending on the quadrant in which the intervention is focused, various system-level functioning must be assessed. Our knowledge of human behavior and the social environment enables us to assess and understand these multilevel systems. Based on this assessment, these systems—individuals, families, groups, organizations, and communities—might be engaged. Where we begin to intervene would depend on the identified purpose of the intervention. Wherever we begin, our ultimate goal is to prevent the incidence, as well as the impact, of social problems. Preventive intervention would ultimately lead to activity in any or all of the four quadrants.

Promotion and Prevention

Social problem intervention is directed toward primary, secondary, or tertiary prevention. Bloom differentiates these three levels from a public health perspective as follows:

> Efforts at primary prevention of disease are designed to prevent the disease from occurring at all—these efforts fall into two major categories. First, and most common, are efforts to decrease people's vulnerability to specific stresses. Second, and considerably less common, are efforts to reduce these stresses at their source. Efforts at secondary prevention are designed to develop techniques for early case finding so that treatment can be applied promptly— finally, tertiary prevention involves limiting the disability associated with a particular disorder, after that disorder has run its course. [1975, pp. 74–75]

Prevention refers to intervention activities that are aimed at reducing the prevalence of dysfunction within a population. Its earliest and perhaps most-extensive application has been in the public health field. As a public health method, prevention can best be exemplified by the use of inoculations to prevent smallpox, measles, and polio. Known as disease prevention, this approach conceptualizes the incidence of a specific disease as an interplay of host, agent, and environment, as depicted in Figure 2.3.

In this configuration, "host" refers to the individual who is vulnerable to illness. Referring back to the quadrant in Figure 2.2, this could be a client or a category of clients. "Agent" refers to the germ or agent that causes the illness. "Environment" refers to the conditions that have to be present for the agent to survive and thrive and the conditions that increase the host's vulnerability to the agent's potential effects.

Prevention intervention based on this disease model involves a series of activities targeting either the host, the agent, or the environment, alone or in combination. Intervening with the host involves strengthening the host's

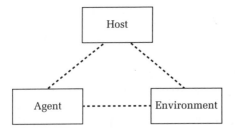

Figure 2.3   Components and relationships in disease prevention

resistance to the effects of the agent as, for example, inoculations strengthen the immune system to minimize the harmful effects of germs. Interventions targeting the agent attempt to eliminate the agent as sterilizing instruments or boiling food kills harmful germs. Interventions targeting the environment attempt to manipulate conditions that may breed harmful agents as in public trash collection.

From Causality to Risk Factors.   More recently, principles of disease prevention have evolved into the development of strategies aimed at preventing social ills such as psychosocial disorders and mental illness. Efforts to prevent school dropouts, delinquency, substance abuse, teenage pregnancy, welfare dependency, depression, and so forth are examples of prevention strategies. When applied to psychosocial disorders, disease prevention encompasses services to prevent the occurrence of specific disorders by using strategies derived from the analysis of the risk factors for these disorders (Bloom, 1981). Preventive social work involves ". . . an organized and systematic effort to apply knowledge about social health and pathology in such a manner as to enhance and preserve the social and mental health of individuals, families, and communities" (Wittman, 1977, p. 1049).

Albee (1982) conceptualized mental dysfunction as a product of organic factors and stress mediated by coping skills, self-esteem, and support systems, as depicted in the following equation:

$$\text{Incidence} = \frac{\text{organic factors} + \text{stress}}{\text{coping skills} + \text{self-esteem} + \text{support system}}[1]$$

In this equation, the incidence of mental dysfunction can be reduced by strengthening organic factors that make individuals susceptible to mental dysfunction and eliminating environmental stress that may precipitate the occurrence of the dysfunction. Coping skills, self-esteem, and support systems can similarly be strengthened to promote the individual's general

[1]From G. Albee, "Preventing psychopathology and promoting human potential." *American Psychologist*, 1982, 37(8), 1043–1050. Copyright © 1982 by the American Psychological Association. Reprinted with permission.

well-being and health. Change in any of these factors affects the incidence, though not necessarily the cause.

Primary-prevention approaches differ in several aspects from other forms of change. First, primary-prevention interventions precede the onset of a specific problem or dysfunction and its early signs. Because they occur before the onset of a dysfunction, these approaches precede the need for intervention. As a result, the disorder or dysfunction is avoided, interrupted, or reversed, and there is a demonstrable reduction of both the incidence of the dysfunction and the need or demand for intervention.

Primary prevention involves lowering the prevalence rate of the incidence of dysfunction in a given population. It does not aim at preventing a specific person from becoming ill. Instead, these measures attempt to reduce the risk for a whole population so that, although some may become ill, their numbers will be reduced (Caplan, 1964).

Because it precedes the occurrence of a dysfunction, primary-prevention social work practice targets populations of "well" individuals, families, and groups. But these target populations are in vulnerable situations such as life transitions, bereavement, or common crises. Preventive social work also incorporates a holistic focus on the person in the situation, such as transacting personal and environmental emphases (Sobey, 1982).

Steps in Prevention.   As with any social work intervention, preventive approaches build on effective assessment. Assessment in prevention focuses on two dimensions. The first is an assessment of the nature of the problem. Are its causes known? If so, can they be eliminated? If the causes are unknown, can the associated precipitating events or factors be identified? The second dimension involves identifying distinguishing characteristics of the affected population. Is there something that sets this population apart from other populations? Does this population share characteristics with the "risk factors" that are associated with the problem?

Having assessed the nature of the problem and the characteristics of the at-risk population, the next step is to identify points for intervention. Do you intervene with individuals, environments, precipitating factors, or all three? Should the predominant strategy be promotion or protection? Do you need to impact behaviors, attitudes, and beliefs, or all three? Should the primary method be education, support or regulation? In which of the quadrants suggested by Wood-Goldberg and Middleman should intervention be focused?

Perhaps the most problematic aspect of developing preventive approaches is evaluation. To evaluate the effectiveness of prevention approaches, indicators of outcome must be clearly identified. It may seem easy enough to determine prevalence rates for any specific disorder before intervention; however, prevention deals with whole populations. In order to reduce incidence rates among a population, the programs must impact substantial numbers of individuals. Most prevention programs are not sufficiently extensive to reach mass audiences. Reaching so many people requires consistent effort over a long period. For example, while we may have made substantial progress in reducing the smoking rate in this country, it has taken over 20 years of concerted public education to do so!

In practice, if we were to propose a promotion-prevention effort to combat the problem of violence, the promotion aspect might include policies to encourage nonviolent solutions to social conflict. Primary-prevention programs might be directed toward the population at large to reduce the number of weapons in circulation. For example, a Catholic priest in Denver regularly asks his parishioners to voluntarily surrender handguns and promise not to buy weapons in the future. Secondary prevention would be directed at specific populations who, based on their demographic profile, would be at higher risk for violence. Finally, tertiary prevention efforts would be directed toward known perpetrators and the victims of violence to ameliorate the impact and reduce recurrence of violent incidents.

While primary prevention is an ideal goal for social problem intervention, many social work efforts are found at the secondary- and tertiary-prevention levels. Deciding when and where to intervene is guided by social problem perspectives and social practice frameworks. All social work intervention, particularly primary- and secondary-level prevention, calls for us to make the public aware of the presence, prevalence, and nature of social problems. We must set the agenda and then communicate it to others in order to mobilize resources to alleviate social problems.

Agenda Setting and Communication

Placing the social problem on the community agenda is done to promote maximum public awareness (Rubin & Rubin, 1992). Such awareness better serves the goal of prevention. This agenda-setting task requires the practitioner to become a skilled communicator, one who can communicate at the interpersonal level as well as at the mass-communication levels. Baker and Anderson (1987, pp. 30–31) have provided a framework for interpreting social problems using the dimensions of "scope of awareness" and "degree of generality." Using a continuum of micro to macro and concrete to abstract, this framework allows a problem to be depicted at several levels (see Figure 2.4).

For example, let us assume that a citizen has learned through a newspaper or television story about a specific abused child (a client) in his or her neighborhood. This level of awareness (micro-concrete) may sensitize the citizen to the fact that this phenomenon happens locally. Learning about the numbers of similar children (a category of clients) in the total community (macro-concrete) would help depict the "social" nature of the problem. In other words, the individual problem would be seen as being repeated throughout the community.

Source. Let us begin with the first box, the ''source'' of the message. Before we begin to interpret the problem to our receiver or audience, whoever that might be, it is vital to examine just who we, the senders, are. If we are to place an issue before the public, we must first establish our credibility. Several questions come to mind. Do we have the credentials to command the attention of our audience? What information or expertise do we have? What is our track record? Why should we be sanctioned to speak out on a problem with more expertise than someone else? Why is our word good? Why is our data credible?

The give-and-take of defining the need for change often involves establishing credibility. Agenda setting is a competitive activity; a contest where one set of ideas is often pitted against others. The sponsors of the ideas are also competing and a demonstration of having done the proper homework may be the difference between simply communicating and being heard.

Receiver. The audiences of human-service agencies are multiple and varied. From micro to macro, at least eight ''publics'' have been identified (Baker & Routzahn, 1947):

1. The agency itself, including its board of directors, committees, and staff
2. Volunteers, those who provide day-to-day volunteer services
3. Clients, those who are the consumers of agency services
4. Co-operators, individuals and organizations that are allied with agency goals and objectives
5. Supporters, contributors of financial or other in-kind support
6. Key persons, leaders and key influentials in business, labor, education, religion, or other social institutions
7. Special publics, including professions, industries, racial and ethnic groups
8. The general public, people at large in any community from the local to national or even international level

The audience or receiver we intend to communicate with will naturally determine the content and shape of our message. Needless to say, there may be reasons to communicate with one audience before communicating with another or even to the exclusion of another. Each potential audience warrants its own assessment; an assessment that answers two basic questions: ''Why do we wish to communicate with them? What do we know about them?''

Message. Assuming that our audience(s) or public(s) have been selected and the two questions have been answered, we are now faced with the task of framing our message. Given that our goal is to elicit some change in levels of knowledge, attitude, or behavior, our message must appeal to audiences in some important aspect of their personal make-up. It may appeal to their motions, their rationality, or to other needs, but it should be coined so that it stands out among other messages in the environment. If the message is memorable enough, the receiver may be open to more messages.

Litwak (1967) has proposed some important principles to recognize in communicating around controversial issues:

1. People do not tend to listen to messages that present a viewpoint that differs from their own.
2. People select facts or parts of messages that are consistent with their previous opinions.
3. There is no necessary relationship between knowledge and action.
4. When an individual holds an opinion different from one held by the group, that individual tends to change it to conform to the group.
5. In changing the views of a hostile group, both sides of an issue must be included.
6. People are more likely to accept a negative message if it is preceded by a view they agree with.
7. Having an emotional involvement with the receiver before giving information is more likely to produce change.
8. A communicator who is perceived by the audience as friendly to their views is better able to give opinion-changing messages.
9. Communicating messages hostile to an audience must be done when the group norms are weakest.
10. Messages should be pitched to relate to the multiple value systems of groups.
11. When people's public actions differ from their public opinions, there is a tendency for the attitude to change to fit the action.

The practice implications of these principles are quite obvious and reinforce the importance of analyzing the receiving audience before shaping the message.

First, a change agent should be conversant with other viewpoints and able to argue a case from several perspectives. To be able to appreciate various perspectives of a change objective demonstrates openness and greater willingness to communicate. This, in itself, is empowering.

Second, knowing a client system's opinions helps the agent develop messages that can better relate to those points of view. Hostile messages can be softened and friendly messages can be strengthened.

Third, and perhaps most important, being willing to listen to an opposing point of view and communicate about that point of view opens the door to emotional involvement, an important ingredient in creating change.

Channel. The channel is the mode or the medium through which messages are sent. In the final analysis, the audience, the message, and the action sought will dictate which channels will be utilized. Generally speaking, however, mass audiences are reached through mass communication—the print and electronic media. Specialized audiences are reached through smaller scale approaches such as newsletters, closed-circuit television, and speaker's bureaus, whereas individuals are more likely to be informed through "hands-on" experiences such as open houses, group discussions, and person-to-person approaches that allow for more intimacy. A general rule is that direct communication is more likely to change attitudes and behavior, whereas mass-media approaches arouse public awareness.

Noise. Any message sent is unlikely to reach its receiver in exactly the form it was intended. This is because of "noise." Noise is the ongoing interference caused by poorly conceived messages, environmental factors, and the receiver's preconceived attitudes (such as bias, hate, and belief systems). The sender must take all this noise into account before sending a message. While the sender cannot overcome all the noise in the communication environment, he or she must make sure not to add to the noise level.

Feedback. Finally, the change agent must develop within the communication process a means of determining whether the message achieved its objective. This is called a feedback mechanism or feedback "loop." It is a way of knowing whether the receiver did anything different as a result of receiving the message. The message should request some action from the receiver. Whether the loop includes calling a hotline, asking for more information, volunteering, or providing financial support, action is the final gauge to evaluate whether the message had the intended impact.

SUMMARY

The social problems that have accumulated at the end of this century will likely extend into the next century as well. In the final analysis, how problems are defined, whether in simple or complex terms, by system blame or victim blame, determines how they will be addressed. Political ideologies —conservative, liberal, and radical—drive our philosophical perspectives for viewing social problems. Historically, problems have been explained through six theoretical orientations: social pathology, social disorganization, value conflict, deviance, labeling, and the critical perspective. Social problem analyses include definition of the problem, etiology of the problem, and consideration of norms and values regarding the situation. Social work and non–social-work operations and their consequences are compared with the ideal of which interventions might work and how. This problem analysis enables the practitioner to plan interventions.

Intervention into social problem dynamics transcends microsystems and macrosystems. Intervention is a political process and requires a high level of political acumen on the part of the practitioners. The integrated practitioner approaches a problem in its totality, rather than focusing only on the victims or carriers.

Consistent with contemporary approaches, practice aims to adjust the environment to suit individual needs and also helps individuals adjust to their situations.

The first step in intervention is to develop an agenda for change from micro to macro through communication and education. Noise between the sender and receiver of communication is created by cultural, gender, and social class differences. Prevention of social problems at the primary, secondary, and tertiary levels is necessary to intervention. While causality is not easily determined, risk factors can be identified, which will provide the basis for planned interventions.

STUDY QUESTIONS

1. Critique the definitions of social problems in this chapter. What would you add or delete? Create your own working definition of social problems.

2. Cite an example of a social problem as depicted from a systems-blame approach. What problems does this approach present?

3. Cite an example of a social problem as depicted from the person-blame approach. What problems does this approach present?

4. Examine a social problem from the political perspectives of the radical, conservative, and liberal points of view. What are the implications of each perspective in dealing with a social problem?

5. Examine a social problem from each of the six philosophical perspectives. Which of these perspectives are most congruent with the conservative political perspective? The radical political perspective? The liberal political perspective?

6. Using Wood-Goldberg and Middleton's quadrant approach, give an example of work that might be done in each quadrant in intervening in a specific social problem.

REFERENCES

Abbott, G. (1930). The county vs the community as an administration unit. *Social Service Review* 4(1), pp. 12–16.

Albee, G. (1982). Preventing psychopathology and promoting human potential. *American Psychologist 37*, pp. 1043–1050.

Baker, H. C., & Routzahn, M. S. (1947). *How to interpret social welfare*. New York: Russell Sage Foundation.

Baker, P. J., & Anderson, L. E. (1987). *Social problems: A critical thinking approach*. Belmont, CA: Wadsworth.

Billups, J. O. (1984 March/April). Unifying social work: Importance of center-moving ideas. *Social Work* 29(2), pp. 173–180.

Bloom, A. (1987). *The closing of the American mind*. New York: Simon & Schuster.

Bloom, B. L. (1975). *Community mental health: A general introduction*. Pacific Grove, CA: Brooks/Cole.

Bloom, M. (1981). A working definition of primary prevention related to social concerns. In M. Nobel, *Primary prevention in mental health and social work*. New York: Council on Social Work Education.

Caplan, G. (1964). *Principles of preventive psychiatry*. New York: Basic Books.

Cloward, R., & Ohlin, L. (1965). *Delinquency and opportunity: A theory of delinquent gangs*. Glencoe, IL: The Free Press.

Cohen, N. E. (1964). *Social work and social problems*. New York: National Association of Social Workers.

Dluhy, M. J. (1981). *Changing the system: Political advocacy for disadvantaged groups*. Beverly Hills: Sage.

Edelman, E. M., & Goldstein, A. P. (1981). Moral education. In A. P. Goldstein, E. G. Carr, W. S. Davidson, & P. Wehr (Eds.). *In response to aggression*. New York: Pergammon Press.

Eitzen, D. S. (1983). *Social problems*. Boston: Allyn & Bacon.

Galper, J. (1975). *The politics of social services*. Englewood Cliffs, NJ: Prentice-Hall.

Gordon, D. M. (Ed.). (1977). *Problems in political economy: An urban perspective*. Lexington, KY: D.C. Heath.

Green, A. (1975). *Social problems: Arena of conflict*. New York: McGraw-Hill.

Kennedy, P. (1993). *Preparing for the twenty-first century*. New York: Random House.

Lipsky, M., and Smith, S. (1989). When social problems are treated as emergencies. *Social Service Review* 63(1), pp. 5–25.

Litwak, E. (1967). Policy implications in communications theory with emphasis on group factors. In E. J. Thomas (Ed.). *Behavioral science for social workers*. New York: The Free Press.

National Association of Social Workers. (1980). *Code of ethics*.

Pierce, D. (1984). *Policy for the social work practitioner*. New York: Longman.

Piven, F. F., & Cloward, R. (1971). *Regulating the poor. The functions of public welfare*. New York: Vintage Books.

Richmond, M. (1917). *Social diagnosis*. New York: Russell Sage Foundation.

Rogers, E., & Shoemaker, C. (1971). *Communication of innovations: A cross-cultural approach* (2nd ed.). New York: New York Press.

Ross, R., & Staines, G. L. (1972 Dec.). The politics of analyzing social problems. *Social Problems.*

Rubin, H. J., & Rubin, I. (1992). *Community organization and development* (2nd ed.). Columbus, OH: Merrill.

Rubington, E., & Weinberg, M. S. (Eds.). (1989). *The study of social problems.* New York: Oxford University Press.

Shannon, C., & Weaver, W. (1949). *The mathematical theory of communication.* Urbana: University of Illinois Press.

Shulman, L. (1991). *Interactional social work practice.* Itasca, IL: F. E. Peacock.

Smith, R. E., & Zeitz, D. (1970). *American social welfare institutions.* New York: Wiley & Sons.

Sobey, F. (1982). Integration of prevention in social work education. Presented April 21–22, 1982. University of Denver.

Specht, H. (1969). Disruptive tactics. *Social Work* 14(1), pp. 5–15.

Vonnegut, M. (1975). *The Eden express.* New York: Bantam Books.

Weick, K. E. (1984). Small wins: Redefining the scale of social problems. *American Psychologist* 37.

Weinberg, M. S., Rubington, E., & Hammersmith, S. (1981). *The solution of social problems.* New York: Oxford University Press.

Wittman, M. (1977). Preventive social work. *Encyclopedia of Social Work.*

Wood-Goldberg, G., & Middleman, R. (1989). *The structural approach to direct practice in social work.* New York: Columbia University Press.

York, R. O. (1982). *Human service planning: Concepts, tools, & methods.* Chapel Hill: University of North Carolina Press.

Chapter 3

◆

Deviance and Labeling

ABSOLUTIST VERSUS INTERACTIONIST VIEWS OF DEVIANCE
Constructing a Social Reality
Functions of Deviance

STEPS IN DEVIANCE AND LABELING: THE CRITICAL PATH
Deviation
Visibility
Identification of Difference
Labeling
Establishment of Deviance
Devaluation
Stigmatization
Discrimination
Oppression
Victimization
Alienation
Powerlessness
Becoming at Risk
Reaction

IMPLICATION FOR INTERVENTION
Intervention at What Stage?
Normalization and Positive Visibility as Early Intervention
Competency-Based Screening

SUMMARY

STUDY QUESTIONS

REFERENCES

74

everal perspectives to social problems were discussed in Chapter 2. In this chapter we will concentrate on deviance and labeling. Because these orientations are processes as well as social constructions, a more elaborate discussion is necessary in order to examine how they contribute to the creation of the adversive environments of many devalued, oppressed populations. Society has great power to fix blame for social conditions either through persons or systems. If the person-blame point of view prevails, society can establish the standards from which deviance is measured, police the deviant behavior, negatively label the deviants, and make that label stick. Such blaming and labeling is applied to diverse social groups, including racial minorities and women.

The interaction that takes place between the labeler and the labeled presents all the inherent dangers that occur when one social group imposes its reality and will over another. At the same time, this interaction provides an opportunity for the labeled to examine their own standing in terms of values, power, and influence, and here lies the potential for self-empowerment and social action.

ABSOLUTIST VERSUS INTERACTIONIST VIEWS OF DEVIANCE

Perhaps no issue exemplifies the application of deviance and labeling more sharply than the homosexual community's struggle to come out of the confines of the so-called closet and become recognized as a mainstream community.

In Colorado, over a period of years and through the political efforts of the gay and lesbian community, the cities of Boulder, Denver, and Aspen enacted ordinances to protect the rights of homosexuals in such areas as housing and employment. These ordinances drew the attention of a community organization known as Colorado for Family Values. The group managed to obtain enough voter signatures to place an amendment on the ballot to void these ordinances. The amendment, now well known as Amendment Two, stirred a debate between those voters who maintained that homosexuals were seeking "special protections" and those who believed these ordinances were vital to assure guaranteed civil rights.

Colorado for Family Values ran an aggressive campaign, which became more targeted as the election drew near. Letters to newspaper editors became the medium for labeling homosexuals as sinners, perverts, and violators of God's will. Their behavior was described as disgusting, frightening, sick, and immoral. Although right up until election eve public opinion polls reflected that Amendment Two would be defeated, the measure passed by

54% to 46%. Court action blocked implementation of Amendment Two and the matter is under review by the Colorado Supreme Court.

What happened in Colorado is nothing new. Our society has invented numerous negative labels to ascribe sanctions to people whose skin color, ethnicity, culture, values, religion, gender, sexual orientation, or behavior might be used to set down exclusionary measures. Depending on the degree and scope, such exclusion can become outright oppression.

Constructing a Social Reality

We need to ask ourselves, "Does any one person or group of persons have a corner on reality?" As human animals, we are unique in having the capacity to observe what goes on around us, paying particular attention to what concerns us most. We think about this phenomenon, talk about it, and draw conclusions. These conclusions become our "truth." In short, we extract meaning from our observations and in the process determine that certain things "matter." Thus, we concern ourselves with the practice of social work (or teaching and writing about it) and we define it as "important" or "significant." Or we read about the sexual practices of others and find them wanting. As we incorporate day-to-day observations and conclusions into our lives, we each construct a "social reality" (Berger & Luckman, 1967). This is quite different from the notion that there is one objective reality that some people may or may not discover.

These reactions to homosexuality are notable, not just in terms of their depiction of a stigmatized form of sexual expression as being inherently evil or bad. Within the social reality of Colorado for Family Values, the behaver as well as the behavior is adjudged repugnant.

Functions of Deviance

Sociologists have different opinions on whether deviance is a function of society's need for consensual or shared values or whether it is a phenomenon that reflects the natural conflict of a heterogeneous society (Pfuhl, 1986). To the degree that there is a consensual social reality, there is a strong driving force for individual members of society to condemn those who deviate from that reality. There is very little choice. To say that "nothing matters" or "nothing has meaning" is to consign ourselves to an anomic world without norms for behavior. With the construction of a broadly agreed-on social reality, people ultimately determine that some things "do not go." This determination is accompanied by actions to impose social controls and police behaviors that violate those loosely construed consensual norms.

Society members communicate to other members what is right or wrong, and these injunctions become part of the everyday thought processes that lead toward behavioral constraints. Goode maintains that deviance is universal:

> Not only do people everywhere set rules detailing what constitutes appropriate and inappropriate—or conventional and deviant—behavior, but also groups of people everywhere experience deviance in their midst. And everywhere some sort of punishment is meted out for non-conformity. No society experiences absolute conformity from all of its members. Deviance is implicit in social organization. In order to render human existence viable and workable, rules have to be set. And when rules are set, it is inevitable that they will be broken by some people at some time. The social organization of the condemnation of deviant behavior is universal. And the behavior itself—that is, some sort of behavior that touches off condemnation—is also universal. [1978, p. 14]

The only universal in deviance is its very existence. Deviance appears to be a natural process: one that the social order, with varying degrees of efficiency, uses to indoctrinate and socialize its individuals.

Yet deviant behavior is prevalent. Linton (1952) notes that practically all societies disapprove of incest, adultery, promiscuity, cruelty to children, laziness, disrespect for parents, murder, rape, theft, lying, and cheating. Yet in the United States incest is often described as an epidemic; the much-criticized *Hite Report* (1987) contends that adultery and promiscuity are commonplace. Child abuse continues to defy solutions, laziness is blamed for our nation's failure to compete in an international economy, elder abuse becomes an increasing aspect of domestic violence, and murder and rape continue to plague society. Coincidentally, theft, lying, and cheating have often been promoted as "necessary" at the highest levels of government, and the practitioners of these actions have even been extolled as "national heroes." It is an understatement to say that some individuals do not conform to the proposed standards. Given their differential levels of power, some people may be punished for their lack of conformity, while others are ignored or even admired. For those who are punished, being labeled as a deviant constitutes part of the punishment. We negatively label people as criminals, drug addicts, religious fanatics, mental patients, street people, or prostitutes.

As a way of explaining differential treatment by the more powerful society, we also negatively label members of stigmatized and devalued groups merely for their group membership. Members of devalued groups assume a position of marginality as they are socialized to identify with their group. They understand the punishments that may be associated with such identification and the rewards for leaving the group to join the mainstream of society. Norton's (1978) dual perspective explained this marginality for members of racial minority groups. She suggested that while people may be valued as members of their racial group by other group members (what she called the nurturing environment), they may be devalued by the larger environment (the sustaining system) simply because of their membership. Such labeled, devalued people often become the "clients" or "consumers" of social services.

The environment in which social work clients live and in which social work is practiced is often regulated in large measure by the public opinions expressed by Colorado for Family Values. This school of thought is sometimes referred to as the *absolutist school* (Hills, 1980). It maintains that fundamental human behavior may be classified as inherently proper or self-evidently immoral, evil, or abnormal; a proposition that most social work practitioners would find unacceptable.

An alternative view of the social reality of sexual expression emerged from the Amendment Two debate. This view emphasized the inherent diversity in sexual behavior, placing it on a continuum from homosexual to bisexual to heterosexual. It challenged the sin, and sexual disorder conceptualizations, calling on voters to be more open to a larger inclusionary view of community.

Most social workers would find this school of thought more compatible with their social reality. Known as the *relativist* or *interactionist* view of deviance, this view is constructed on the premise that society is in a continual struggle over values (Hills, 1980, p. 9). Within this context, deviance becomes more of an issue of how people value, evaluate, and control each other. It is perhaps best expressed by Kai Erickson:

> Deviance is not a property inherent in certain forms of behavior; it is a property conferred upon these forms by the people who come into direct or indirect contact with it. [1966, p. 6]

Thus in the relativist or interactionist view of sexual expression, homosexuality would be explained as a matter of preference between male or female sexual partners; a preference that varies with individuals. Neither the behaver nor the behavior would be judged.

The social reality of the interactionist is one of continuums, whereas the absolutist's reality is dichotomous and arbitrary. The questions facing the social work profession include the following: Can helping efforts directed toward devalued people be delivered in an interactionist mode while the receiver of the assistance lives in a world of absolutism? Can we change criminal behavior while we punish it? Shall we treat, shun, pray for, or allow homosexuals to live in the mainstream with straights? Shall we consider members of the Unification Church to be cultists needing deprogramming or as legitimate practitioners of a religion? Shall mental patients be managed as cases, hospitalized, deinstitutionalized, or left to street predators?

The school of thought that you use to construct a reality to explain deviance will also be used to provide answers to these questions. For how you evaluate behavior will ultimately determine how you intervene, where you intervene, and perhaps most important, whether you intervene at all.

STEPS IN DEVIANCE AND LABELING: THE CRITICAL PATH

The integrated-practice perspective of deviance is an interactionist one. It is our premise that deviance occurs in a world largely populated and shaped by absolutists who have the power to promote their dominant view. The process of deviance and labeling occurs in a series of steps or stages comprising a chain of events wherein the deviant gradually becomes devalued, stigmatized, and disempowered. It is this structural chain of events that must be broken. For this to happen, the absolutists or labelers must become the target of change as much as the labeled and devalued. We have much work to do in facilitating the valuation and celebration of difference as it pertains to ethnic, gender, and age-based groups.

Each stage that the deviant passes through strengthens the process of negative labeling, but each stage also provides opportunities for proactive and preventive intervention as well. These stages are illustrated in Figure 3.1 and will be discussed in the following paragraphs.

Deviation

Matza discussed deviation in terms of straying, as from a path or standard:

> Since deviation is a common feature of society, since it is implicit in social and moral organization, it needs no extraordinary accounting. Straying from a path need be regarded as no less comprehensive nor more bewildering than walking it. Given the moral character of social life, both naturally happen, and thus are pondered and studied by sociologists and others. [1969, p. 14]

To be sure, deviation is not unusual. People who speak or think faster or slower than the norm deviate, yet their behavior is not usually punishable. In Garrison Keillor's fictitious Lake Wobegon, all the children deviate in that they are "above average." "Norwegian bachelor farmers" deviate from the expected norm of marriage as well as from certain standards of hygiene, yet they are incorporated into the community life and may even command considerable respect within the Lutheran church (Keillor, 1985).

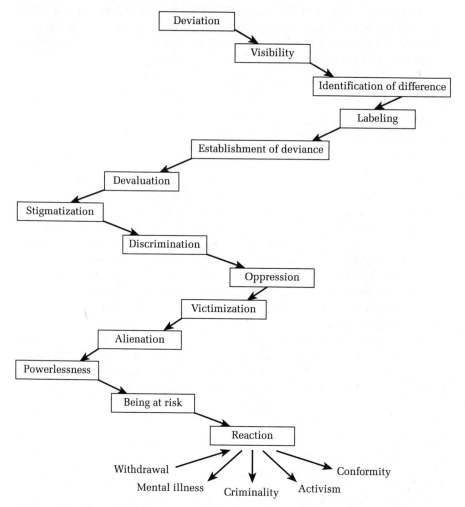

Figure 3.1 Steps in deviance and labeling: the critical path

Through their dress and other forms of symbolic communication, the Amish and Hutterites deviate from a larger societal standard. This deviation is largely expressed within the relatively closed society of a colony, however, and it does not become the concern of the larger society. Furthermore, when the difference becomes apparent to society in general, it is not necessarily offensive.

Being a member of a stigmatized group does not in itself set up deviance. When that membership creates a difference between the group and society, however, it may become more visible and vulnerable to the labeling process.

Drinking or becoming intoxicated are deviations from the norm of sobriety, yet they are unlikely to warrant high levels of concern in the absence of other more objectionable behaviors. Campaigns against drunk driving focus much more on the driving than the drinking.

Deviation can best be thought of as the beginning step in the process of deviance. It can include the way one looks, acts, or thinks, but deviation does not place an individual on the path to deviance. The deviation must somehow be called to the attention of a larger audience. That is, it must be given visibility.

Visibility

Whether deviation is given visibility is one factor in whether the behavior will ultimately be considered deviant. Goode proposed that the "contexts of deviance include audience, actor, and situational relativity" (1978, pp. 32–36).

Homeless mental patients will find that their presence on the street creates a greater public reaction than when they are ensconced in a psychiatric ward. In spite of pedestrians' attempts to ignore them, their public hallucinations and delusions are forced into the public's consciousness. To the extent that this deviation becomes a regular experience to more diverse audiences, it naturally creates a greater stir than when it is not observed. Mentally ill patients who take up residence on the same block with the so-called mentally healthy are provided a prominent stage from which their new audience can view them. On the other hand, the mental state of the Norwegian bachelor farmer is kept under wraps and thus is relatively inoffensive to the larger community. He can act crazy and live undetected in an unsanitary state, while the urban mental patient becomes a public concern.

Discrimination against gays and lesbians has not just been due to the repugnance of their sexual choice to some straight people, but to the fact that they choose to expose their sexual orientation, normalize it, and even promote it. "Coming out of the closet" and the honesty of that expression is as disturbing to society as the actual behavior of homosexuality.

"Black is beautiful" is a statement of visibility and power. Its message is that not only is black skin different than white skin, it is also beautiful, of positive value, and is increasingly becoming a part of the environment of *all* people.

Identification of Difference

Once the deviating population has become visible, the next step toward creating full-fledged deviants will be to identify them as "different." At this juncture a label may or may not be applied, but there is an implicit message of exclusion. "They are not one of us" or "they differ from us" are statements designed to establish a degree of social distance. These messages inform the deviators they don't "belong" or "fit in" or they are "strange." Many immigrant populations have been the targets of such identification. An 1896 speech on immigration, delivered in the U.S. Senate by Massachusetts Senator Henry Cabot Lodge, made the point:

> If a lower race mixes with a higher race in sufficient numbers, history teaches us the lower race will prevail . . . In other words, there is a limit to the capacity of any race for assimilating and elevating an inferior race and when you begin to pour in unlimited numbers of people of alien or lower races of less social efficiency and less moral force you are running the most frightful risk that a people can run. The lowering of a great race means not only its decline but that of civilization. [Goodwin, 1987, p. 101]

The key words in Lodge's speech are *lower, inferior, alien, less social efficiency,* and *less moral force.* The tone of his speech, while benign, makes it very clear that he, as a member of the "higher race" is the definer, and the "inferior races" are being defined as such because of their inherent characteristics. He has established distance, difference, and a power differential. Such distance and difference are often applied to racial and gender groups in order to justify and explain why diversity is devalued in this society rather than celebrated.

Labeling

Once identification of difference has been established, a negative label is often applied to the deviators: The label emphasizes the difference. A litany of hurtful names may come to mind: *pervert, sicko, crazoid,* and *drugger.* All of these labels depict special meaning and create the resulting social distance between the labeler and the labeled.

Of relevance here is the concept of symbolic interactionism. Blumer (1969) offered three basic premises to define this perspective. First, "human beings act toward things on the basis of the meanings things have for them" (Blumer, 1969, p. 5). In this statement, the terms *meaning* and *things* are used in their broadest sense. A thing's meaning embodies all the complex images and attitudes that the thing elicits for a person. Things, or objects, include everything that can have meaning for a person. Things are not limited to the inanimate, they include people; that is, the actor and others. People have images and attitudes about other people and about themselves (Heiss, 1981).

Blumer (1969) contended that to understand human behavior one must know how the actor defines the situation because behavior emerges from these definitions. The key for interactionists is people's perceptions. How a person defines a situation or others is crucial because, regardless of the facts, people act on their perception of a situation (Heiss, 1981).

Second, the meanings of things are derived from, or arise out of, the social interaction that one has with others. That is, the definitions that an individual applies to a situation are based on previous interactions and on experiences in the earlier stages of the present encounter (Heiss, 1981).

Third, "the actor selects, checks, suspends, regroups, and transforms the meanings in the light of the situation in which he is placed and the direction of his action" (Blumer, 1969, p. 5).

The significance of labeling should not be minimized, because inherent in the negative label is a repertoire of behaviors that is inferred to be a property of the labeled person. Once the label is applied, the labeler begins to ascribe certain behavioral expectations to the labeled, which legitimize subsequent discrimination and oppression.

The playwright Cervantes demonstrated the potency of labeling in the interaction between his main character, Don Quixote, and the harlot, Dulcinea (Cervantes, 1964). Don Quixote, who is crazed, refuses to define Dulcinea as a harlot but rather as a queen. Unable to conceive of herself as anything but a whore, Dulcinea begs for her more familiar label only to be recast time and again as a queen. At the time of Don Quixote's death, Dulcinea has abandoned the harlot role, moving in the direction of Don Quixote's positive label. As readers, we are left to wonder about the boundaries that define the sane and the insane.

Establishment of Deviance

Up to this point, the definer (the more powerful) has established a role for the defined (the less powerful). What must happen next is for the defined to occupy that role. This involves an element of coercion. Conrad and Schneider spoke to this point.

> What is considered deviant in a society is a product of a political process of decision making. The behaviors or activities that are deviant in a given society are not self-evident; they are defined by groups with the ability to legitimate and enforce their definitions. [1980, p. 22]

This enforcement results in the establishment of both law enforcement and treatment "industries." Akers wrote:

> To gain some idea of what behavior exceeds the tolerance limits in a social system we can observe how it is defined and related to by those who support this normative system. We can see that major concern about certain kinds of deviance has been expressed by large or powerful elements of society when: laws are passed; programs are initiated; money, time and personnel are

allocated; and organizations are created to combat or control the occurrence of specified behavior or to punish, treat or "cure" those who engage in it. [1985, p. 9]

Role theory posits that once a role has been established, embellished with the accompanying behaviors, and held out to the labeled individual, there are powerful resulting forces for the individual to occupy it. If the choice is to gain affirmation by occupying a role or to receive no affirmation or disconfirmation by rejecting an assigned role, there is little choice but to submit, assume the role, and act out the accompanying behaviors.

In the popular *One Flew Over the Cuckoo's Nest* (Kesey, 1962), the all-powerful Big Nurse spells out in detail how mental patients are supposed to act, administering appropriate punishments when prescribed behaviors are violated. McMurphy, the hero, deviates from these norms, becomes a deviant among deviants, and ultimately is given a lobotomy. Martini and most of the other patients survive by conforming.

This scenario is a self-fulfilling prophecy in that the "good" deviants behave in a way that fits Big Nurse's expectations, thus reaffirming her original prescriptions for their behavior. Women and racially diverse groups are often guided into assuming socially prescribed roles by the administration of a system of rewards and punishments that shape the taking of socially inferior positions. Establishment of deviance is much like being fit with concrete shoes; the longer one wears the shoes the harder they get, and finally they become impossible to remove!

Devaluation

If the newly defined deviant is to remain under control, he or she must recognize who is doing the controlling. This is accomplished in part by the more powerful reminding the deviants of their lack of value. To some extent, the assigned label provides these reminders, since negative labels infer not only expected behavior but the relative value of the individual as well.

Beyond that there are other symbols that make statements about a deviant's value. The nature of social service delivery often gives a message of devaluation. For example, a "welfare mother," waiting for a social service worker to keep an appointment, has to sit in a waiting room policed by an armed sheriff's deputy. She is given a number and told to be available when it is called. The message is clear: "Your time is less valuable than mine, you have potential for violence, and in relating to this agency, you are merely a number." In short, and through nonverbal communication, she is reminded that she is of lesser value.

A client, Mrs. Morris, describes the experience of sitting in a social services waiting room with her children for eight hours as she is being processed for financial assistance:

> I approached the receptionist again to find out why I hadn't been called. She told me flatly, "Everyone has to wait their turn; they will call you when they get to your name." I tried to explain that my two older children hadn't had breakfast or lunch and I couldn't afford to purchase them anything from the snack bar. She looked up from her scratch pad and said, "What do you expect me to do? I hear this kind of thing all day long." I quickly took my seat hoping too many people hadn't heard our conversation. [Compton & Galaway, 1989, pp. 260–261]

Stigmatization

Devaluation is compounded by having to manage the accompanying stigma, another source of discrediting the individual. Higgins and Butler described it in this way:

> It is a negative discrepancy between virtual and actual social identity. A virtual social identity encompasses the characteristics that we expect others to possess. Those who fall short of what we expect are stigmatized. We generally expect people to be conventional, able bodied, and of sound mind. Deviants, however, diverge from these expectations. They are stigmatized. [1962, p. 206]

Stigmatizing goes beyond devaluing in that the devalued individual is negatively marked. In many respects, the mark is indelible. In any event, it is not easily removed. To warn of her adulterous nature, for example, Hester Prynne, in Nathaniel Hawthorne's *The Scarlet Letter*, was marked with an "A." While society doesn't brand foreheads today, it still can prevent devalued citizens from escaping into anonymity. Food stamps stigmatize the poor and render shame. Thanksgiving and Christmas dinners, eaten in the glare of television cameras, stigmatize the homeless. Newspapers reports of the location of paroled convicts under the guise of the public's "right to know" further stigmatize this category of deviant. Publication of names of delinquent youth and delinquent taxpayers serves no useful purpose other than shaming. Stigmatizing is a form of ongoing punishment, designed to last beyond the original punishment of labeling. Stigmatizing keeps the label as well as the labeled in place.

One of the consequences of prolonged stigma is role engulfment. Pfuhl saw this phenomenon as the result of people relating to the deviant in terms of a "spoiled identity":

To the degree that social interaction is restricted by reason of a person's deviant identity; that is, as people respond to the actor more in terms of the master status of deviant and less often in terms of socially acceptable identities, the master status becomes more salient for the actor. Becoming engulfed in one's deviant status, then, is a cumulative process, the outcome of which is that people may define themselves in the same negative way that others do. A person's "I," or essential/substantial self, becomes that of deviant. [1986, p. 134]

Role engulfment does not allow for escape from the deviant role because the individual's identity is already invested. Thus the deviant seeks and obtains affirmation of his or her existence from the deviant role to the exclusion of other prosocial roles.

Discrimination

Devaluing and stigmatizing prepare the way for yet another phase—discrimination. In this phase, the social institutions make the processing experience more aversive and less rewarding for the deviant than for the rest of the population. The end results are limited access to resources that would otherwise be available—such as housing, education, or employment—and more severe treatment by criminal justice agencies. Discrimination may not necessarily be an intentional attempt to harm. The discriminating agent may be carrying out a policy or law, but a bias or prejudice in the law may have evaded examination for scores of years. Such forms of "institutionalized" discrimination have deep roots in our society and have been reflected in such things as poll taxes, housing covenants, segregated facilities, and lower wage scales. This legalized discrimination was tolerated for long periods in U.S. history under a "separate but equal" justification.

Social systems incorporate processes, procedures, or structures that affect the distribution of control, authority, and influence to individuals. This distribution constitutes a political economy; that is, how a system distributes power and its various vestiges to its members. As a society, this differential distribution of power, influence, goods and services, prestige, and status contributes to the development of conditions that discriminate among populations within society and that are at the heart of social problems.

While a social-systems view of clients and their environments assumes mutual reciprocity between social systems, there are power differentials inherent in those reciprocal interactions. That is, social institutions, communities, and organizations tend to hold and use much more power than groups, families, and individuals. So, while clients of social workers are engaged in mutual interaction with political economic forces, they have comparatively little power in relation to those forces.

An example of the differential effect that social problems have on select populations can be seen in a comparison of the socioeconomic status of minorities and nonminorities, and women and men. DiNitto and Dye (1991) cited that on average, African Americans do not live as long as whites, are in poorer health, earn less, and are overrepresented in public assistance programs. They further cited 1988 census data that 34% of African American families earn less than $10,000 annually compared with 24% of Hispanic Americans and 15% of white families. Poverty rates are 10% for whites, 32% for African Americans, and 27% for Hispanics. Even after controlling for education, differences in poverty levels for these three groups are apparent (DiNitto & Dye, 1991). Although women constitute a majority of the population, they are the object of economic and other forms of discrimination. Women's wages were just 70% of men's in 1987. Single mothers who are heads of households experience less than half the income of all families (Longres, 1990, p. 83). Discrimination against members of stigmatized groups is a common, pervasive condition that leads to oppression.

Oppression

To the extent that discrimination permeates the individual's life and is experienced as specific to his or her particular population, the deviant now feels the weight of this force in the form of severe oppression. Oppression is the cumulative result of long-standing discriminatory actions that are not successfully contested. People who feel oppressed believe that they are always at the bottom or are in situations that they know they will lose. Such a state has been described as "learned helplessness," the idea that an individual's actions have no influence on or relationship to the outcomes of events and experiences (Hooker, 1976).

Oppressors, often unaware of their oppressiveness, are surprised to learn they are experienced in this way and may become defensive. In the deviant's eyes, felt oppression is the stress of living in a bipolar world. The power structure, which in the words of poor African Americans, consists of "the man" and those who are the less powerful. In prison the correctional office may be "the man," an extension of the ultimate white male, while inmates may refer to themselves as "brothers." Felt oppression is when the individual measures his or her power against the "powers that be" and concludes that it is insufficient to establish parity. In this situation, the individual recognizes that he or she has become a victim.

Victimization

While a case might be made that many victims may not be aware of their plight or may deny it, our discussion is about the people who come to believe in their victimized status. Prolonged loss of self-esteem is usually followed by depression and a state of self-pity. Self-pity is one of the most destructive human emotions because it allows the deviant to become disempowered. In the process of self-pity, there is little room for self-empowerment. In this state, people surrender responsibility for themselves, in many instances, to the powers of society at large. Having surrendered responsibility, they can now justify nearly any behavior, no matter how irresponsible that behavior might be, on the ground that it is the fault of the oppressor. The victimized deviant accepts a robotlike identification and, in so doing, surrenders the self. Under the domination of self-pity, an individual can justify medicating social and psychological pain with alcohol and other drugs. Escape from oppression can be justified in instant pleasure. A rejecting society holds no social bonds for the deviant, and actions can thus be taken without a sense of communal or community responsibility. The paradox, of course, is that by accepting victimization as a reality, it is now easier for the individual to justify making victims of others (Gilliland & James, 1992). This justification will in large measure be informed by the degree of alienation present.

Alienation

Alienation reflects the degree of breakdown occurring between the remaining bonds that exist between society and the deviant and the degree to which the deviant breaks away from the community as a source of social satisfaction. Alienation may be a gradual deterioration with no conscious decision to break away, or a deliberate decision in which society is defined as an enemy. Breaking away may be psychological or physical or both, but in the end alienated deviants feel no investment in the power structure and their participation in community life becomes minimal and marginal. Socially, the deviant may find rewards through participation in the lives of similarly alienated people. Social systems that emerge from such participation may be known as gangs or cults, and their boundaries may be defined by the race, ethnicity, or religious beliefs of their members.

The world of alienated deviants is increasingly "us" versus "them." As alienation is more deeply felt, the conflict becomes charged to the point where the battlelines are drawn even sharper; "us" against "the world."

Powerlessness

A natural consequence of prolonged alienation is a sense of powerlessness; that is, the deviant feels that there are no options and therefore no real choices to be made. Powerless people no longer think of themselves as deciders; they see themselves as reactors. Faced with reacting to events rather than controlling them and determining their outcome, they discover they have little to lose, regardless of their actions. With no vested interest in society and thus no responsibility toward it, these powerless deviants have few consequences to consider. One response is as good as another. In this state of mind, deviants have a higher potential for becoming violent. Rollo May noted convincingly that the chief source of violence lies in felt powerlessness, impotence, and apathy:

> As we make people powerless, we promote their violence rather than its control. Deeds of violence in our society are performed largely by those trying to establish their self-esteem, to defend their self-image, and to demonstrate that they, too, are significant. Regardless of how detailed or wrongly used these motivations may be or how destructive their expression, they are still the manifestation of positive interpersonal needs. We cannot ignore the fact that no matter how difficult their redirection may be, these needs themselves are potentially constructive. Violence arises not out of superfluity of power, but out of powerlessness. [1972, p. 23]

Becoming at Risk

When powerlessness becomes a fact of life, there is greater likelihood that the powerless will develop into a population at risk. People who feel powerless and vulnerable to societal forces present a risk to society and themselves because their reactions to their environment are more desperate, unpredictable, and chaotic.

At-risk individuals present a much greater likelihood of striking out at and preying on the society from which they feel alienated. Because of their risk to others, they require more societal resources and, in the process, become more dependent on the alien social order.

They may surrender their lives through suicide or forfeit control to the criminal justice or mental health industries. They may extract a cost by venting their rage through terrorist or revolutionary behavior or become fair game for cults and religious fringe elements.

To be at risk then is to live on the edge of organized society, to be most vulnerable to social change, to feel endangered, and to become endangering. An at-risk population demands an inordinate amount of resources for its care and control.

Reaction

Ultimately, at-risk individuals react to the circumstances that confront them. Halleck pointed out four basic ways of reacting to helplessness and powerlessness: "mental illness or psychopathology, activism, conformity, and criminality'' (1967, p. 81). Added to the above we might include a fifth: withdrawal or rejection of society. While there is some overlap among these reactions, we will discuss them separately in terms of their implication for social work.

Mental Illness. Mental illness as a form of deviance has provided social work clinicians and other helping professionals with ample employment over the years. Even so, we do not know exactly what this disease is or even if it is a disease at all. Szasz (1961) has called the phenomenon a "myth." While providing descriptions for categories of behavior, the *Diagnostic and Statistical Manual of Mental Disorders, Revised* (1987) or DSM III-R, published by the American Psychiatric Association, does not depict it in other than a medical context.

As tools for categorizing psychiatric patients, diagnostic labels do not necessarily have the same meaning among psychiatrists. Mechanic (1969) asserted that the disease concept is meaningful in that it has reliability in diagnosing a condition and prescribing treatment. He further noted that psychiatric disorders have a lower level of confirmation among psychiatrists than other medical theories.

We are left to ponder some questions. What if mental illness is only an assumption? Could it be simply a political consensus arrived at by medical professionals? Homosexuality, once within the domain of *DSM III-R*, was finally expunged after much political pressure (Conrad & Schneider, 1988). If homosexuality can be eliminated (by vote) as a disease and normalized, would the world be any worse off if some of the others were eliminated as well?

A well-known psychiatric syndrome, melancholia, happens to be fairly commonplace in Scandinavian culture (Hendin, 1964). The related frequency of suicide among Scandinavians might indicate that Scandinavians have many things to be sad about or that they enjoy being melancholy, or that the culture places high value on sadness. In fact, if one were Scandinavian and enjoyed getting in touch with his or her melancholy, he or she might resent being considered pathological. Yet it is there among other syndromes to be "treated."

If an individual has been labeled, stigmatized, devalued; become the object of discrimination and oppression, and feels powerless, there is probably ample reason to become depressed and even lose touch with a harsh reality. What is the nature of the mental health that the mentally ill are alleged to have lost? At the very least, if we are to describe behavior as pathological, it would seem imperative that we be able to separate out pathology—that is, what is wrong inside the head—from those behaviors that are culturally driven or possible attempts to cope with society. It is very tempting to classify someone's personal construction of reality as "impoverished thinking," particularly if the classifier has more power than the classified. The high level of concern about the mental health of immigrants and other citizens of marginal membership gives cause to question whether their "disease" was not "powerlessness" rather than psychopathology (Szasz, 1970).

Criminality. Crime and delinquency are illegitimate responses to society, which easily lead to deviance and the many labels that categorize the behavior. Although criminals and delinquents have also provided employment for the social work profession, social workers have been less comfortable practicing with this clientele, particularly since rehabilitation has lost favor in the criminal and juvenile justice systems (Martinson, 1974). It is not as easy to deliver services to people who are defined as "bad" as it is to people who are considered "sick" and can be dealt with as "patients in need of treatment."

As a deviant role, criminality is likely to bring about incarceration at some point unless the criminal is successful at it (which many apparently are). However, there is a limit to how many people can be incarcerated, given the current costs of prison construction, the high cost of incarceration once prisons are built, and the dismal record of success in "correcting" the deviant. As this is is written, there is a waiting list for convicted criminals to enter many state prisons, and the most lengthy sentences are reserved for the most predatory. As a reaction to helplessness, criminality seems to be increasingly popular and largely immune to society's attempts to curtail it.

Activism. Activism, which on the surface would appear to be one of the more positive reactions to powerlessness, has had its bleak side as well. For example, political activists include the Ku Klux Klan, Aryan Nations, and, more recently, the Skinheads. Many such activists have been convicted of criminal offenses, yet still enjoy varying degrees of popular support.

On the positive side, however, activism is a powerful force in the self-help and mutual-aid movement, as is evident in the mobilization and empowerment of gays and lesbians. "Black is beautiful" is a social movement with a self-definition of competence. Individuals with disabilities have used their activism to sensitize public transportation authorities to the need for better access. The American Association of Retired Persons has mobilized elders. Women's rights movements have become a focal point for women's issues. Social action can mobilize and empower at-risk populations. It can provide a direction for energy that might otherwise go unharnessed.

Conformity. Conformity, a reaction that follows the path of least resistance, would seem to provide society with one of the more favored options for powerless people. Although conformity contributes to law enforcement, it also has a negative side. People who join cults are willing to surrender their independence and their identity to powerful leaders in exchange for care and control. Religious cults promising salvation or an alternative society have a ready audience among many powerless people. Members of the Branch Davidians in Waco, Texas, looked to their leader, David Koresh, for leadership even to the point of joining him in a fiery death.

Conformity, while helping large numbers of people identify with ideas and ideals, does not necessarily provide an atmosphere where people can learn to assert themselves by saying "No."

Withdrawal. Since humans are social animals, withdrawal or noninvolvement holds little promise over the long run. While perhaps providing a temporary solution for some deviants, the fact is if people can't live within society, they also can't live without it. This is also true for the powerless.

Communes, numerous during the 1960s, were often based on rejection of and withdrawal from society at large. Most of them experienced a short life span. The lesson to be learned here is that whatever the basis of an alternative community, withdrawal from society is not enough of a principle on which to build a social system. A community must produce some output, which can input to another system, if the community is to be viable. Apparently we cannot live indefinitely behind closed boundaries without paying a heavy personal price.

Group withdrawal is not the only way in which people escape from society. Individual withdrawal into drugs and alcohol are epidemic. This form of withdrawal can provide a circuitous route to criminality, mental illness, conformity, and ultimately into social work practice arenas.

IMPLICATION FOR INTERVENTION

It may be helpful to apply the above 14 stages to a carrier or survivor of an actual social problem. The school dropout problem was discussed earlier. When students drop out of school, there is a negative impact on society, so the behavior is labeled as deviant. Such labels usually emphasize the student's lack of competence and relegate him or her to membership in a devalued group.

Since at least three-quarters of the population have a high school diploma, the minority who don't (deviation) tend to stand out (visibility). The identification of difference is made clear in employment want-ads where a high school diploma or the GED are requisite. The affected youth now feel the impact of the label"dropout" and are more likely to establish deviance and the devaluation of being rejected in the employment market as reality. This devaluation stigmatizes the individual, particularly if he or she is a member of a minority group. At this juncture, the youth may feel that the inability to get a job is as much a function of ethnicity or race as of lack of education. In any event, a feeling of oppression follows and the dropout is more likely to lapse into the role of victim. Alienation and powerlessness follow, and the youth is more prone to be at risk for reacting dysfunctionally.

Intervention at What Stage?

Traditionally, social work intervention has occurred at the final point in the chain of events: the point of reaction. By design, social service agencies are programmed to serve people who react in ways that threaten the welfare and safety of themselves and others. Until someone becomes a ''case,'' he or she usually remains ineligible for services. This of course produces a workforce oriented to caseloads and casework. It is one of the central factors in our seeming inability to move forward in this chain of events to a point where there would be more potential for education and prevention and less need for the huge expenditure of resources associated with remediation.

From an integrated-practice perspective, we wish to think in terms of preventive social work practice. We must conceive of interventions that can be made as early as possible; interventions that are proactive, positive, and designed to promote well-being. Primary, secondary, and tertiary prevention strategies can be implemented at various points in this chain of events.

Normalization and Positive Visibility as Early Intervention

A view of behavior from a normative environmental context instead of from a normal/abnormal dichotomy attempts to decrease devaluation of difference. Three factors are considered in a normalized view of behavior (Ingleby, 1980). First, behavior viewed in its environmental context becomes understandable in its specific circumstance, and given that specific set of circumstances, behavior is a normative response. Second, behavior is purposive. It is intended to convey a message about the specific situation. It can be viewed as a form of protest against environmental press or as a way of coping with the environment. And finally, behavior is understandable when viewed in its cultural code of conventions.

The authors have had occasion to observe a group of developmentally disabled young people who work in a nearby cafeteria. Their training, based on ''normalization'' (Wolfensberger, 1973), gives them a type of visibility that emphasizes their similarity to other people rather than their differences.

This normalizing principle emphasizes the common bonds shared by all people and stresses positive visibility and positive labeling.

The impact of positive visibility is that the population at large develops higher thresholds of tolerance for the devalued population. A feature story on television depicting convicts living in a halfway house reflects the normal striving of people everywhere. Giving visibility to their neighborly acts, such as raking leaves and shoveling snow for elderly citizens, pairs positive labeling with positive behavior. The message is that devalued people can perform valuable acts.

Positive visibility, then, detracts from the tendency to focus on people's differences. While there have been and always will be differences among people, focusing on the potential for positive social exchange sets the stage for valuing diversity rather than devaluing it. Affirmative action has helped place minorities and women in situations where they have more visibility. Although affirmative action has had the force of law, it also demonstrates the valuable social exchange inherent in this practice. It provides positive labels for devalued populations and makes it much more difficult to return to the old practices of exclusion. In that same vein, once gays and lesbians began to display their political clout, their visibility became a positive force that could not be reversed.

Competency-Based Screening

As an antidote to labeling and devaluation, competency-based screening in assessment emphasizes strengths, not deficits. In what Maluccio (1981) referred to as a new/old approach to social work practice, competence-based social work is defined as ecological competence containing three interactional components: the client's capacities and skills, the client's motivation, and the significant environmental qualities impinging on the client's functioning. Capacities, skills, and motivation are often overlooked in problem analysis in deference to the negative factors that are impinging on clients. Albee's (1982) equation for prevention, described in Chapter 2, suggests that competency in clients can be identified in self-esteem, coping skills, and social supports. This approach focuses on the clients' strengths and competencies as a focus for promotion and enhancement, rather than on deficits or weaknesses.

To the extent that normalization, positive visibility, positive labeling, and competency-based screens are promoted, the establishment of deviance can be weakened and devaluation will be less likely to occur. To the extent devaluation is reduced, the next links on the chain, discrimination and oppression, will be curbed, reducing feelings of oppression, alienation, and resulting powerlessness. If people can become empowered rather than disempowered, their at-risk status will be lessened as will the likelihood of reacting adversely.

Obviously social work cannot change its emphasis overnight. At best, these changes—moving toward promoting and preventive interventions—will be evolutionary. They will require new constructions of reality and new conceptual and interventive tools. We discuss these tools in Chapter 4 as we consider empowerment, competency assessment, habilitation, and promotion as practice principles that counter devaluation and oppression.

SUMMARY

Two competing schools of thought dictate which reality will prevail in explaining deviant behavior. The absolutist view, which maintains that fundamental human behavior can be classified as inherently proper or self-evidently immoral, evil, or abnormal, is in direct opposition to the relativist or interactionist perspective, which in essence explains deviance as a struggle over values. In this view, the more powerful elements of society evaluate and control the less powerful ones. Social work is practiced from an interactionist value perspective in an absolutist environment.

The process of deviance consists of 14 stages that the labeled goes through: deviation, visibility, identification of difference, labeling, establishment of deviance, devaluation, stigmatization, discrimination, oppression, victimization, alienation, powerlessness, becoming at risk, and reaction. The forms of reaction open to the deviant are mental illness, criminality, activism, conformity, and withdrawal; each reaction has specific liabilities.

For the social worker, the significance of these 14 steps is that while each has its downside, they also provide opportunities for earlier intervention through normalization, positive visibility, competency-based screening, positive labeling, competency building, and empowerment.

STUDY QUESTIONS

1. What is the difference between the absolutist and interactionist views of deviance? Provide an example of each.

2. Trace a particular member of a specific population through the 14 steps in deviancy and labeling. What observation did you make as you traveled the "critical path"?

3. Think of some ways in which you might intervene with this population earlier in the critical path. What would these interventions look like? How would they differ from traditional interventions?

4. What does normalization mean and how does it apply to poor people, and to oppressed groups such as ethnic minorities, gays and lesbians, or women?

REFERENCES

Albee, G. (1982). Preventing psychopathology and promoting human potential. *American Psychologist 37*, pp. 1043–1050.

Akers, R. J. (1985). *Deviant behavior: A social learning approach*. Belmont, CA: Wadsworth.

Berger, P., & Luckman, T. (1967). *The social construction of reality*. New York: Doubleday.

Blumer, H. (1969). *Symbolic interactionism: Perspective and method*. Englewood Cliffs, NJ: Prentice-Hall.

Cervantes, S. M. (1605/1964). *Don Quixote of La Mancha*. New York: New American Library.

Compton, B., & Galaway, B. (1989). *Social work processes* (4th ed.). Pacific Grove, CA: Brooks/Cole.

Conrad, P., & Schneider, J. W. (1988). *Deviance and medicalization*. St. Louis: C. V. Mosby.

Diagnostic and statistical manual of mental disorders. (1987). Arlington, VA: American Psychiatric Association.

DiNitto, D. M., & Dye, T. R. (1991). *Social welfare: Politics and public policy* (3rd ed.). Englewood Cliffs, NJ: Prentice-Hall.

Erickson, K. (1966). *Wayward Puritans*. New York: Wiley.

Gilliland, B. E., & James, R. K. (1992). *Crisis intervention strategies*. Pacific Grove, CA: Brooks/Cole.

Goode, E. (1978). *Deviant behavior: An interactionist approach*, Englewood Cliffs, NJ: Prentice-Hall.

Goodwin, D. K. (1987). *The Fitzgeralds and the Kennedys*. New York: Simon & Schuster.

Halleck, S. L. (1967). *Psychiatry and the dilemmas of crime*. New York: Harper & Row.

Heiss, J. (1981). *The social psychology of interaction*. Englewood Cliffs, NJ: Prentice-Hall.

Hendin, H. (1964). *Suicide and Scandinavia: A psychoanalytic study of culture and character*. New York: Grune & Stratton.

Higgins, P. C., & Butler, R. R. (1962). *Understanding deviance*. New York: McGraw-Hill.

Hills, S. L. (1980). *Demystifying social deviance*. New York: McGraw-Hill.

Hite, S. (1987). *The Hite Report women and love: A Cultural revolution in progress*. New York: Knopf. (p. 922).

Hooker, C. E. (1976 May). Learned helplessness. *Social Work 21*(3), pp. 194–198.

Ingleby, D. (Ed.). (1980). *Critical psychology*. New York: Pantheon Books.

Keillor, G. (1985). *Lake Wobegon days*. New York: Viking Press.

Kesey, K. (1962). *One flew over the cuckoo's nest*. New York: Signet, New American Library.

Linton, R. (1952). Universal ethical principles: An anthropological view. In Ruth N. Anshen (Ed.), *Moral principles of action*, pp. 645–660. New York: Harper & Row.

Longres, J. F. (1990). *Human behavior and the social environment*. Itasca, IL: F. E. Peacock.

Maluccio, A. N. (Ed.). (1981). *Promoting competence in clients*. New York: Free Press.

Martinson, R. (1974 Spring). What works? Questions and answers about prison reform. *The Public Interest 35.*

Matza, D. (1969). *Becoming deviant.* Englewood Cliffs, NJ: Prentice-Hall.

May, R. (1972). *Power and innocence.* New York: Norton.

Mechanic, D. (1969). *Mental health and social policy.* Englewood Cliffs, NJ: Prentice-Hall.

Norton, D. (1978). *The dual perspective.* New York: Council on Social Work Education.

Pfuhl, E. H., Jr. (1986). *The deviance process.* Belmont, CA: Wadsworth.

Szasz, T. (1961 Feb.). The myth of mental illness. *American Psychologist 15,* pp. 113–118.

Szasz, T. S. (1970). *Ideology and insanity.* Garden City, NY: Doubleday.

Wolfensberger, W. (1973). *Normalization in the delivery of human services.* Toronto, Canada: National Association for Mental Retardation.

Part Two

Concepts for Deciding What to Do: Goal Setting, Planning, and Evaluating

This section deals with knowledge that guides practitioners in deciding what to do. Through a series of actions and interactions, social work practice involves phases of activity that move from initial engagement to intervention to termination. These phases encompass activities such as assessment, problem solving, planning, and evaluation and are a part of change and role taking.

Empowerment is the key process in this framework. Chapter 4 defines and develops empowerment as both an outcome and a process. Sources of powerlessness and components of empowerment from the social science literature are discussed. Implications for empowerment-based practice are developed. An example of an empowerment-based intervention is presented.

Social workers are constantly dealing with the change process. To facilitate purposeful change, they assume a variety of practice roles. Chapter 5, "Role Taking in Social Work Practice," examines the dynamics of assuming practice roles when engaging a client system. Professional roles are categories of activity or functions that social workers take on during the intervention process. The process of role taking is presented within the framework of the worker's orientation to change, the organization climate, the client system, professional values and ethics, and the political environment. Each of these aspects, in combination, determines the nature of the goals and objectives of interventions, resources, and sanctions, and of the available knowledge base. All of these factors form a context within which a social worker operates. Ultimately, the nature of practice demands influences the selection of professional practice roles.

This section concludes with Chapter 6, a discussion of evaluation of practice. Evaluation is a means of objectively assessing role performance in professional practice in terms of its efficacy and efficiency. It is a systematic process of monitoring progress toward outcomes during phases of intervention and of assessing the overall efficiency and effectiveness of intervention outcomes. Specific evaluation approaches appropriate to integrated practice, action research, and goal-attainment scaling are described and illustrated.

The chapters in this section build on the conceptual foundation developed in the first section. Both change and role-taking processes build on habilitation and empowerment principles that promote competence building and person/environment perspectives to practice. Later chapters will incorporate these principles in discussion of specific practice roles.

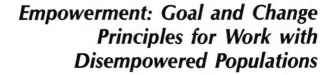

Chapter 4

Empowerment: Goal and Change Principles for Work with Disempowered Populations

POWERLESSNESS AS A TARGET OF SOCIAL WORK INTERVENTION
Internalization of Powerlessness
Sources of Powerlessness

EMPOWERMENT AS A PROCESS AND AN OUTCOME
Necessary Components for Empowerment-Based Intervention
Empowerment as a Developmental Process
Summary

EMPOWERMENT AS A PRINCIPLE FOR SELECTION OF PRACTICE STRATEGIES
Strategy Selection
Specific Strategies
Large-System Strategies
Differences Between the Empowerment Approach
and More Traditional Approaches

SUMMARY

STUDY QUESTIONS

REFERENCES

Many social work clients are caught in the downward spiral of labeled deviance and devaluation. They see themselves as powerless to make changes in their lives. In particular, at-risk disempowered populations are impacted by the devaluation ideology of differences. This chapter defines the goal of social work practice with oppressed populations as facilitation of empowerment. We describe empowerment-based practice and give an example.

From the friendly visiting programs to the settlement house movements and social reform activities, the focus of concern in social work has been disenfranchised and oppressed populations. Defined as intervention in the transaction between individuals and their environments, the overriding goal has been (1) to enable people to overcome those conditions that keep them from participating in the benefits of the society, and (2) to find ways to meet their needs so they could develop and function within their environment to the best of their potential.

Beyond these general agreements about purpose and goal, commonalities in the profession have been harder to define. How to facilitate that transaction has not been as clearly defined. As a result, social work activities have been directed toward the individual, family, or group end of that transaction (helping those microsystems and macrosystems change their understanding and coping skills, as well as toward the organizational and community end (engaging in change in environmental system structures, organizations, and communities so that individual and family needs are met more readily).

The enormous breadth of such intervention has created a great disparity in methodology, tools, and knowledge and a breadth of disciplines from which these are borrowed. We have emulated specializations in both ends of the transaction between people and their environments. In our efforts to become competent in adapted methods, we have often lost or forgotten our profession's goal and purpose. Moreover, we have split into functional groups around these methods and even argued that one or the other was more viable and more primary as a social work activity. This chapter tries to define the common goal of social work activities as empowerment of client systems and suggests using that goal as a focus to guide the selection and use of methods and strategies, regardless of which end of the transaction is involved.

POWERLESSNESS AS A TARGET OF SOCIAL WORK INTERVENTION

Excessive powerlessness felt by the general population has been a source of much discussion and commentary in recent decades. Groups that are discriminated against by the general society—such as lower socioeconomic classes, ethnic minorities, women, the aging population, and people with disabilities—are particularly vulnerable to perceived powerlessness (Kieffer, 1984; Torre, 1985). The diversity and difference represented by these groups are often viewed as "deviant" and therefore devalued. The difference could just as well be valued and celebrated but instead it is often labeled as a problem, creating the potential processes described earlier.

Degrees of powerlessness are present at various levels on the deviance and labeling spiral, but powerlessness is viewed as a problem of stigmatized groups as well as the general population (Berger & Neuhaus, 1977; Nisbet, 1953). Berger and Neuhaus suggest that the "mediating structures" through which individuals negotiate relationships to the larger environment have been eroded. The resulting cultural value claims the efficacy of individual autonomy in the face of a sociopolitical reality of overwhelming social forces (Simmel, 1977).

The weakening of the American community through increased industrial specialization and a mobile work force (Warren, 1978) has eroded such standard "mediating structures" as community organizations, churches, and families that could previously be relied on for support, mutual aid, and joint problem solving. People's capacities to be influential in the sociopolitical environment have also eroded. Therefore, many people perceive themselves to be powerless in the face of the economic system, the political system, religious and educational systems, legal and justice systems, and, even on a more immediate level, the family and peer group system. This lack of power, noted by Sennet and Cobb (1972) and Conway (1979), is based on several factors: economic insecurity, absence of experience in the political arena, absence of access to information, lack of fiscal support, lack of training in abstract and critical thought, and physical and emotional stress (Cox, 1988, p. 112).

Internalization of Powerlessness

As individuals experience powerlessness in relation to the social systems that impinge on them, they may internalize that feeling and come to see themselves as helpless. This concept has been described as alienation (Seeman, 1985), learned helplessness (Seligman, 1972), or "surplus powerlessness" (Lerner, 1986). Lerner describes it as a process in which people contribute to real powerlessness by allowing their own emotional, intellectual, and spiritual mind-set to prevent them from actualizing possibilities that actually exist. For example, while AFDC (Aid to Families with Dependent Children) recipients are somewhat powerless to change these programs and benefits, their perception of themselves as powerless vis-à-vis the bureaucracy increases their actual powerlessness. Perceived powerlessness can be viewed as a "construction of continuous interaction between the individual and his/her environment . . . and combines an attitude of self-blame, a sense of generalized distrust, a feeling of alienation from resources for social influence, and a sense of hopelessness in sociopolitical struggle" (Kieffer, 1984, p. 9). As a result of this process, many social work clients perceive themselves as powerless and may blame and devalue themselves as a result. Membership in a stigmatized group increases the likelihood of such a process. The spiral sequence suggests that powerlessness may lead to oppression and alienation.

However, power is thought to be a critical component in functioning. William Ryan summarized the concept of power in helping disadvantaged groups in his powerful book *Blaming the Victim* (1972). He suggested that a sense of power is essential to self-esteem and survival. Mentally healthy persons must be able to perceive themselves as at least minimally powerful—that is, capable of influencing the environment to their benefit—and this sense of power must be based on the actual experience of exercising power. An internalized sense of powerlessness or a sense of locus of control (Phares, 1965; Rotter, 1966) results in a dynamic of debilitation and self-blame.

Sources of Powerlessness

Solomon (1976), in her important contribution to the concept of power in social work, identified three potential sources of powerlessness: negative self-valuation, negative interaction with the environment, and larger environmental systems that resist action by smaller systems.

Negative Self-Valuation. Powerlessness may come from the negative self-evaluation attitudes that oppressed people hold. For example, women or ethnic minorities may feel less powerful simply because they were socialized to see themselves as not having equal power in society.

Negative Interaction with the Environment. Powerlessness may also come from negative experiences in the interaction between the victims of oppression and the outside systems that impinge on them. For instance, women or ethnic minorities may attempt to influence their organizations or groups to hire more women and minorities and find that their goals or values are not reinforced by the organization and their power to change that situation is limited.

Larger Environment. Powerlessness may also result from larger environmental systems that consistently block and deny effective action taking by powerless groups. In the same example, institutionalized policies that inherently discriminate against women and minorities may still serve as governing policies in the agency or organization.

Any one of these sources or combination of sources may set up perceived powerlessness and subsequently a self-blaming dynamic in an individual. Low self-esteem, so often viewed as a primary problem in troubled clients, may be a result of this interactional dynamic around powerlessness, not the cause of it. This screen of understanding the process of powerlessness represents an interactional perspective of social problems with elements of value conflict, deviant behavior, and the labeling perspectives.

To intervene in the downward spiral of devaluation, empowerment-based practice is needed for work with oppressed populations. Social work intervention takes place in the transaction between individuals and their environments. The power differential between individuals and environmental systems is often so great that individuals cannot perceive themselves as competent to take action on their own behalf. This marginalized status may increase from the simple labeling of difference by society to deviant and devalued. When client groups blame themselves for the situation, perceived helplessness occurs and empowerment as a goal seems obvious.

But, what is the empowerment process? What is involved in the process of assisting people not only to *believe* they are more efficacious in the face of their problems, but also to assist them to *act* in resolution of those problems? Does the process merely imply a change in attitude? Or must attitude change on the clients' part be accompanied by a change in outcome for the client population as well? Does one or the other create greater empowerment for clients, or are both components necessary? Although it has become a byword of the 1980s, the clarity and understanding of empowerment are not as widespread as its use. Rappaport said:

> Empowerment is easy to define in its absence; powerlessness, real or imagined; learned helplessness; alienation; loss of a sense of control over one's life. It is more difficult to define positively only because it takes on a different form in different people and contexts. [Hegar & Hunzeker, 1988, p. 3]

The next section will explore the meaning of empowerment both in terms of a *process* and as a *product* and its implication for empowerment-based practice.

EMPOWERMENT AS A PROCESS AND AN OUTCOME

"Empowerment is like obscenity; you have trouble defining it but you know it when you see it" (Rappaport, 1986, p. 69).

Webster's New World Dictionary (1982) defines the word *empower* as "to give power or authority to; to give ability to; enable; permit." These definitions assume the act of power is given to someone by someone else. However, power is rarely given away. When it passes hands, it is usually taken or at a minimum shared but not simply given or handed over. In an intervention, social workers do not own power that they can give to clients. Power exists within the clients, not outside them. In an important contribution to the concept, Staples (1987) used the prefix *em* with the word *power* to create a definition of empowerment as the process of gaining power, developing power, taking or seizing power, or facilitating or enabling power. This definition more accurately reflects social work intervention.

Human services literature is quite diverse in the conceptualization of empowerment. Torre (1985) identified at least three major themes in the literature defining empowerment.

1. A developmental process that begins with individual growth, and possibly culminates in larger social change

2. A psychological state marked by heightened feelings of self-esteem, efficacy, and control

3. Liberation resulting from a social movement, which begins with education and politicization of powerless people and later involves collective attempts by the powerless to gain power and to change those structures that remain oppressive

Based on a vast amount of literature, covering a wide disparity of viewpoints from the political left to the right, Torre concluded in her synthesis that empowerment can be defined as

> a process through which people become strong enough to participate within, share in the control of, and influence events and institutions affecting their lives, [and that in part,] empowerment necessitates that people gain particular skills, knowledge, and sufficient power to influence their lives and the lives of those they care about. [1985, p. 18]

Similarly, Kieffer (1981) reported a convergence of three components within the concept of empowerment: citizenship competence, sociopolitical literacy, political competence or participatory competence (p. 26). He listed the requisite conditions of these components as follows:

1. A *personal attitude* or sense of self that promotes active social involvement

2. *Knowledge and capacity* for critical analysis of the social and political systems that define the environment

3. An *ability to develop action strategies* and cultivate resources for attainment of own goals

4. An *ability to act* in an efficacious manner in concert with others to define and attain collective goals

Furthermore, these components are compatible with Solomon's definition of empowerment as a "feeling, conviction, or perception of intrinsic or extrinsic value which manifests itself as achievement of self-determined goals through the use of personal resource and skill'' (1976, p. 19).

In summary, empowerment is a process of change in which people come to see themselves as able to take action in the face of impinging problems. What is involved then in this process from the standpoint of a helping professional? Social workers don't own power to give to clients but try instead to help them tap their own empowerment process. How is this accomplished? How does this process come about?

Necessary Components for Empowerment-Based Intervention

Literature on empowerment is generally consistent that the process is initiated by interaction with others, and it is through this interaction that support, mutual aid, and validation for one's perceptions and experiences are received. This begins the initial process for targeting internalization of powerlessness. Validation and perception of commonality are critical to the development of heightened self-esteem and self-confidence and the perception of personal efficacy (Torre, 1985). For example, many social work programs that deal with women's issues of sexual abuse and domestic violence found that the use of groups is necessary to help women perceive their experiences as common to others and to regain self-esteem.

If the process of empowerment comes initially through interaction with others, it helps guide the selection of concepts to be used in a practice framework, and of methodologies and strategies to attain the desired goal. The following practice components must be present in social work practice for the intervention to contribute to the empowerment of clients:

♦ Power-shared relationships
♦ Competency-based assessment
♦ Collectivity for mutual aid
♦ Education for critical thinking, and knowledge and skills for finding resources and taking action

Power-Shared Relationships.   Our discussion of the development of clients' power and influence would not be complete without touching on the power differentials that exist between worker and client and how they impact empowerment practice. Social workers often have a negative view of having or using power. We deny our power in relation to clients because we don't like it. However, power differentials are a natural part of the work. We need only ask our clients about their perception of how egalitarian our past work has been to get a sense of the power differentials that exist.

Even when social workers operate from an egalitarian value system in relation to clients, service delivery systems create power differences between workers and clients. The subtle processes that disempower clients are influenced by the profession's ideological perspectives and guiding principles. Some theories are expert based and do not give credence to the client's view. Many practice techniques do not seek mutuality in the intervention process. We often label clients as "resistant" when they do not accept our definition of their problems. We label clients who do not get "better" as a result of our prescribed treatment as "nonamenable" to treatment.

The agency and organization base of practice also creates power differences between worker and client. Services may be designed to have a disempowering effect on the client population. Social workers have to recognize the power they have in relation to clients and use that power carefully and critically to create empowerment-based practice.

In power-shared relationship, clients are viewed as having equal and legitimate expertise on their own problems and solutions. Gutierrez (1990) suggested that accepting clients' definitions of their problems is a critical part of empowerment practice. A worker brings expertise regarding social problems, problem definition, and assessment to the collaborative process.

Goal setting, planning, and doing are also a collaborative effort. Workers must share their power and facilitate it within their clients. Workers need to recognize the clients' skills, expertise, and competency and bolster these attributes through mutual sharing and education.

Competency-Based Assessment. Much of the social work literature concerns itself with knowledge and assessment tools. What kind of assessment is appropriate with collective dialogue, mutual aid, and collective action? To counter internalized powerlessness, we use *competency-based assessment* done jointly by worker and client. At a minimum, this kind of assessment assumes potential competency on the part of clients. That is, clients generally know what they need and, with heightened self-awareness and support, will choose a good alternative for action on their own behalf. Clients are competent to identify and understand their problems and to choose adequate solutions (see Kopp, 1989). Strengths and coping skills rather than deficits in coping are assessed in relation to impinging stress (see Albee, 1980; Saleebey, 1992). Maluccio's (1981) competency-based practice model suggested that competency-based assessment include motivation for change, capacity for change, and opportunities for change. Gutierrez (1990) suggested that client and worker should engage in a power analysis, which looks at the conditions of powerlessness affecting the situation, the power resources, and the effects of the social-structural context. Social workers need to look for desire, perceived hope, the belief that change can come about, knowledge and skills for making change, and environmental impingements that facilitate or hinder change. Intervention strategies that emanate from competency assessment include building support networks and systems to capitalize on the present strengths for coping. Teaching coping and problem-solving skills should follow a competency-based assessment.

For professional helpers, competency assessment may present an anomaly to the traditional deficit-based or pathology perspective of social problems. By definition, professionals are experts in their areas. Human services professionals are often socialized and expected to be experts in the clients' psychopathology, or individual deficits. To facilitate empowerment, we need to be experts in social problems, but we also need to learn from individual clients about their particular experiences, issues, problems, and coping skills. The expertise that human services professionals assume regarding clients' deficits and pathologies has been criticized as "disabling help" (McKnight, 1977, pp. 69–71) and is the opposite of empowerment-based social work. Perspective deficits are not ignored in a competency assessment, but they are of secondary focus in deference to the strengths. Given time, trust, and opportunity, clients often express their own deficits and self-concerns, which can be a powerful process toward change.

Collectivity for Mutual Aid.   The idea of building collectivity is central to the helping process. Collectivity involves merging the energy of the individuals into a whole. While self-help groups such as Alcoholics Anonymous have been successful as treatment modalities, the formation of collectives for empowerment goes beyond treatment in a group to focus on the social basis of identity. The experience is designed to reduce isolation (Rese, 1990). Collectivity contains William Schwartz's (Lee & Swenson, 1986) notion of providing a mediating or third-force function to help people who need to separate their situations from impinging systems and who in turn must shape those systems and assist in their functioning. The development in clients from powerlessness to personal autonomy and from alienation to interdependent mutual aid and political power requires a blending of reflection and action (Anderson, 1992). The collective provides an opportunity for support, consciousness raising, mutual aid, developing skills, and action on behalf of the whole.

Small groups give clients an opportunity to interact with other people who have similar problems and concerns. If single, low-income parents are to be helped in their role as mother, for example, the best strategy is to create an opportunity for them to interact with and receive validation from others in their situation.

The need for collectives in empowerment exists exclusive of the strength of society's basic mediating structures. The creation of collectives for action may or may not strengthen those mediating structures referred to earlier. However, through collective interaction and validation, members gain the support to act on their own behalf.

Education: Critical Thinking, Knowledge, and Skills for Finding Resources and Taking Action.   Paulo Friere (1972) contributed to the conceptualization of empowerment with a concept called *critical consciousness* or critical thinking. He proposed that for people to consider their situations in a normative, sociopolitical context, they must learn to critically examine them in relation to environments. Dialogue, interaction, and education with others in similar circumstances help individuals develop a critical consciousness regarding their own subjective condition of powerlessness.

Members of the collective effort come to see themselves as part of a common problem in the larger sociopolitical and economic context. Acquisition of knowledge and skills for common problem solving most often occurs through the group process. The power of group cohesion in building collectivity and providing education in problem solving cannot be underestimated. Gutierrez (1990) identified the learning skills and mobilization of resources as necessary techniques in empowerment practice. Gutierrez went on to suggest that the group process is ideal for these activities to take place. Specific information regarding the problem at hand and specific skills for handling it are important parts of empowerment. When working with low-income single parents for example, dialogue around being poor and raising children alone can provide an opportunity for parents to tell their story to people who will understand their plight, to listen to others, to find out about resources, to discuss ways to deal with children, or to share skills. But, perhaps most important, the parents receive a "critical education" by broadening their understanding of their problems from an inward context to a socioenvironmental context and back to a focus on the self and how to proceed. Acquisition of critical thinking skills, knowledge regarding resources, and skills for taking action are necessary for any of us to become self-advocates and advocates for others.

Empowerment as a Developmental Process

In his comprehensive study of the process of empowerment, Charles Kieffer (cited in Maze, 1987, p. 5) analyzed the development of indigenous grassroots organizers. He observed the following four phases of the empowerment process:

1. *Entry.* In this stage an individual realizes the imminence of an immediate threat to self or family and sees the limits of his or her ability to act, thereby becoming engaged in some type of activity to change those limitations.

2. *Advancement.* The individual establishes ties with an enabling and supportive peer group and becomes critically aware of the external causes of problems and of the interrelations of social, economic, and political structures.

3. *Incorporation.* This stage shows maturation of self-concept, strategic ability, and critical comprehension. Here the lessons and concepts learned during the previous phase become internalized, and the individual becomes a shaping influence on the environment.

4. *Commitment.* The individual continually applies empowerment skills and abilities to change the environment and enable others to empower themselves in a similar process.

An entry event, as described by Kieffer, may be a blatant sociological event such as being evicted from an apartment building without cause or a psychological event such as a major life transition or joining a political movement. Any event that creates crises can serve as the basis of the entry phase of empowerment.

In Denver, a neighborhood in the inner-city was being destroyed to make way for a new convention center. Within the targeted neighborhood, an empowerment project with elderly residents was operating in one of the buildings, where a cohesive group of elders met on a regular basis. The threat of their building being destroyed and their group splitting apart provided an entry event for their pulling together and taking collective action. The group of elderly residents demanded that the city move them together to a common site where their supportive empowerment group could continue. The city complied. As a result of their new collective strength, they worked with the landlord in the new building to screen new people who might move into the building, creating a supportive community environment. Much collective strength comes about due to collective problem solving around an entry event.

Social workers often set goals for increasing clients' self-esteem and coping ability (what Kieffer called the incorporation phase), without engaging in that critical linkage to supportive peer groups (described by Kieffer as advancement). Social workers who provide that linkage role testify to the strength and critical influence of the collective on the individual's self-esteem, self-perception, and willingness to act.

The development sequence is a significant reminder that the process of tapping into one's internalized powerlessness may take a longer route than current interventive strategies and modes of intervention. Torre concluded from her study that empowerment is a complex process involving the following components:

♦ Positive perceptions of personal worth, efficacy, and internal locus of control

♦ Recognition, by self and others, that some of one's perceptions about one's self and the surrounding world are indeed valid, and therefore legitimate to voice

♦ The ability to think critically about macro-level structures—namely, the social, political, and economic systems—as well as about one's position within such systems

♦ Knowledge and skills necessary to more successfully influence micro, mediating, and macro system structures

♦ Reflective action directed toward achieving better balanced power relations; action directed toward responsible social change [1985, pp. 42–43]

Creation of these components in practice is complex. It cannot be understood by studying the individual process exclusively or focusing only on the influence of the social structure on the individual. Rather it involves the following: personal perception, interpersonal interaction, interaction between microsystems and mediating structures within communities and neighborhoods, and interaction with the larger environmental system, the political, social, economic, and cultural ideology. It is a cyclical process and perhaps, like labeling and deviancy, may be viewed as a spiral. Empowerment-based intervention is a counter to the downward spiral of labeling, deviancy, and devaluation.

Summary

In summary, the process of empowerment involves developing attitudes and beliefs about one's efficacy to take action; developing critical thinking about one's world, acquiring the knowledge and skills needed to take action, receiving the support and mutual aid of one's peers in any given situation, and taking action to make changes in the face of impinging problems. Empowerment has both a process and an outcome. It is a process in which individuals become critically aware of their relation to the environment and interact with it. Empowerment occurs not only on the individual level, but on the group or collective level as well. Changes may take place within the individual, within the collective itself, or within the larger environment. The critical question is not which end of the transaction between individuals and their environment the empowerment activity is directed toward, but on what that activity is focused. The focus is on the components of empowerment.

EMPOWERMENT AS A PRINCIPLE FOR SELECTION OF PRACTICE STRATEGIES

The components of empowerment guide the selection of strategies for role taking. Strategies have to be chosen carefully so that the empowerment process can develop.

Strategy Selection

The empowerment process takes place most easily in a collective. No literature on empowerment suggests that the process occurs only in a worker-client relationship. Although one-on-one work may augment the development of self-esteem and self-efficacy, it is not the primary strategy of intervention. However, not all social work interventions can take the form of collectivity. Some interventions begin and end with one-on-one intervention. Individually based interventions can, however, link clients to others in similar situations and provide knowledge, education, and skills for understanding problems and taking action. Similarly, social planning, community organization, and other macro-interventions can be directed toward building the client skills that social planning and advocacy models attempt to impact. Social work intervention activities on behalf of client groups such as influence campaigns, legislative lobbying, policy development, and creation of resources may augment the clients' activities but cannot take the place of their involvement in change efforts on their own behalf. This self-help process creates a change in the clients' ability to think and act on their own behalf.

Specific Strategies

Specific strategies for practice with small systems such as individuals and families include those that can be shared with clients for their use in the absence of the social worker. Education and task-oriented methods as well as group methods are important.

Education and Task Models.   Many empowerment-practice advocates suggest that the most critical strategy in empowerment consists of teaching, training, and education. (See, for example, Gutierrez, 1990; Solomon, 1976; Cochran, 1993.) A task-centered approach is a relevant strategy for empowerment because clients can learn and employ it for future use without professional help. Educational and communication models are appropriate family methods for similar reasons. In any microsystem intervention, clients must be educated about their situations and the situations of others like them. Furthermore, they must be linked with others in similar situations for validation of their experience and mutual help and support. This often occurs through group methods.

Group Methods.   Group methods may be the key client system in empowerment-based practice. First and foremost, strategies for empowerment include mutual aid (Gutierrez, 1990) through self-help groups, support groups, network building, education groups, and social action groups. Such strategies provide the opportunity for the dialogue that is needed to develop critical thinking, knowledge and skill building, validation, and support. Mutual aid provides necessary linkage to larger systems that impinge on the group and its defined common problem. These methods may include educational structured groups and mainstream model groups (Papell & Rothman, 1980).

Large-System Strategies

Large-system strategies appropriate for empowerment practice include models of campaigning, legislative lobbying, policy development, community organization, and social planning, which include both consultation and building the victims' skills. Providing services on behalf of clients without their input may provide more resources, but it may or may not enhance the client population's perceived power and efficacy. More specific strategies include conflict management, communication, and problem-solving strategies that clients of diverse functional states can learn. Because conflict is inherent in change of any kind, particularly in brokerage and advocacy types of activity, skills for dealing with conflict are critical to empowerment.

In summary, clients are seen as competent to understand their own situations and to choose, in concert with others in similar situations, appropriate strategies for action. They are viewed as capable of learning knowledge and skills for action and as capable of acting.

Engagement with clients to facilitate their empowerment to solve problems may well be social work's unique position in the wide array of human service programs and approaches in the service community. While current policies and programmatic structures such as third-party payments mitigate against such practice strategies, many opportunities for this kind of intervention still exist. When empowerment is accepted as the goal of intervention, contexts for such intervention are readily available. One such example is described in the following case study. This intervention took place in a Head Start agency.

CASE STUDY: *Single-Parent Support Group* ◆─────────

The Approach

A social worker assigned to a Head Start agency in an inner-city housing project was asked to intervene with the mothers of specific children in the program. For a variety of reasons, these children were having difficulty in school. The problems, which were related to lack of discipline, showed up in the classroom, thus becoming the teachers' concern. The Head Start teachers went on to identify the mothers as single parents who seemed to have some problems with their children's discipline.

The social worker approached each woman to discuss her child and any parenting issues and to assess specifically identified concerns regarding discipline. While some women identified discipline as a specific problem, others seemed to view parenting in stride with other stress-producing situations. The women identified environmental conditions that contributed not only to parenting issues but impacted their lives in general. The social worker did not identify each woman as having a discipline problem with her child, but instead asked each woman if she would like to join a group of women much like herself who had children in the Head Start Center. The worker said the purpose of the group would be to share parenting hassles and solutions. Seven women agreed to come to the group and try it out.

The Group

The group initially consisted of seven members; all but two were Hispanic. One woman was severely scarred from multiple birth defects and subsequent surgeries. Another was illiterate. Their ages ranged from 30 to 45. All were single parents in practice. Two were involved periodically with the father of their children. All were low income, living either on AFDC or at a similar subsistence level. All lived in a public housing project in the same neighborhood. Lupe, a teacher's aide in Head Start, also joined the group. She identified with the other women as a single parent, living at a low level of economic security and being in a similar situation. Her presence encouraged the other women to participate in the group.

The Contract

The social worker began the group by supporting all of the women for being a part of a support group that would share common problems and common solutions about parenting. The group followed a mutual-aid model and was left open for development by members. The model could be characterized as a mainstream model in its allowance for the group to set goals and processes for achieving them (Papell & Rothman, 1980).

The worker reached for the commonality of the group members, including, but not exclusive to, parenting concerns. Although members were willing to share parenting concerns, many other concerns were also voiced. These concerns included many stresses associated with single parenthood, such as low incomes, housing problems, problems in the housing project itself, ex-husbands, boyfriends, relationships with men in general, and general feelings of anger about their lives. The anger seemed to be about being left by the men in their lives to raise children by themselves with no support and no economic base. Quickly, the group turned to venting and sharing their feelings. They needed to have their feelings and perceptions validated and supported.

The social worker facilitated this environment. The members quickly perceived themselves as having common feelings, problems, and experiences, and their feelings about their circumstances were heard and validated. The group's contracted goals expanded beyond dealing with parenting to supporting each other in dealing with the stresses of being poor and a single parent.

The Group Process

Members were reluctant to trust one another with confidentiality due to their close living proximity. They were also reluctant to trust the social worker who was from a different social class and lifestyle. Acceptance of the worker as a leader came about partially because of Lupe's presence. Because Lupe was a teacher and a community resident, her presence bridged the gap between the worker and the group, at least until trust could be developed. However, the trust issues still had to be dealt with. As trust began to build and members felt supported by one another, and expressed feelings about their situations, they were ready to move on to learning more specifically about the context of their situations and about solutions.

The worker brought expertise to the group in the form of information about income and other resources, the housing project system, the city and its resources, and parenting techniques. As members began to voice common problems, they were targeted for work. The members and the worker shared problem-resolution knowledge and skills.

The "Environmental Context" of Single Parenthood

As group members began to share both problems and expertise, they identified many common environmental conditions. These included the following:

♦ A teacher in the neighborhood school whose racist attitudes were a source of irritation to their children and to them
♦ The local grocery store owner who charged an exorbitant fee to cash monthly checks
♦ The local city recreation center director who was selling drugs
♦ Broken-down playground equipment
♦ Poor lighting in the projects that made it unsafe for women and young girls to walk at night for fear of sexual assault
♦ The housing manager who dealt unfairly and capriciously with many residents in the projects

All these issues were integral to parenting and to the environmental contexts of discipline problems between a single parent and her child.

Implementation

One by one, these problems were put on the group's agenda. The worker and the members themselves educated each other about these issues. As action strategies were developed, group members became more convinced that they could take effective action on the problems that impacted their lives.

The group intervened in the school system regarding the racist teacher. They intervened with the city about the recreation center director. They confronted the housing manager about his behavior, and a liaison was appointed from the housing office to work directly with the community residents. When the local grocery store owner refused to lower his prices for cashing a check, the group led a boycott of the store and organized transportation to a major supermarket to buy groceries at a lower price and to cash checks for free.

Linkage with Others.   As successes piled up, and some failures, the group began to observe that there were other entities both within their community and outside that were concerned with similar problems. They began to join forces. For example, group members joined the local community interagency/citizens' action council, which was concerned with the whole community. Through that council, they became members of task forces working on specific community projects. They were able to get the community council to write grants for playground equipment and better lighting. They joined with the community council to get a stoplight at the corner to protect schoolchildren crossing the street. And, eventually, as representatives from the community action council, they began to serve on citywide task forces for various projects.

Becoming Proactive.   Although the group achieved success in collaborating with other community groups, they wanted to continue their group for support and for discussion of parenting and relationships with men. They worked as a subgroup of the community action council for specific community projects. One project was to raise the awareness of the counselors at the local community mental health center regarding the community. They were concerned about their friends, depressed women who were suicidal and abusive to their children. They observed that when these women went to the community mental health center for help, they rarely went back again. Thus, they decided to intervene with the community mental health center itself. They asked counselors to come to the women's homes to see them and to alter their services to fit the culture and needs of the community. They served as liaisons for the community mental center, setting up meetings between specific women and counselors.

Overall, the group lasted approximately three years. Membership changed, but a core group remained active throughout. Discipline was a running theme in the group's discussions, but it was viewed in its environmental context and as related to many other parts of the members' lives. The women's self-esteem as parents and as partners in relationships with men improved remarkably. Consequently, so did their parenting skills.

Discussion

Initially, the group served as a place where the members could be heard and validated, where they could affiliate and experience commonality with others like themselves. Then a second common theme—negative feelings and experiences with men in their lives—emerged and became part of the group agenda. That issue gave the women an opportunity to voice feelings that they needed to let go of in order to relate more effectively to their children and to get on with other issues in their lives. This began the process of targeting the internalized powerlessness perceived by the group members.

Those two aspects of the group gave the women a stronger feeling of *commonality,* increased their ability to *think critically* about their situations, and helped them share *knowledge* and skills regarding their common problems. Then, one by one, they experienced success in *collective problem resolution,* and continued to target subsequent arenas for action. The ability to act collectively increased each woman's *self-esteem* and *self-efficacy,* making her stronger both as an individual and as a group member. Eventually, they were able to function without a professional leader, and the group continued in some form for several years.

───◆

While the initial problem was identified as an individual problem belonging to each woman, the group provided a place for the commonality of those problems to emerge and for collectivity to occur for resolution. If these clients had not linked with others in similar situations, the same results would likely not have occurred. This empowerment-based intervention countered the perceived helplessness, powerlessness, and self-blame of the group members.

Differences Between the Empowerment Approach and More Traditional Approaches

Because the identified problem centered around parenting, many social work interventive strategies would have assessed each parent's parent/child relationship, diagnosed the parenting deficits, defined the situation in terms of individual parent deficit and contracted around goals to improve each woman's parenting skills. Empowerment-based practice emphasizes the social problem focus, which was parenting in the context of single parenthood, low-income households, and other socioenvironmental conditions. Instead of ignoring the context of the problems, it was seen as primary in the assessment. Exploration of the problem included the sociopolitical, economic conditions that affected the parent/child relationship and the parent's views of the child. Assessment included a power analysis and focused on the strengths of the single parent, how she managed to parent successfully, the knowledge and skills she brought to the parenting situation, and her areas of vulnerability.

While many interventive strategies may have called for one-on-one worker/client contracts to work on each mother's parenting ability, empowerment-based practice strategies call for linkage with others in a common situation in order to share, tell stories, receive validation, and confirm their world views and experiences. The collective interaction provides opportunities for transferring knowledge and skills, building self-esteem, and developing a basis for collective reflection and action.

In a more traditional perspective of social work, even if a group were the method of choice, the leadership style would likely have been either structured around learning parenting skills, such as a parent effectiveness group (PET) or psychotherapy-based intervention in which each parent is viewed as having an individual problem that is at the heart of the parenting issue. Empowerment-based social work intervention suggests that it is critical to link the mothers around their common psycho-social-political issues, all of which affect their ability to parent.

In traditional and non–empowerment-based social work, if the socioenvironmental problems were identified as a point of focus, the most likely means of addressing them would be to use the means and structures already existing and outside the client group itself; for example, in the problem with the drug-dealing recreation center director, a more traditional approach might have been for the worker to intervene with the city parks and recreation office to discuss the perceived problem. A more traditional approach to the poor lighting in the projects might have been to refer the problem to the housing authority. Problems with the housing project manager might have been handled by the worker's complaining to the city housing department about the management of the projects.

An empowerment-based approach to the identified problems called for collective action by the problem's recipients. That collectivity included learning about the problems and resources, acquiring skills to act, and finally acting. It called for the social worker to facilitate communication and training for problem solving. Taking action on one's own behalf increases the knowledge, skills, and self-esteem to know what the situation is and to use that knowledge next time. The process of empowerment took place in the collective context. Intervention was directed toward both microsystems and macrosystems, with the group collectivity as the focal point of intervention. Individual change resulted from new roles obtained from group action and from increased self-esteem and increased knowledge obtained through the group experience. Macro-intervention resulted from the group's social action strategies and from other community activities in which the members participated. This collectivity-based intervention resulted in both the process and product of empowerment.

SUMMARY

Empowerment is an appropriate goal for social work intervention at both microlevels and macrolevels. Client populations and people in general may feel powerless to do anything about the problems that confront them. When this feeling is internalized, learned helplessness may occur. Perceived powerlessness comes from negative self-valuation, negative interactive processes with the environment, and powerful, rigid environmental structures that act as closed systems in response to change efforts.

Empowerment is both a developmental process and an outcome of a psychological state or liberation. Its component parts include personal efficacy, the knowledge and skills for critical analysis, the capacity for development of action strategies, and an ability to act. Empowerment-based practice involves competency-based assessment, a normalized view of behavior, education for critical thinking, knowledge, skills, and collective action. When empowerment is a goal, specific strategies become more useful and relevant than others.

While few strategic interventions could be characterized as "pure" empowerment-based or "pure" non–empowerment-based practice, there is a fundamental difference in the way a social worker defines and focuses on problems when empowerment is the goal of intervention. This goal is to build knowledge and skills for problem solving and to create self-efficacy to act on one's own behalf and on the behalf of others.

STUDY QUESTIONS

1. Select a client population that is devalued in our society and discuss the specific sources of powerlessness.
2. For the same population, identify "mediating structures" that exist or don't exist for problem solving.
3. Summarize the components of empowerment as suggested by the literature presented in this chapter.

4. Characterize the key differences in an empowerment-based practice approach as compared to traditional approaches in social work.

5. Explain how empowerment-based practice fits with the deviancy-and-labeling perspective of social problems.

REFERENCES

Anderson, J. (1992). Between individual and community: Small group practice in a generalist perspective. Paper presented at Annual Program Meeting, Council on Social Work Education, Kansas City, KS.

Albee, G. (1980). A competency model must replace the defect model. In L. A. Bond & J. C. Rosen (Eds.), *Competence and coping during adulthood.* Hanover: University Press of New England.

Berger, P. L., & Neuhaus, R. J. (1977). *To empower people.* Washington, DC: American Enterprise Institute for Public Policy Research (p. 2).

Cochran, M. (1993). Parent empowerment: Developing a conceptual framework. *Family Science Review, 5*(1 & 2). pp. 81–92.

Conway, M. (1979). *Rise gonna rise.* New York: Anchor Books.

Cox, E. (1988). Empowerment interventions in aging. *Social Work with Groups, 11*(4), pp. 111–125.

Friere, P. (1972). *Pedagogy of the oppressed.* New York: Herder & Herder.

Gutierrez, L. M. (1990). Working with a woman of color. *Social Work, 35,* pp. 149–153.

Hegar, R., & Hunzeker, J. (1988). Moving toward empowerment-based practice in public child welfare. *Social Work, 33*(6).

Kieffer, C. H. (1984 Winter/Spring). Citizen empowerment: A developmental perspective. *Prevention in Human Services, 3,* pp. 9–36.

Kieffer, C. H. (1981). *The emergence of empowerment: The development of participatory competence among individuals in citizen organizations.* Doctoral dissertation, University of Michigan.

Kopp, J. (1989). Self-observation: An empowerment strategy in assessment. *Social Casework: The Journal of Contemporary Social Work, 70*(5), pp. 276–286.

Lee, J., & Swenson, C. (1986). The concept of mutual aid. In A. Gitterman & L. Shulman (Eds.), *Mutual aid groups and the life cycle.* Itasca, IL: F. E. Peacock.

Lerner, M. (1986). *Surplus powerlessness.* Oakland: Institute of Labor and Mental Health.

McKnight, J. (1977). Professionalized service and disabling help. In I. Illich (Ed.), *The disabling professions.* London: M. Boyars.

Maluccio, A. (Ed.). (1981). *Promoting competence in clients.* London: Free Press.

Maze, T. (1987). Empowerment: Reflections on theory and practice. *Aging Network News, 4*(5), pp. 4–9.

Nisbet, R. (1953). *Community and power.* New York: Oxford University Press.

Papell, C., & Rothman, B. (1980). Relating the mainstream model and social work with groups to group psychotherapy and the structured group approach. *Social Work with Groups, 3*(2), pp. 5–23.

Phares, J. (1965). Internal control as a determinant of amount of social influence exerted. *Journal of Personality and Social Psychology, 2* (5), pp. 642–647.

Rappaport, J. (1986). Collaborating for empowerment: Creating the language of mutual help. In H. C. Boyle & F. Riessman (Eds.), *The new populism: The politics of empowerment,* pp. 64–87. Philadelphia: Temple University Press.

Rese, S. M. (1990). Advocacy/empowerment: An approach to clinical practice for social work. *Journal for Sociology and Social Welfare, 17*(2), pp. 41–51.

Rotter, J. (1966). Generalized expectancies for internal vs. external control reinforcement. *Psychological monographs 80.*

Ryan, W. (1972). *Blaming the victim.* New York: Random House.

Saleebey, D. (1992). *The strengths perspective in social work practice.* New York: Longman.

Seeman, M. (1985). Alienation studies. In A. Inkeles, J. Coleman, & N. Smelser (Eds.), *Annual review of sociology* (pp. 91–123). Palo Alto, CA: Annual Reviews, Inc.

Seligman, M. (1972). *Helplessness.* San Francisco: Freeman & Co.

Sennet, R., & Cobb, J. (1972). *The hidden injuries of class.* New York: Vintage Books.

Simmel, G. (1977). The metropolis and mental life. In R. Warren (Ed.), *New perspectives on the American community* (3rd ed.). Chicago: Rand McNally.

Solomon, B. (1976). *Black empowerment: Social work in oppressed communities.* New York: Columbia University Press.

Staples, L. (1987). *Powerful ideas about empowerment.* Unpublished manuscript.

Torre, D. (1985). *Empowerment: Structured conceptualization and instrument development.* Doctoral Dissertation, Cornell University, Ithaca, New York.

Warren, R. (1978). *The community in America.* Chicago: Rand McNally.

Webster's New World Dictionary. (1982, 2nd college ed.). New York: Simon & Schuster.

Role Taking in Social Work Practice

S ocial workers are change agents. Through a variety of strategies and tactics, based on such factors as their style as a change agent, approaches to managing conflict, and agency goals and sanctions, social workers pursue various forms of change in a planned systematic way.

In pursuing change the worker enters into one of the six professional interventive roles: conferee, enabler, broker, advocate, mediator, and guardian. In later chapters, we will examine the activities that accompany each of these roles. This chapter, however, explores the dynamics that lead to the decision of which role to assume.

In deciding what to do in relation to social problems, and more specifically client problems, social workers constantly consider change and the change process. Whether engaged as a conferee or enabler, working one-on-one with individuals toward personal growth, or engaged as an advocate working to change larger systems on behalf of a class of individuals, social workers are involved in either trying to initiate, guide, or prevent change from happening.

A field practicum student with whom the authors worked several years ago returned from his field placement in a residential child care facility and sought out one of the authors. He was deeply troubled by what he had seen. In the student's opinion, the leader of the treatment team to which he had been assigned had gone out of his way to cause a resident to cry during a group therapy session. Thinking there must have been a professional therapeutic reason, the student sought out the team leader after the session to gain some insight. The team leader said there was no particular reason for his being so aggressive. He simply ''liked to try things out.''

The point is that professional role taking is not a matter of ''trying things out.'' There must be both a rationale and an intent for what we do. Role taking is the conscious use of the professional self; there is nothing casual or random about it. Professional roles help us categorize professional activity. In a sense, role taking is a form of shorthand that provides concise understanding of the professional activity that will be called for. Just as the role of Hamlet predicts how he will act, so too the role of advocate gives guidance to how it should be played out. The analogy has limits, however, that are imposed by the nature of the social welfare system. This theater of operations is much more complex and has many more directors and actors than the ordinary playhouse. Thus more goes into role taking than the social worker's intent, as important as that intent may be.

A FRAMEWORK FOR ROLE TAKING

Social services are generated from a series of complicated interactions. Just as the delivery of a newspaper requires the involvement of many people, so too does the delivery of a social service. Unlike the delivery of a newspaper, however, social services are tailored to the needs of each receiver; thus they differ in their make-up from individual to individual. Because they are designed to maintain or promote the well-being of unique populations, social services are seldom uniform in their design and in the way they are perceived at the individual level. This characteristic prescribes that they be provided through a variety of professional roles.

First of all, what is meant by the term *role*? Compton and Galaway (1989, p. 506) defined role as "a set of expected behaviors." When these expected behaviors are translated into actual behavior, they are defined as "role enactment." Interventive roles are depicted as client and worker behaviors, which are related to the goals specified in a service contract. This delineation is important because it helps us separate out personal roles from professional roles.

A framework for role taking is depicted in Figure 5.1. As can be seen, the practitioner operates within a multitude of forces originating from (1) the agency of service or change, (2) the client (consumer), and (3) the profession. The social worker (change agent), responding to the restraining and driving nature of these forces, engages in a course of action that involves performing at a certain level of competence in the six identified professional roles. This all takes place in an ever-changing political environment. Let us examine how this operates in more detail.

POLITICAL ENVIRONMENT

Social work service is political. Earlier we discussed political perspectives and their implication for social work practice. While the word *political* is generally considered synonymous with governmental action, the term as used here is more inclusive. We know there is a political aspect to all human systems. But what is it? The root of the term *politic* suggests that political considerations would take into account such factors as what is prudent, diplomatic, discrete, and expedient. Thus for our purposes, the term *political* relates to the prudent, discreet, diplomatic, and expedient delivery of social services. There is, of necessity, a certain amount of built-in conflict among these terms. For example, what may be prudent may not necessarily be expedient. The political environment, then, relates to how hospitable the environment is for social work and social welfare.

In this sense, the profession of social work and its clientele have a common bond in that they both exist in a generally hostile task environment (Weinbach, 1990). For social agencies whose constituencies are often powerless and devalued, the political reality is that social work practice is often considered tainted. Like the consumers of social services, the deliverers are also suspect. Providing social services to populations at risk is seldom

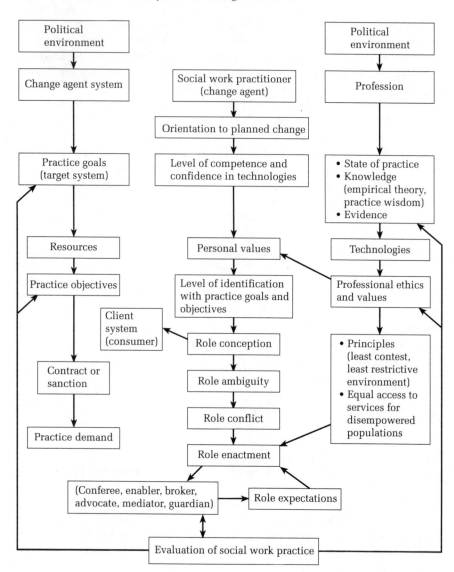

Figure 5.1 Framework for role taking

politically popular, because devalued people usually come from disempowered populations, nonconstituencies, in a sense.

Social welfare programs, like buildings, reflect necessary compromises between the visions of their architects and the resources of their engineers. The former Speaker of the House of Representatives, Tip O'Neill, once said, "All politics is local." That is, political actions at any level have ramifications at the local level. The delivery of social services, a political act, is no exception. It is often a trade-off between the ideal of what should be done and the pragmatics of what can be done. In other words, what is expedient? The disparity between the promise and the practice of social work has often been determined by the relative popularity of politicians, their programs, and the ramifications in terms of rewards and punishments.

The political environment doesn't necessarily imply only partisan politics or only conservative-liberal-radical ideology. Although political discussion often takes place within such an ideological context, political agreements also emerge out of convenience or necessity.

If "all politics is local," then the profession of social work certainly is not immune, whether at the local chapter level or at national headquarters. It, too, is besieged by factions representing its many interests, and all demand an audience and a voice. The implication is that social workers who are planning a career combating social problems will soon discover that political astuteness is a primary requirement.

While political and economic dynamics are often presented as applying exclusively to macro practice and policy arenas, these concepts really apply to all levels of social work practice. Because social work practice is predominately agency based, it is directly affected by the dynamics of political economies. To practice effectively, social workers must understand how organizational dynamics affects them. As formal organizations, agencies are themselves political economies in the sense that they have formal and informal processes and structures that differentially distribute power and influence to their members. Clearly, there are positions within any agency structure that are vested with differing authorities and responsibilities. Similarly, there are differences in how prestige and rewards are distributed within any organization. What is critical to understanding the effect of organizational dynamics is understanding the various external and internal forces at play in any organization.

External forces are generally thought of as policy directives, resources, and social ideology. How social problems are defined in the political arena, what resources are allocated toward addressing these problems, and how social ideologies converge to determine what approaches are "acceptable" for intervention influence to a large extent the nature of the programs that agencies develop. The nature of these programs in turn influences what individual practitioners do or don't do in regard to their practice.

Internal forces are organizational ideology, goals, structure, administrative leadership style, communication patterns, staffing patterns, and individual affiliations. The interplay between internal and external forces creates the dynamics that makes social services delivery a political process.

CHANGE AGENT SYSTEM

In our view, a social welfare agency can be viewed as an agency both of service and of change. The agency as a change agent system is from Pincus and Minahan's (1973) conceptualization of social work intervention as involving four systems: the change agent system, the client system, the target system and an action system. The *change agent system* consists of the worker's, or change agent's, employing agency. The *client system* represents the individual or group of individuals who have sanctioned the change action system to intervene with them or on their behalf. The *target system* is that system that will need to be affected in order to bring about the change objectives of the intervention effort. The *action system* is that system that is mobilized in alliance with the change agent and client systems to influence the target system.

At times, each of these systems will be separate and distinct. In other instances, the client, target, and action systems may coincide and become the same. Whether client, target, and action systems coincide or are distinct, the intervention process involves a series of problem-solving and decision-making steps. At each phase, the social worker engages in problem solving in terms of the appropriateness of specific outcome goals and necessary process goals. That is, there is a constant decision-making and evaluation process that focuses on how best to achieve desired intervention outcomes. Often called strategizing or intervention planning, this process evaluates the alternative change processes to select the one that can best accomplish the change outcome.

There are certainly legitimate questions about whether human service organizations are the ideal entities for providing services, to say nothing of creating change. At the moment, however, they are all that we have to work with and to work within. Social systems or organizations develop their own climate, norms, and behavior (or misbehavior) over time. They become remarkably resilient, if not always efficient or effective, and their impact on employees can be dramatic.

Public social welfare organizations currently operate on the periphery and usually far down on the priority scale of governmental decision makers. This invariably makes their futures uncertain and they become susceptible to means-end displacement (Weinbach, 1990, p. 59) when the processes intended to facilitate goal achievement become goals themselves. Many mental health and correctional agencies have experienced this displacement when they try to place offenders and chronically mentally ill patients in residential halfway houses. Ultimately, they are forced to use their energy to ward off bad publicity and community pressure. The goal of resocializing patients and offenders in all likelihood becomes a secondary effort and is sometimes abandoned altogether.

Caught up in the realities of its political environment and the priorities of its actors, the change agent system, the service delivery organization, guided by whatever history it has developed, its culture, and its leadership nevertheless attempts to respond to human need. That response is often tentative because by the time public policy is enacted into legislation, it may well be contradictory. The "legislative intent," presented as if it is in the "public interest," may miss its mark. Then by the time the act has been interpreted by a board of directors and further interpreted by an agency executive, it may even be further removed from its original intent. Nevertheless, it forms the guidelines for practice goals.

Practice Goals

Goals are global, timeless, and even "fuzzy" at times (Mager, 1972, p. 22). At worst, goals provide a hazy direction for an organization to proceed. At best, they provide the parameters for more specific practice objectives. Goals that are too vague are subject to misinterpretation, thus setting up situations that allow the "public interest" to be misinterpreted or "legislative intent" to be violated.

Perhaps the most damning observation is that often goals are not shared with the people who are supposed to make them happen—the change agents themselves. We have discussed this issue with social workers who frequently admit that they have no knowledge of the agency's mission or its goals. It may be safely tucked away somewhere in a policy manual, but staff are not necessarily privy to it. A social worker who doesn't know what the agency's goals are is certainly in a difficult position to actuate them.

Then there are those goals that are, in reality, unachievable. We are aware of one agency goal that reads: "To transform the social order with particular attention to minorities." Such an ambitious goal leaves staff pondering the outer limits of the "social order" and what specifically within that social order is to be transformed.

Neugeboren wrote of a phenomenon that he described as "bureaupathology." This is a malady of dysfunctional organizations that are ineffective because their structures are inappropriate for their goals. The individual working within this type of organization is susceptible to a condition Neugeboren called "bureausis"; namely, "the pathological behavior of individuals who cannot function within a large complex organization because of unreal expectations that their personal needs can be met within the organizational situation" (1985, p. 98). Neugeboren saw the need for a worker, the "good bureaucrat," who "functions effectively in a bureaucracy because of his or her understanding of the opportunities and constraints of the system" (1985, p. 98). Obviously, he did not view bureaucracies as places for workers to self-actualize!

Critical to any discussion of practice goals is what has been referred to as the "target system" (Pincus & Minahan, 1973). Once practice goals have been formulated, someone or something must be changed if the goal achievement is to be successful. For example, if the goal is for residents of a housing project to reclaim their neighborhood from street gangs, targets for change may include the housing authority administration, the police, and the gangs themselves. Although the client system may be an appropriate target for change, the target system may often impact the client's life and, in some cases, the change agent system itself.

Resources

Given that staff formulate and understand practice goals, they cannot be achieved unless the required resources are allocated. The organizational budget is a political document in that it is usually a trade-off between diplomacy, discretion, prudence, and expediency. It reveals just how much relative value the organization places on its stated goals.

A mental health center that has no budget item for its stated goal of "community outreach" is probably giving lip service to this goal rather than resources. The child welfare agency whose goal is to "provide foster care for at-risk youth" but whose budget for this goal is depleted halfway through the fiscal year will need to return children to their at-risk homes. In this case, the goal is not achieved and the money expended for the aborted effort is wasted as well.

Practice Objectives

Unlike goals, objectives are specific, time oriented, measurable, and visible. They represent outcomes. Professional role taking is enhanced if objectives are presented as the way the situation will look *after* a planned intervention. Role taking becomes blurred when, as is often the case, objectives become confused with process, activity, or method.

For example, one objective of a grant proposal was in reality an activity: "to serve 400 single-room occupancy elderly during the next fiscal year." What are the elderly being served: soup, sandwiches, or human services? There is no notion of what they will be like after they are served, because the outcome is not stated. The specific role that a worker assumes is contingent on objectives that provide mental pictures of results, not merely statements of activity.

CLIENT SYSTEM

In our diagram, we have placed the client system in a position directly between the worker and the change agent system. This depiction reflects the power differentials that exist between the worker or change agent and the client. Such discussions are often uncomfortable for social workers since we have a negative view of using power in our work, and we like to see ourselves as working benevolently and altruistically on behalf of our clients. The reality, however, is that whether we realize it or want it power differentials are a natural part of our work. The organizations that employ social workers represent society's power to intervene in the lives of its citizens. We need only ask our clients about their perception of how egalitarian our work has been to get a sense of the existing power differentials.

In spite of our best intentions, subtle processes influence the exercise of power in our work with clients. It is not that power by itself is bad. It is how that power is put to use that matters. We often have a view of power as *might*; that is, our ability to coerce our will onto others. There is another view of power illustrated by the Spanish word *poder*, "to be able to." Power that imposes might is disempowering. Power that facilitates a person's "being able to" is empowering. It is how we use our power in practice that matters.

The subtle processes that disempower clients are influenced by some of the ideological perspectives and guiding principles that inform social work practice. To what extent do the theories that inform our practice give credence to the client's view of the problem? To what extent do they set the worker up as the "expert" and definer of the client's problems? To what extent do workers allow mutuality in all aspects of the intervention process? To what extent are clients labeled "resistant" if they do not accept our definition of their problems? To what extent are clients labeled "nonamenable" to treatment if they do not get "better" as a result of our prescribed treatment?

How we answer these questions is a clue to how we exercise power in client/worker relationships. Oftentimes we tend to be unaware of the subtle processes that we use to exercise power over our clients. This does not apply to those times when we have to impose our power and authority over clients in their own behalf. Situations of guardianship and mandated interventions are examples where social workers must intervene regardless of the clients' wishes because they are a danger to themselves or others. Such situations, however, are a deprivation of individual liberties and should never be exercised without appropriate due process and advocacy on the client's part.

Contract or Sanction

The objectives, the methods, and the activities needed to achieve them should be derived from some type of formal or informal contract with the client. A contract details what the worker is willing and able to do, contingent on the client's awareness and sanction. In the spirit of empowerment, it also specifies what the client agrees to do. The contract should also set the parameters for terminating the services or for recontracting them.

As previously noted, there may be instances when a client is unable to contract. Incompetence, immaturity, or loss of rights might authorize the practitioner to provide services through the authority of some formal sanction. Whether the worker is committed through a voluntary contract or an outside sanction, the contract is always a prerequisite for what ultimately becomes a practice demand.

Practice Demands and Professional Roles

Integrated practice involves role taking based on practice demands that result in six concomitant professional roles. Although these roles are presented as distinct, it is not uncommon for workers to find themselves in more than one role simultaneously. Let us look at how practice demands determine priorities in role taking.

Demand #1.   When the consumer or client demands that the social worker serve as the primary source of assistance in problem solving, those demands create the professional role of *conferee.* The word *conferee* is derived from the word *conference.* The role of conferee calls for worker/client collaboration to explore and assess the problem, formulate goals and objectives, and plan for mutual work on problem intervention. If the plan calls for the worker to continue as the sole source of problem solving (i. e., as a counselor or therapist), the role would take on a more clinical context. If, as the principle of empowerment would dictate, the worker moves into any of the other five roles, the conferee role might be seen in retrospect as a data-gathering springboard to other practice demands.

Demand #2.   When the practice demand is for the social worker to structure, arrange, and manipulate events, interactions, and other environmental factors in order to facilitate and enhance system functioning, the demand signals the need for the *enabler* role. Activity might range from conducting family or group therapy to facilitating education, medical aid, and self-help to most of the management functions. The word *manipulate,* as we use it, should not be viewed in a negative sense but rather as a neutral activity undertaken within the context of social work values and ethics.

Demand #3.   When the practice demand is that the social worker link the client (consumer) with existing goods and services and control the quality of those social goods and services, the worker moves into the role of *broker.* Activity might include case management, networking, and interorganizational linking.

Demand #4.   When the practice demand requires the social worker to secure needed services or resources on behalf of clients (consumers) in the face of identified resistance by those who control the resources, or when resources are unavailable and must be developed, the role of *advocate* is created. Activity could include both case and cause advocacy, grant writing, and social planning.

Demand #5.   When the practice demand is for the social worker to reconcile opposite or disparate points of view and engage the disputants in unified action, the role is known as *mediator.* Activity ranges from behavioral contracting to several forms of third-party peace making and other conflict resolution.

Demand #6.   When the practice demand calls for the social worker to perform in a social control function and act on behalf of clients (consumers) when their competency level falls below minimal standards, the role of *guardian* is established. Activity might include initiating a mental health hold, seeking court control of abused children, or returning probationers to court and parolees to prison.

These six demands are congruent with Wood and Middleman's (1989, p. 20) four categories of social work activity (see Figure 2.2 in Chapter 2). Quadrant A, for example, includes all activity in which the worker directly engages a particular sufferer out of concern for his or her plight. Here we would include the four roles of conferee, enabler, broker, and guardian.

Quadrant B includes activity in which the worker engages a specific sufferer out of concern for all clients in a category of clients. This quadrant would include the roles of enabler and mediator.

Quadrant C includes activity in which the worker engages nonsufferers out of concern for a category of sufferers. In this quadrant, the roles of broker and cause advocate would be most appropriate.

Finally, in Quadrant D the activity engages nonsufferers out of concern for a specific sufferer. Here case advocacy, brokerage, and the guardian role would be applied.

THE PROFESSION

While operating within the agency's driving and restraining forces, the social worker is also reacting to similar forces emanating from the profession itself. It is not unusual or unexpected for the worker to experience conflicting demands from these two reference points. However, these demands must somehow be reconciled before role taking can occur or the worker will perform under considerable role strain or conflict.

State of Practice Knowledge

Because there has been greater emphasis on research in graduate social work programs, the modern-day practitioner is a better consumer of research and more adept at evaluating his or her practice (Meyer, 1987). The increase in doctoral-level education has gradually increased demand for theory based on empirical evidence rather than on practice wisdom.

Technologies

Beyond research, there has been a veritable explosion of knowledge in the social sciences in general. Because of social work's practice of borrowing and applying knowledge from other disciplines, in the space of three decades we have found ourselves buried in an avalanche of knowledge and technology, much more than we are capable of applying. If such an over-supply of knowledge is threatening to the social work educator, it is over-whelming to the practitioner, whose practice demands often do not leave time to read the information.

Although many technologies have developed in the past quarter century, some have proved more faddish than scientifically sound. Eclipsing all of these, however, the computer has revolutionized the delivery of social services. The event has been of such magnitude that it impacts how social work will be practiced in the future. At the least, the future of social work practice, whatever it will be, will certainly be augmented by the computer and may even be driven by it.

As new technologies emerge, regardless of their degree of computerization, the modern-day practitioner is in a race to stay abreast of current development. Specialists, depending on how narrow their specialization, may be able to develop proficiency with their practice technologies. Generalists, however, are faced with a more ominous task; how to stay abreast of the whole as well as the parts.

Professional Ethics and Values

At a time when the national confidence is strained by the violation of professional ethics by public officials and in some professions, the profession of social work has striven to maintain its code of ethics by screening its technologies and policing and regulating the behavior of its practitioners.

Equally as important, social work values and ethics continue to provide reference points from which important practice principles have emerged. For example, the principles of least contest, least restrictive environment, habilitation, normalization, and empowerment are all linked to and supported by our values and ethics.

Despite professional values and a code of ethics, the profession of social work is not immune to society's differential treatment of diverse population groups. Practice interventions often vary from one group to another. Studies have revealed that factors such as socioeconomic status, ethnicity, education, gender, and the social worker's subjective attitudes may be powerful determinants of the amount and type of treatment clients receive (Hollingshead & Redlich, 1958; Jones & Seagull, 1977; Copeland, 1982; Cobb, 1972; Gurin, Veroff, & Field, 1960; Vail, 1978; Broverman et al., 1970; Jayaratne & Irey, 1981; Fischer et al., 1976).

Lum (1992) documented the historical prejudicial treatment of diverse groups by social workers and social service programs, and lack of attention in social work education and journals to diverse populations. Lum found the following barriers to accurate assessment and interventive approaches with diverse groups:

1. Lack of trust in social agency representatives on the part of some ethnic minority groups
2. Differences in language and culture
3. History of demeaning skills and contact with social service agencies
4. Services located too far away from the community they are intended to serve
5. Lack of bilingual and bicultural staff
6. Lack of effective outreach programs to identify and locate members of diverse groups
7. Culture of agency setting alien to culture of diverse populations
8. Social service agencies not linked to ethnic minority organizations for information and collaboration (1992, pp. 111–117)

Practitioners have to be aware that the agencies and organizations that deliver services to diverse client populations often become ineffective and even hinder client groups by employing discriminating assumptions and practices toward group members. Therefore, in order to practice within the profession's code of ethics, social workers must often initiate change within the agency to remove barriers to services to oppressed and disempowered groups.

SOCIAL WORK PRACTITIONER

Suspended in the political environment and operating within the field of client/agency/profession, the practitioner is the primary actor in professional role taking. Central to assuming a professional role is the worker's orientation to planned change. The worker's competence in change technologies, personal values, skills, and role conception will also influence role taking.

Orientation to Planned Change

Chin and Benne (1969) suggested that there are three fundamental types of strategies that people use in attempting to bring about planned change in human systems. The three types of strategies are rational-empirical, normative-reeducative, and power-coercive.

Rational-Empirical Strategies.   These strategies are based on the assumption that people are basically rational and, while some may have personal quirks, most make decisions primarily on logical grounds. People follow their rational self-interest. They will adopt proposed changes if they can be rationally justified and shown to be in the best interests of the individual, group, or organization. People will adopt a change if they have something to gain. Change agents using this approach maximize the use of empirical data and evidence to support the need for change and the benefits to be realized by the change. For example, if a coalition of agencies was trying to influence a legislative body to provide programs for early childhood and family support, a rational-empirical approach would be to present facts and figures about the cost savings of these programs compared to the need for future resources like residential care and foster care if early childhood and family intervention were not funded.

Normative-Reeducative Strategies.   These strategies build on different assumptions about human motivation than rational-empirical approaches. Changes in normative orientations involve changes in attitudes, values, skills, and significant relationships. This approach does not deny people's rationality and intelligence but presumes that patterns of action and behavior are supported by sociocultural norms. People have complex motivations; that is, varied mixtures of cognitive, affective, and social motives. People will change the way they do things when all of these motives—ideas, feelings, conventions—are affected. Change agents using this approach pay attention not only to people's ideas but also to their feelings about and commitments to certain practices and to the effects that group pressures and norms might have. Using the same example, members of the legislature would have to be educated and sensitized to the situation of children and families in order to support such programs. This might involve accompanying social workers in their day-to-day work.

Changes in a pattern of practice or action will only occur when the persons involved are brought to a point where they change their normative orientations to old patterns and develop commitments to new ones.

Power-Coercive Strategies.   Power-coercive strategies are based on the application of power in some form. The change process is basically one of compliance by those with less power to the plans, directions, and leadership of those with greater power. Power may be legitimate authority or it may be political or economic. Individuals in positions of power are seen as basically motivated by political and economic interests. They will act in ways that either gain greater power or at least maintain existing power. Change strategies involve uncovering underlying sources of power and motives in order to use them to get people to change and convincing persons with power to back the proposed change. Change strategies may also involve coercive tactics aimed at minimizing the power differentials between actors affected by the change. Such tactics would include confrontational and pressure strategies such as demonstrations and sit-ins or legal action. In the earlier example, pressure groups would be used to force a change in the legislators' behavior and less emphasis would be placed on how they might think or value such a change.

Because human systems are complex, it will be difficult to find any one individual or organization that strictly complies with the characteristics of any one of these approaches. Although most individuals hold a mixture of assumptions about change and human motivations, each tends to operate from a predominate orientation. Any successful change effort needs to accurately assess this orientation toward change and develop approach strategies to respond to that orientation. Normative-reeducative change may be the most comfortable for social workers, but it may also take more time to implement. Power-coercive change may be uncomfortable for many social workers, but it is at times a necessary tactic.

Competence and Confidence in Technologies

Competence and confidence in available technologies are critical to the practitioners' choice of role taking. Being competent is difficult enough, but practitioners must also have confidence that the methods they employ are appropriate to the tasks at hand. In practice, this means being able to use a specific problem-solving method when it is called for rather than because the worker is proficient in its application. As a social planner, for example, what are the arguments for and against certain techniques for forecasting? Which approach should be used in program budgeting? In work with groups, is a structural approach more valuable than a process approach? Is a structural family technique as useful as a communication model? While no one worker can be an expert in all the available techniques, generalist practitioners need to be aware of a general array of strategic interventions and when to go more in one direction than another.

Personal Values and Identification with Practice Goals and Objectives

Even when there is congruence between competence and confidence, there may still be a deficit in terms of a worker's identification with agency goals and objectives. This may be a matter of personal values. This point was demonstrated clearly by a child welfare worker in a rural community. She was unable to carry out the agency policy of allowing parents to sign a temporary release of their children to the agency, even though she understood the rationale for that policy. The rationale was that parents who have the option of temporary release would tend to feel less pressure and would be less likely to abuse their children. This worker's personal values would not allow her to take temporary releases. Her own personal "tape" kept playing the message "Parents shouldn't release their children." In short, her values forced her into a guardian role when the enabler role was required.

Role Conception, Role Ambiguity, and Role Conflict

In the final analysis, expectations of how to perform in a given role are the major determinants in how the worker eventually fulfills that role (Biddle & Thomas, 1966). Of course, there may be a built-in difference of opinion on the part of the agency, the consumer, and the profession as to how a role should be carried out. When role expectations are diverse and conflicting and thus unable to be fulfilled, the result is likely to be role conflict and possibly paralysis and inaction.

CASE STUDY: *The Parole Officer* ♦

A professional social worker employed in a parole agency revealed the consequences of this type of impasse in a recent discussion:

> The legislature has no respect for our department and the Director of Corrections has no respect for parole services. We are on the bottom of the totem pole, nevertheless, we are expected to keep the public safe while our staff has been reduced by ten percent; this while our caseloads have been rising. Fifty percent of my time is spent pushing paper to justify our actions in case a parolee goes off the deep end. When one does, the media goes crazy and we spend half our time being interviewed by television and newspaper reporters. I live in fear of the day when somebody on my caseload kills somebody, and I know it will eventually happen. I've given up any thought of rehabilitating offenders.

The worker then went on to spell out a professional dilemma:

Being a social worker is impossible in this agency. I conceive of my responsibility as reintegrating these offenders back into the community, but the fact is the community wants them out of sight and certainly out of their community. I'm ridiculed as a "bleeding heart" if I advocate for them. When I refer them to social service or mental health agencies, they're turned away as "unmotivated" and maybe they are. The parolees themselves are ambivalent about me because while they are told I am there to assist them, they also know I have the power to arrest them. I am a quasi–parole officer and a quasi–social worker.

The worker concludes:

It's stressing me out. I conceive of myself as a facilitator and am forced to be a combination clerk-cop. I'm not motivated to be either. Nobody really can agree on what our objectives should be with these people or how we should go about it. Even if they did, we don't have the resources. I'm getting out because my only future here is to develop ulcers.

♦

What is graphically displayed in this account is how role performance is influenced as the worker is bombarded by the opposing forces in the work environment and how these forces come into conflict, creating chaos and demoralization. This situation is further complicated by the worker's own role conception (as facilitator) and the role expectations of others. It is even further compounded by the lack of consensus about how the job should be handled. This ambiguity adds to the difficulty the worker experiences in the ultimate selection of a role and in producing the required behaviors (role enactment).

The predicament is quite common for a social worker in corrections agencies, but it is not unusual in other settings, particularly those where social work services are being offered as an auxiliary service such as in medical social work, school social work, industry, and other secondary settings. The worker's approach to dealing with the problem may lead to leaving the field as this worker eventually did or operating under considerable role strain as do many people with high stress levels. Neither, of course, is a solution.

Role Enactment

As has been emphasized in this chapter and throughout the book, fundamental to being an integrated practitioner is the ability to integrate the six professional roles across the five client systems (namely, the individual, family, small group, organization, and community). This was illustrated earlier in the form of a role matrix in Figure 1.1. This matrix is illustrated in the following case study of professional role taking in attacking the problem of domestic violence. Social worker roles can be understood as functions. Functions are not discrete and exclusive but relate to each other much like colors in a rainbow. They fade into each other through blurring and meshing as is illustrated in the following case example.

CASE STUDY: *Kay Britton* ◆

Kay Britton, M.S.W., is the chief social worker at Ridgeway Battered Women's Shelter, a facility for 14 women and their children. The shelter serves as a safehouse, providing a range of services to assist battered women in their decision making about their future. The shelter is part of a larger array of services provided by the host agency, Women's Initiative. These services are geared to the prevention of domestic violence. Funding is provided by the Brinkley Brown Foundation. Ms. Britton's job description calls for her direct or indirect involvement in all agency services as deemed appropriate.

In her role as intake worker, Ms. Britton interviews newly admitted arrivals, making assessments regarding the degree of endangerment in which the women find themselves at the time of arrival. She also acts as a primary resource in emergency problem solving during the crisis that commonly accompanies entrance into the shelter (conferee role with the individual). As Ms. Britton continues her work with these women, she involves them in goal formulation and objective setting (enabler role with the individual), makes referrals to community resources, and monitors the use of these resources as a part of case management (broker role with individuals). These clients often experience internal conflict regarding the direction of their lives, and Ms. Britton consequently involves them in intrapersonal decision making (enabler role and mediator role with individuals). In those instances where court action follows, she regularly accompanies the women to court for social support and victim (case) advocacy (advocate role with the individual). In circumstances where a spouse makes life-threatening gestures, Ms. Britton, as required by agency policy, reports such behavior to the police (guardian role on behalf of the individual).

When children accompany parents to the home, as they often do, Ms. Britton completes a brief family history, provides basic casework services, and orients the family to the program as a unit (conferee role with the family). In some instances, because of the family crisis that occurs with the family uprooting, she provides family crisis intervention and family therapy (enabler role with the family). Ms. Britton often refers families to other family agencies (broker role with the family). She is also sometimes called on to mediate issues of custody in divorce actions (mediator role with the family) and regularly appears in court on matters of suspected child abuse to speak out for the need for guardian ad litem for children (advocate role for the family) and to offer expert testimony on the degree of endangerment of the family (guardian role on behalf of the family).

Ms. Britton runs group class sessions for shelter residents (conferee role with a small group) to provide information. These classes take various forms as the groups identify their needs. Some groups request help in assertiveness training, decision making, anger management, and other skills training (enabler role with the group). Still others are referred to various self-help and mutual-aid networks (broker role with the group).

At times, conflict has broken out between racial and ethnic groups that develop within the shelter. Such conflicts are usually settled through Ms. Britton's mediation efforts (mediator role with small groups). As a part of the public education thrust of Women's Initiative, she makes regular presentations to community groups on the dynamics and scope of domestic violence as a social problem (advocate role with small groups). Recently, Ms. Britton served as a co-facilitator for a group of battering men who had been ordered by the courts to participate in coerced group therapy as an alternative to a jail sentence. This involves monitoring attendance and reporting violations to the court (guardian role with a small group).

In addition to her role as a direct service provider, Ms. Britton provides administrative supervision to two graduate social workers and three counselors in the organization. She is also a designated consultant for all staff regarding endangerment (conferee role with the organization). She facilitates team-building sessions for the board of directors of the Brown Foundation (enabler role with the organization). She is the Women's Initiative's representative to a network of related agencies known as the Federation of Domestic Violence Agencies (broker role with organizations). As a member of this federation, she has been called on to do third-party peace making between rival agencies (mediator with organizations). Currently, she is writing a federal grant proposal to secure training monies for public education on domestic violence (advocate role for the organization). She also acts as the agency liaison to the prosecutor's office when criminal charges are being filed against domestic violence perpetrators (guardian for the organization).

Ms. Britton is called on to give expert testimony before country commissioners and members of the city council and state legislative committees (conferee with the community). She chairs a subcommittee on shelter care as a member of the State Coalition on the Prevention of Domestic Violence (enabler role with the community). This committee was responsible for conducting a community needs assessment and developing a state case-management plan (broker role with the community).

The plan resulted in the location of a small group home for battered spouses in a neighborhood that was not zoned for this purpose. Ms. Britton mediated a settlement between the neighborhood group and the city council. A variance was granted for the group home in exchange for commitments from the home regarding parking, noise violations, and other matters of concern (mediator role with the community).

It came to the attention of the agency that the police who were publicly committed to a policy of probable cause arrest had in fact been practicing a policy

of nonarrest and mediating domestic violence disputes. Ms. Britton was interviewed by one of the newspapers and appeared on a radio talk show where she
called attention to the inconsistencies between policy statements and practice
(advocate role with the community). This resulted in Women's Initiative's threatening to file a class-action suit, whereupon the police department returned to the
practice of probable cause arrest (guardian role with the community).

♦

Evaluation of Social Work Practice

Evaluation is a systematic process of monitoring progress toward outcomes
during all phases of the problem-solving method and assessing the overall
efficiency and effectiveness of the outcomes. Evaluation starts at the time
of goal setting and stipulates what will be measured and how. It is an ongoing process requiring feedback into the next phase of action or decision
making. Evaluation involves judgment by some rules or standards of a given
activity or set of activities. It also is a feedback mechanism for goals, objectives, and other components of role-taking decisions.

SUMMARY

Role taking is a deliberate process of responding to practice demands and
acting in accord with these demands to fulfill the six professional roles (conferee, enabler, broker, advocate, mediator, and guardian). These roles are
generally played out within a hostile political environment that impacts
the change agency system, the profession, the client, and ultimately the
social worker, determining the efficacy of his or her role enactment. In integrated practice, role taking includes a blurring of social work functions
across all client systems with a focus toward reduction and management
of the problem.

Evaluation of outcomes is a necessary part of goal-setting and role-taking
behavior. Chapter 6 elaborates on this topic.

STUDY QUESTIONS

1. What is meant by the statement "Social work service is political"? What
   is an example from your previous professional experience?
2. Differentiate the concepts of change agent system, client system, target
   system, and action system. Cite an example of each from your previous
   professional experience.

3. Give an example of Neugeboren's term *bureaupathology*. Cite an example from your past professional experience.

4. How do objectives differ from goals? Write an example of each.

5. What are the major differences between rational-empirical, normative-reeducative, and power-coercive orientations to change? Give an example of each orientation.

6. How does role conflict impact a social worker's role enactment? Cite an example of role conflict that you have experienced in your practice.

REFERENCES

Biddle, B. J., & Thomas, E. J. (1966). *Role theory: Concepts and research.* New York: Wiley.

Broverman, I. K., Broverman, D. M., Clarkson, F. E., Rosenkrantz, P. S., & Vogel, S. R. (1970). Sex role stereotypes and clinical judgments of mental health. *Journal of Consulting and Clinical Psychology, 34,* pp. 1–7.

Chin, R., & Benne, K. D. (1969). General strategies for effecting changes in human systems. In W. S. Bennis, K. D. Benne, & R. Chin, *The planning of change* (2nd ed.). New York: Holt, Rinehart & Winston.

Cobb, C. W. (1972). Community mental health services and the lower socioeconomic class: A survey of research literature outpatient treatment (1963–1969). *American Journal of Orthopsychiatry, 42,* pp. 404–414.

Compton, B., & Galaway, B. (1989). *Social work processes* (4th ed.). Pacific Grove, CA: Brooks/Cole.

Copeland, E. J. (1982). Oppressed conditions and the mental health needs of low-income black women: Barriers to services, strategies for change. *Women and Therapy, 1,* pp. 13–26.

Coser, L. (1956). *Functions of social conflict.* New York: Free Press.

Dailey, D. M. (1983). Androgyny, sex-role stereotypes, and clinical judgement. *Social Work Research and Abstracts, 19*(1), pp. 20–24.

Fischer, J., Dulaney, D. D., Fazio, R. T., Hudak, M. T., & Zivotofsky, E. (1976). Are social workers sexists? *Social Work, 21,* pp. 428–433.

Gurin, G., Veroff, J., & Field, S. (1960). *Americans view their mental health: A nationwide interview survey.* New York: Basic Books.

Hollingshead, A., & Redlich, F. (1958). Social stratification and psychiatric disorders. In H. D. Stein & R. A. Cloward (Eds.), *Social perspectives on behavior.* New York: Free Press.

Jayaratne, S., & Irey, K. V. (1981, Sept.). Gender differences in the perceptions of social workers. *Social Casework,* pp. 405–412.

Jones, E. E., & Seagull, A. (1977). Dimensions of the relationship between the black client and the white therapist: A theoretical overview. *American Psychologist, 32,* pp. 850–855.

Link, S., & Milcarek, B. (1980). Selection factors in the dispensation of therapy: The Matthew effect in the allocation of mental health resources. *Journal of Health and Social Behavior, 21*(3), pp. 279–290.

Lum, D. (1992). *Social work practice and people of color.* Pacific Grove, CA: Brooks/Cole.

Mager, R. (1972). *Goal Analysis.* Belmont, CA: Fearon.

Merton, R. K. (1968). The Matthew effect in science: The reward and communication systems of science are considered. *Science, 159,* pp. 53–63.

Meyer, C. H. (1987). Content and process in social work practice: A new look at old issues. *Social Work, 32,* pp. 401–404.

Neugeboren, B. (1985). *Organizational policy and practice in the human services.* White Plains, NY: Longman.

Pincus, A., & Minahan, A. (1973). *Social work practice: Model and method.* Itasca, IL: F. E. Peacock.

Schofield, W. (1964). *Psychotherapy: The purchase of friendship.* Englewood Cliffs, NJ: Prentice-Hall.

Specht, H. (1969). Disruptive tactics. In R. Kramer & H. Specht, *Readings in community organization practice.* Englewood Cliffs, NJ: Prentice-Hall.

Vail, A. (1978). Factors influencing lower-income black patients remaining in treatment. *Journal of Consulting and Clinical Psychology, 46*(2), p. 341.

Weinbach, R. (1990). *The social worker as manager.* New York: Longman.

Wood, G. G., & Middleman, R. (1989). *The structural approach to direct practice in social work.* New York: Columbia University Press.

Chapter 6

Evaluation of Integrated Practice

Chapter 5 discussed social work intervention as planned change. Through a variety of strategies and tactics, the social worker pursues change in a planned, systematic way and engages in a variety of interventive roles. The appropriateness of a given role and how well the worker performs in the role is a function of many factors, but ultimately the measure of its success lies in what the client perceives and receives as a social service. Evaluation of practice provides feedback to many facets of the role-taking environment, as depicted in Figure 6.1.

Since integrated practice occurs across systems and engages in multi-system interventions, this chapter focuses on the use of evaluation approaches to assess the worth of interventions at both the microsystem and macrosystem levels. These approaches are presented as tools that practitioners can use to evaluate their practice interventions.

THE EVALUATION PROCESS

In the realities of today's economic and political environments, social work interventions are increasingly being objectively assessed in terms of their efficacy and efficiency. Efficacy refers to the degree to which an intervention produces a desired effect. Efficiency refers to the degree of effort necessary to produce that desired effect. Social work and other human service professions are being pressed to demonstrate that their services are effective and cost efficient. Thus we must develop and use approaches to evaluation that adhere to principles of accountability and research rigor and do not compromise our basic practice principles and client-centered commitments. Integrated-practice evaluation approaches need to be not only appropriate at multisystem levels but also consistent with principles of client/worker mutuality and client empowerment.

Evaluation is a systematic process of monitoring progress toward outcomes during all phases of the problem-solving method. It also assesses the overall efficiency and effectiveness of intervention outcomes. Evaluation begins when the goals are set, by stipulating what will be measured and how. It is an ongoing process requiring feedback into the next phase of action or decision making. Evaluation involves judgment through the application of rules or standards to a given activity or set of activities. In short, evaluation lets us know how we are doing. As a gauge of intervention outcome, evaluation can be equally useful to the client and to the worker and agency.

Why Evaluate?

Evaluation is engaged in for a variety of reasons. We evaluate to determine whether an intervention was worth the effort, whether we or our clients

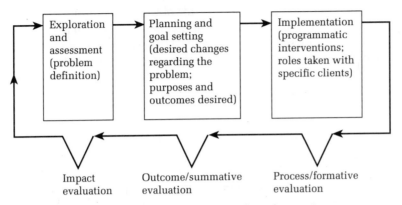

Figure 6.1 Levels of evaluation in social work practice

are satisfied, whether the results were what were expected, and perhaps what was learned as a result of the intervention. We also evaluate to build a knowledge base about our interventions and the nature of problems in order to minimize the need for trial-and-error approaches. Ultimately, we evaluate to maintain accountability in our practice; that is, to demonstrate whether our interventions are effective and what specifically about our interventions contributes to that effectiveness. In a study of the use of evaluation by social workers, Richey, Blythe, and Berlin (1987), found that practitioners engaged in practice evaluation activities because they viewed them as intervention aids.

Regardless of why we engage in the process, the net results of evaluation should allow us to learn about the nature and dynamics of the problems we address, to economize our efforts, and to improve interventions. Evaluation should help answer the following questions: What difference did the intervention make? Who was affected? Why did it happen this way? How consistent and widespread is the effect? Were there any unforeseen side effects? (Solomon, 1977)

Types of Evaluation

There are three types of evaluation: outcome (or goal attainment), process, and impact. *Outcome*, or summative, evaluations determine to what extent intervention goals and objectives were realized. In short, were the desired effects achieved? *Process*, or formative, evaluations assess the activities, methods, or means (or process) used to achieve the desired outcome. They focus on what is actually being done and compare it to the original intervention objectives and plan to determine if activities need to be modified (Schuerman, 1983). *Impact* evaluations assess the intervention's beneficial effects on the recipient's problem(s). Impact evaluation asks, ''Was the social condition of the recipient improved as a result of the intervention beyond what might have been expected had the intervention not occurred" (Washington, 1977)? All three types may be used separately or in combination. They may be applied at differing system levels; with individuals, families, groups, organizations, or entire programs. Figure 6.1 may help illustrate the levels of evaluation in social work practice.

Relationship of Evaluation to Research Methods

Research is generally categorized into two broad types: basic and applied. *Basic* research means research designed to develop or test theory. *Applied* research activities are used for some end. In practice, most applied research has some implications for the development of theory, and basic research has often led to the development of significant applications (Schuerman, 1983). For our purposes, evaluation falls into the category of applied research.

As a research method, evaluation is a systematic investigation of a given phenomenon. For our purposes, that phenomenon involves an intervention or series of interventions. Evaluation uses research procedures and designs to protect against bias or error in analyzing and interpreting results.

Steps in Evaluation

There are several steps in formulating evaluations. First, the evaluator must decide what information he or she is trying to attain. What purpose will the evaluation serve? What questions about the intervention will the evaluation answer? Given the nature of the presenting problem and intervention, is it more important to assess effectiveness, efficiency, impact, or all three?

Each of these purposes will set the stage for the design of the evaluation and the procedures used in carrying it out. Effectiveness or outcome evaluations focus primarily on measures of effect. Efficiency evaluations focus on effect plus measures of the efforts expended to bring about that effect. Impact evaluations necessitate measures of effect as well as a comparison with what might have been the effect without the intervention.

Second, the evaluator must state the interventions to be evaluated in the form of clear, concise, measurable objectives. This is important because all evaluations ultimately focus on the goals and objectives of the intervention.

Third, the evaluator must decide on the indicators of progress. These are estimates, gauges, or measures of progress made toward accomplishing goals. Assessment of progress involves comparing measures of current conditions against desired outcomes. Measures might include worker assessments of client progress, client self-reports, observations of behavioral manifestations of change, or standardized evaluation tools such as psychological tests. For comparison purposes, some baseline measure of preintervention conditions is always necessary.

Fourth, the evaluator needs to establish the appropriate procedures for data collection and monitoring. Intake and termination assessments and case-recording documents can be important sources of data. However, data collected through these methods must relate to the objectives being evaluated. If not, supplemental or alternative methods of data collection may need to be devised.

Finally, the evaluator needs to address how that data will be analyzed and conclusions drawn based on the findings. In other words, what does it all mean? How do we examine the data in order for it to be informative? Such examination may take the form of a simple comparison with preintervention measures, or it may involve more complex statistical operations and testing.

The steps in evaluation can be summarized as follows:

1. What questions do we want to have answered?
2. What data do we need in order to answer those questions?
3. How can we collect that data in a reliable, valid, and orderly fashion?
4. How do we organize and examine that data in order to answer those questions?
5. What conclusions can we draw based on our examination of that data?

Figure 6.2 illustrates the steps of the evaluation process as they relate to steps in the problem-solving process: exploration, assessment, goal setting, planning, implementation, and evaluation. This figure illustrates that evaluation can be an integral part of the intervention process. It informs and shapes each step of intervention. Rather than being conducted at the end of an intervention effort, evaluation, as an extension of problem solving, begins in both the planning and goal-setting phase and has a cyclical effect on the process as it further redefines the problem. Evaluation also impacts the intervention process in that it requires intervention goals and activities to be developed in ways that are unambiguous, measurable, and subject to evaluation.

Conceptualized in this manner, the questions that guide the evaluation process can be restated as questions that also guide the intervention process. How is the presenting problem defined? What objectives does the intervention need to achieve to resolve the problem? What data are needed to demonstrate success? How can these data be collected? How can

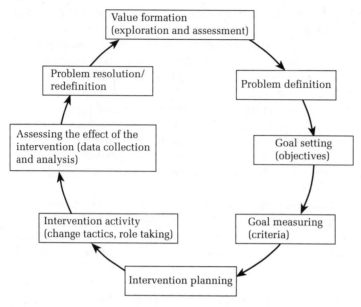

Figure 6.2 Evaluation process

intervention activities be structured and documented to monitor movement toward the objective? How do these data need to be analyzed to determine how well the objective has been achieved? If the problem has not been fully resolved, can we refine our definition and redirect the intervention? At this point the cycle repeats, leading to a further refinement of the problem and the intervention process until the objectives have been achieved satisfactorily.

Validity and Reliability

Of critical importance in any evaluation effort are the concepts of validity and reliability. *Validity* refers to the degree to which a particular instrument or process reflects what it is supposed to measure. *Reliability* refers to the degree to which the same instrument or process yields the same description of a given phenomenon on repeated application (Babbie, 1989; Grinnell, 1988). Said another way, validity refers to whether we are measuring what we think we are measuring, and reliability refers to whether the measurements are consistent if administered over time or by different individuals. A thorough explanation of these two concepts is beyond the scope of this discussion. Suffice it to say that measures that lack validity or reliability will not produce accurate findings and may lead to faulty conclusions. To be useful in evaluation, measurement instruments must be both reliable and valid.

Applications of these concepts to social work interventions can be seen in the manner problems and intervention outcomes are assessed. Typically, in direct practice interventions with individuals and families, problem definition involves some type of data collection such as a social history, a client level of functioning assessment, level of perceived powerlessness, competency assessment, or some other baseline data. This data-collection process leads to a joint decision in problem definition and goal setting. Similarly, there may be periodic practitioner and client assessments to evaluate movement toward goals throughout the intervention process or at the end of the intervention. Depending on agency protocol or the nature of the assessment, these assessments may involve varying degrees of input from the client.

In these situations, validity issues may be present to the extent that the procedures used accurately reflect dimensions of the client's presenting problem or gains realized as a result of the intervention. Using nonstandardized measures, while perhaps generating data specific to the unique circumstances of the agency and client population, will frequently compromise the validity of the assessments. Validating measurement instruments is a methodologically rigorous process that practitioners seldom undertake in the development of client documentation. Conversely, using a standardized instrument that may not have been validated on a population similar to the client population and with presenting problems similar to those that are the focus of the interventions will also compromise the validity of the assessments. Generally we can increase our confidence in the assessments' validity by using multiple or concurrent measures of the presenting problem or client gains. The more coherence there is across different but related instruments, the greater our confidence in the assessments' validity.

Reliability issues in these situations may be present in the repeated assessments of client progress toward goals. The extent to which these repeated assessments reflect consistent results is an indication of test-retest reliability. The extent to which more than one practitioner and the client assess the situation similarly is an indication of inter-rater reliability. Measures and procedures that are unstructured or require a high degree of subjective interpretation or judgment generally have less reliability than those that are more objective and structured. The clearer and more specific we are in our goals and measures, the more reliable our assessments will be.

FRAMEWORKS FOR EVALUATION

Often, social work agencies are reluctant and lack the capacity to design and implement comprehensive summative evaluations. Formative or input evaluations are usually the chosen level of evaluation. Agencies often assume that if the interventions are completed and delivered, then the desired outcomes must have been achieved and the hoped-for impact on the identified problem must have occurred. Or, agencies often engage in broad-based program evaluations that assume that the intended inputs occurred, the desired changes identified in the goals and objectives were achieved, and the question for study is what impact the program had on the problem. In Figure 6.1, you can see that it is necessary to evaluate at various levels or at the end of the problem process. For agencies and practitioners to be accountable to funders, to themselves, and to clients, all levels of evaluation are necessary. Compton and Galaway (1989) suggested that the gap between practice evaluation and program evaluation is not, and should not be perceived as being as wide as it is, but one should be linked to the other.

Specific Approaches

This section discusses a series of approaches to evaluation that integrated practitioners can use in evaluating their practice and their programs. Numerous approaches to practice evaluation have been developed that are applicable at both the individual case level and at the program level. Among these are action research, single-subject designs, client-functioning assessments, client-satisfaction surveys, postintervention surveys, and goal attainment scaling. While not exhaustive, these approaches are representative of the range of available evaluation tools. Two of the approaches are appropriate to integrated practice: action research and goal attainment scaling. They can be adapted to a variety of interventions and settings and do not require a great deal of research sophistication or resources. They are appropriate for integrated practice because they are fluid and responsive to the worker's multiple roles and to multiple-system interventions. Additionally, they are implemented through principles of mutuality more than some other evaluation approaches.

Action Research

Originally conceived as an approach to organization change efforts (Clark, 1972), action research is a quasi-experimental approach to data collection and analysis. It focuses on providing information for making decisions rather than for generating knowledge, although that may be a by-product. Its primary focus is to improve the quality of information used in decision making by participants involved in a change effort and to examine the effectiveness of a change effort to help make modifications while the effort is still ongoing. Its singular distinguishing characteristic as an evaluation tool is that the intended beneficiaries of the intervention are an integral part of

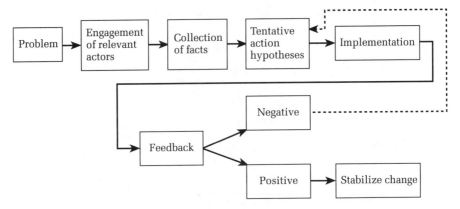

Figure 6.3 The decision process as presented by action research

the evaluation process. This is an important attribute for empowerment-based interventions.

Action research is characteristically less methodologically rigorous than experimental research. It is practitioner initiated and operationalized and focuses much more on the immediate application of data to decision making. It is based on the assumption that the question that underlies all research is "*What level of evidence is needed for what purpose?*" Based on this assumption, action research emphasizes the practitioner's and client systems' expertise and knowledge of the presenting problem and the interventive process and provides systematic ways of gathering information. The ultimate outcome of more effective decision making is to improve the effectiveness of *this* specific intervention for *this* specific client system, rather than to be accountable to the agency or a funding source or to generate new knowledge. For this reason, action research stresses different kinds of data such as qualitative interviews, subjective judgments, and participant satisfaction.

While it is quasi-experimental in that it typically lacks a control group and random assignment and standardized, validated instruments, action research is nonetheless systematic. It builds on the blending of the problem-solving and scientific methods and focuses on decision making. Figure 6.3 illustrates the steps in action research as related to decision making.

As illustrated in the figure, action research uses the scientific method as a guide to decision making. The initial step involves identifying a presenting problem and engaging relevant actors. Relevant actors are those individuals who are affected by the problem or have resources that can be used in a proposed change effort. Relevant actors would include the client system and any appropriate action system.

Assessment consists of collecting data related to the presenting problem and to perceived desired outcomes. At this point, tentative-action hypotheses

Table 6.1 Research Levels in Relation to Decision Making

Research Type	Focus	Temporal Characteristics
"Pure"/scientific	Knowledge testing/ building	Ultimate
Program evaluation	Evaluating outcome of specific program or case	Intermediate
Action research	Monitoring (process) evaluation of program or case	Immediate

Source: Landon, 1980.

are formulated to guide intervention. Action hypotheses are different from causal hypotheses. Causal hypotheses are statements concerning relationships between input and outcome, typically associated with traditional research hypotheses. Action hypotheses are statements about how an action will affect the behavior or condition the worker is seeking to modify. They are tentative because they will be revised in light of anticipated feedback as a result of their implementation. If the feedback is positive, as indicated by movement toward the desired outcome, the process affirms the action hypothesis and continues to the next level of intervention, or stabilizing the change effort. If the feedback is negative, indicating that the implementation did not have the desired effect, the intervention effort is assessed and the action hypotheses are modified based on that information. The relation of action research to other research levels can be seen in Table 6.1.

As an approach to evaluating a worker's practice, action research excludes summative research such as program evaluation and focuses on the immediate aspects of decision making in the intervention process For some, this is often seen as settling for "quick-and-dirty" research. However, an experienced practitioner can use action research to systematically make decisions where otherwise "practice wisdom" tends to predominate. Thus, it can be a valuable tool in presenting a much cleaner picture of intervention decision making. Action research used in combination with other summative data collection is a valuable tool in integrated practice.

CASE STUDY: *Lewis High School* ◆——————————————

An evaluation of the Lewis High School Dropout Prevention Program first introduced in Chapter 1 will help illustrate practice evaluation. The program had as its goals:

1. To increase the graduation rate of at-risk students at Lewis High School
2. To aggressively identify and reach out to students who are at risk of dropping out of school
3. To identify each at-risk student's barriers and difficulties to school achievement and success
4. To involve parents of at-risk children in ensuring school attendance and involvement
5. To programmatically employ a "multisystems" approach in intervening with potential dropouts

Program Services and Activities

The program engaged in the following services and activities to achieve its goals:

1. A community volunteer mentor program
2. An interorganizational network of agencies to share resources and expertise
3. A brokerage (case-management) model of service delivery
4. An informal monthly activity for all participants
5. A self-help network of parents and students
6. An after-school tutoring program

Several approaches were used to evaluate these interventions, employing both summative and formative evaluation schemas. Data were collected on goal accomplishment, the impact of the problem, and the process of the interventions. An action research approach was employed in order to involve students, families, school staff, and community in the setting and testing action hypotheses.

In the four years prior to year one of the dropout prevention program, 720 students dropped out of Lewis High, ranging from a low of 160 during the first year to a high of 210 the last year. During the project's first year, only 82 students dropped out of school. If this rate were to continue over the next three years, 328 students would drop out of Lewis High, a 55% reduction in the overall dropout rate.

Mentor Program

Of the 97 mentor-student matches, 81 survived the full year. Of the 16 matches that did not last, 3 were discontinued at the request of the mentor due to personality clashes, 4 ended when the students were committed to correctional institutions and left the Lewis High District. Another 4 matches were terminated at the request of the student due to personal issues. Three matches were terminated when the team learned of sexual advances made by the mentors. One match ended with the death of one of the mentors. Another ended when one of the students was killed in an auto accident.

The 81 completed matches were evaluated at the end of the one-year period. Client-satisfaction data were used to determine the effectiveness of mentoring. Of most importance, outcome data showed 75 of the students in these matches were still in school. Their absenteeism was reduced by 22% over the previous years, while their mean grade-point average had been raised from 1.9 to 2.7 on a 4.0 scale. Of the 75 in-school students, only 8 were suspended during the year, compared with 24 who were suspended during the previous year.

Each student was asked to rate the importance of the mentor program in terms of its impact on the student during the match year. The outcome of this survey was as follows:

Very Positive	51	Somewhat Negative	5
Somewhat Positive	24	Very Negative	1

Interorganizational Network

The consortium agencies were highly used by the students involved in the dropout program. Twenty students were contacted in some way by the police and 9 made at least one court appearance. Another 9 students were referred to social services, 6 to Big Brothers/Big Sisters, 10 to Partners, 15 to Street Smart, 7 to "Drop In." The two church leaders were active in working with several of the youth but kept no records of their contacts.

During the first year of the project, two agencies were added to the consortium: Prospect Heights Community Center, which proved to be a vital resource for recreational opportunities and meeting places, and Park North, a drug education and treatment program. This program conducted several drug education sessions at Lewis High during the academic year.

Case Management

Brokerage consisted of case management of services provided by the interagency network and the volunteer mentors, and the effectiveness of this role was demonstrated. It was not easy for the three social workers to leave the task of counseling to the mentors. Initially, the workers found themselves infringing on this role and consciously backed away when program participants became confused with multiple counseling relationships. As the program proceeded, the workers found the case-management function to be more natural.

Monthly Activities

The impact of these activities was difficult to measure. Because of the informal nature of the activities and the fact they were attended by mentors, participants, and their parents but were not controlled by Lewis High, the workers were only able to speculate as to their value.

Based on the survey of 81 participants, 75 said they had been involved in at least one monthly activity. Forty-five students had attended all of them. They rated the activities as follows:

Very Positive	50	Somewhat Negative	4
Somewhat Positive	25	Very Negative	2

These data helped confirm the action hypothesis that monthly activities would be useful to this goal.

Self-Help Network

All 15 participating parents responded to a survey of the effectiveness of self-help groups. Eleven felt the groups were helpful, 2 felt they were somewhat helpful, 1 said they were not helpful, and 1 didn't respond. Interestingly, of those who considered the network helpful, 10 had used the telephone tree and rated this feature as very helpful.

Forty-seven participants indicated they had attended self-help groups. All had used the telephone tree (a list containing the name and telephone number of each group member). With the exception of one student, they considered this an important dimension of the program.

Tutoring Program

During the year of the program, 62 tutors were recruited. All were used either for the weekly tutoring sessions or for assignment to particular students.

All program participants used the tutoring services. With the exception of two students, they endorsed the program as having a generally positive impact on increased attendance rates and improved grades. The mental health team attributed much of the average increase in grade-point averages to the efforts of the tutors, although this could not be substantiated.

General Conclusions of the Evaluation

The mental health team concluded that overall the program had been moderately successful. A potential reduction in dropouts of 55% was considered encouraging, although whether this reduction would eventually translate into a higher graduation rate was an open question.

The team noted that by and large, the targets of intervention were the students and their parents. The school itself had not really been targeted for any change, even though the needs assessment had identified deficiencies in its operations.

At the end of the academic year, the social workers were meeting with the principal regularly on team proposals to sensitize all school personnel to the results of the dropout prevention program. In view of the program's positive results, the principal was supportive of the venture.

There were also plans being formulated for a meeting of the workers and the principal with the school board to discuss the project. At the behest of the workers, the principal planned to broach the subject of a reexamination of all curriculum in terms of how it could be presented more creatively for all students.

Summary

The evaluation conducted of the Lewis High Dropout Prevention Program illustrates the use of action-research strategies and summative-outcome data to determine the effectiveness of interventions. These approaches allowed for flexible, multisystem-level measurement of reduction in the identified social problem. The problem was not solved by the actions of the social workers, although the evaluation does suggest that it was ameliorated significantly. The sources of this problem are multiple. For that reason, interventions must also be geared toward multiple systems and methods of evaluating interventions must also be multisystem. The workers recognized this. As the evaluation indicates, they were aware that much more work needed to be done and were in the process of planning more changes as the academic year came to an end.

What is encouraging, however, is that even though the interventions were directed primarily at the carriers of the problem—the students and their parents—the outcome was a most favorable one. The goals, in large measure, were achieved.

―――――――――――――――――――――――――――――――――――――――◆

Goal Attainment Scaling

A tool used frequently to measure client and worker goals and objectives is *goal attainment scaling* (GAS) (Kirusek & Sherman, 1968). This process involves the development of specific evaluation criteria for each client, based on his or her intervention goals. Evaluation is based not on a dichotomy between success or failure in reaching goals but on a 5-point scale, with the target goal at the center of the range, the most favorable expected outcome at one end, and the least favorable outcome at the other end. The client's progress toward attaining each goal is measured, resulting in a score that is related to each goal and a summary goal attainment score that weighs the average of scores on each individual scale (Lewis, Lewis, & Souflee, 1991).

There are five possible outcomes on this scale. Each outcome is defined by a specific set of behaviors that indicate a measure of progress toward the goal. The five outcomes are scored as follows:

-2 = The most unfavorable outcome level of success

-1 = Less than the expected level of success

0 = The expected level of success

$+1$ = More than the expected level of success

$+2$ = The most favorable outcome thought likely

This type of scale is used both to set client objectives and to assess whether the objectives were met. GAS involves four steps: collecting information about the person or organization, specifying the problem areas where change is desired, making specific predictions for a series of outcome levels for each problem area, and scoring the outcomes, by a set date, as they have been achieved (Grinnell, 1988).

A predetermination of success behaviors between worker and client or clients allows for client-centered practice evaluation of the outcome and builds data for an overall programmatic evaluation. Goal setting from this practice perspective takes place at various client and system levels. Goal attainment scaling lends itself to measurement of goals at a variety of client intervention levels, from the individual to the organization and the community. Kirusek and Lund (1978), for example, have used goal attainment scaling for both clinical and organizational evaluation.

CASE STUDY: *Kay Britton* ♦——————————————————

Table 6.2 is an example of multilevel intervention goals directed at a single problem, based on the role-taking example from Chapter 5 of Ms. Kay Britton, social worker at the Ridgeway Battered Women's Shelter. In this example, the client Ms. Jones is a resident of the shelter. As a resident, she can measure her relative success in three areas: increasing her assertiveness, increasing her support networks, and increasing her knowledge of domestic violence. The five behaviors listed clearly distinguish between failure and success and also depict levels of failure and success. In this sense, attained goals are clearly recognized and unattained goals are still visible.

Table 6.3 demonstrates the use of goal attainment scales at the macro (community) level as applied by the Ridgeway Battered Women's Shelter. In this instance, the organization wanted to improve its performance by increasing interagency

Table 6.2 Multilevel Intervention Goals Directed at a Single Problem

Level of Attainment	Goals		
	Increase Assertiveness	**Increase Support Networks**	**Increase Knowledge of Domestic Violence**
Least Favorable Outcome	Unable to recognize her needs	Rejects idea of network as helpful	Does not attend education sessions
Less-Than-Expected Outcome	Occasionally recognizes her needs, but does not express them to others	Recognizes need for network, but does not seek out support	Does not connect her problem with larger social problem
Expected Outcome	Occasionally expresses her needs to shelter staff/residents	Becomes a member of an ongoing support group	Acknowledges her situation as part of larger problem, utilizes resources
More-Than-Expected Outcome	Regularly expresses needs to shelter staff and seeks solutions	Becomes a member of three support networks	Articulates dynamics of domestic violence, shares knowledge of resources with others
Most Favorable Outcome	Helps others to become more assertive	Helps others to form support networks	Teaches new residents about domestic violence, develops a resource list

Table 6.3 Use of Goal Attainment Scales at the Community Level

Levels of Attainment	Goals		
	Increase Interagency Collaboration	**Increase Level of Police Knowledge and Domestic Violence**	**Secure City Funding for Shelter**
Least Favorable Outcome	Federation of agencies does not develop, agency behavior is self-oriented.	No training program initiated, police remain hostile to the idea.	City council rejects idea of providing funding for shelter.
Less-Than-Expected Outcome	Federation meets irregularly, attendance sporadic.	Training set up, 10% of police attend.	Funding rejected, selected members show future interest.
Expected Outcome	Federation meets quarterly, exchanges information, 50% attendance.	Half of police attend training sessions, ask relevant questions.	City council gives a one-time grant for shelter funding.
More-Than-Expected Outcome	Federation meets bimonthly, develops action plan for increased collaboration.	Police regularly seek consultation from federation of agencies.	City council provides a grant and considers future funds.
Most Favorable Outcome	Federation has representation from 75% of agencies, increases collaboration by 75% over starting point.	All city police receive 15 hours of training, increase knowledge of domestic violence on a pretest and posttest.	City council builds annual appropriation into budget.

collaboration, increasing the level of police knowledge of domestic violence, and securing city funding for the shelter. Again the five positions reflect the various possibilities of failure and success, thus providing measurable indicators or controls for the agency's use in evaluating its efforts.

Goals attainment scaling is a client-centered outcome measure applicable across multilevel client systems and useful for evaluation of integrated practice.

◆

SUMMARY

Evaluation of intervention efforts is a necessary part of professional practice. Evaluation addresses various questions in the problem-solving process: Were the intended services delivered and received? Were the services effective? Did the desired changes occur? Did the changes have the desired impact on the problem? Types of evaluations include process, outcome, and impact. Action research and goal attainment scaling are methods for evaluating individual practice as well as broader program efforts.

STUDY QUESTIONS

1. In the evaluation process, what is the difference between the terms *efficacy* and *efficiency*? Give an example of each.

2. Discuss some of the major reasons for evaluating our practice. Think of an example from your professional practice when better evaluation procedures might have improved your intervention.

3. What are the three types of evaluation? Give an example of each.

4. What is the major difference between basic and applied research? Give an example of each.

5. List the steps involved in evaluation. How are these steps related to the steps in the problem-solving process?

6. Distinguish between the concepts *validity* and *reliability*. Give an example of each.

7. How does action research differ from experimental research?

8. How would you use goal attainment scaling as an evaluation tool? Devise a scale that might reflect client behavioral outcomes.

REFERENCES

Babbie, E. (1989). *The practice of social research.* (5th ed.). Pacific Grove, CA: Brooks/Cole.

Clark, P. (1972). *Action research and organizational change.* New York: Harper & Row.

Compton, B., & Galaway, B. (1989). *Social work processes* (4th ed.). Pacific Grove, CA: Brooks/Cole.

Grinnell, R. M. (1988). *Social Work Research and Evaluation* (3rd ed.). Itasca, IL: F. E. Peacock.

Kirusek, T., & Lund, S. H. (1978). Goal attainment scaling. In C. C. Attkisson, W. A. Hargreaves, M. J. Horowitz, & J. E. Sorensen (Eds.), *Evaluation of human service programs.* New York: Academic Press.

Kirusek, T., & Sherman, R. (1968). *Community Mental Health Journal,* 4(6), pp. 443–453.

Landon, P. (1980, April). Impact, action, and research. Lecture given at the University of Denver.

Lewis, J. A., Lewis, M. D., & Souflee, F. (1991). *Management of human service programs* (2nd ed.). Pacific Grove, CA: Brooks/Cole.

Richey, C. A., Blythe, B. J., & Berlin, S. B. (1987). Do social workers evaluate their practice? *Social Work Research and Abstracts* (Summer), pp. 14–20.

Schuerman, J. R. (1983). *Research and evaluation in the human services.* New York: Free Press.

Solomon, D. D. (1977). Evaluating community programs. In F. M. Cox, J. L. Erlich, J. Rothman, & J. E. Tropman, *Tactics and techniques of community practice.* Itasca, IL: F. E. Peacock.

Washington, R. (1977). Alternative frameworks for program evaluation. In F. M. Cox, J. L. Erlich, J. Rothman, & J. E. Tropman, *Tactics and techniques of community practice.* Itasca, IL: F. E. Peacock.

Part Three

SOCIAL WORK ROLES

The following six chapters present detailed discussions of the professional roles—conferee, enabler, advocate, broker, mediator, and guardian—that result from six distinct practice demands. These demands flow from the nature of the planned change being considered, the agency and the agent of change, the action system directing the change, the target of change, and the sanction of the client, who is the presumed beneficiary of the change.

Each role is taken in order to create a particular kind of change. Thus these roles go to the heart of the intervention; that is, moving the client system away from a problem state toward a desired outcome.

Although the roles are presented here as distinct and tidy, this is usually not the case in practice. The world of the social work practitioner is seldom tidy. It is far more likely to be complex and ambiguous, in part because more than one practice demand is often imposed on the worker at once. For example, brokerage and advocacy may be required simultaneously. Similarly, a worker might be assuming the protective role of guardian while also acting as an advocate.

Just as practice demands are multiple, so too are the roles and functions that follow. Thus workers find themselves acting as broker/advocates or guardian-advocates or mediator-enablers. As often as not, one role tends to overlap another. Indeed, a worker may begin to move into a new role while still in the previous one. Although the roles definitely overlap, the focus here is on what makes each role specific and how each role is played out in terms of its relevance to the client's well-being.

The conferee role is the role that is assumed when the worker and client begin their work together. In many respects, this role is a springboard to the other five roles in that the worker gathers data, considers with the client what is to be done, and contracts for future action. In short, in the conferee role, the worker receives the sanction to proceed.

The enabler role means just that, to enable. It is informed by the concept of empowerment and as such focuses on client competency, capacitation, and self-help so that clients are able to act on their own behalf and take responsibility for changes in themselves and in their environment.

Brokerage, analogous as it is to stock brokerage, focuses on linking the client to goods and human services and networking among providers for conservation and judicious use of services while controlling for the quality of these services.

Advocacy, as it is conceived here, is a role that can go in many directions. In the absence of needed services, the worker becomes a program developer. In the presence of services, the worker overcomes resistance to providing these services to at-risk populations. Being an advocate can result in actions taken on behalf of people as individuals, as families, or as groups—namely, case advocacy or cause advocacy, where issues are addressed as they affect society as a whole.

The mediator role is taken to resolve conflict. The principle of empowerment is fundamental to this role. Contestants are enabled to become problem solvers who are capable of finding solutions to end the conflict and ultimately join in unified action.

The guardian role is sanctioned for social work, usually by law. In this role, the social worker protects vulnerable, incompetent, and at-risk people through social controls and the use of authority.

Chapter 7

THE CONFEREE ROLE

T he conferee role is perhaps the most familiar role to both newcomers
to the profession and to outsiders. Many people see social work as
an activity in which a single worker and a single client deliberate
about problems and solutions. In a general sense, this is the conferee role,
although it may be taken with any size client system across the breadth of
the generalist practice. This chapter defines, describes, and conceptualizes
the conferee role. Using the problem-solving process, a framework is provided, necessary skills are identified, and an example is given.

DEFINING THE CONFEREE ROLE

Webster's New World Dictionary (1968) defines conferee as "a participant
in a conference" and to confer as "to have a conference; compare; and exchange ideas or to bring together, compare." Implied here is the mutuality
of the conference and decision making around solutions. The conferee role
in social work is often described as the individual counseling role, crisis
intervention, casework, consultation, or therapeutic role. As was pointed
out in Chapter 5, the conferee role meets the client's demand that the social
worker serve as the primary source of assistance in problem solving. In the
practice situation, the social worker as a conferee may have the most primary
role in the helping process. In some theoretical versions, the social worker
may be considered more of an "expert" than in any other role. The conceptualization of the role here includes the expertise of the worker and of
the client as well. Because mutuality is an important part of the professional relationship, expertise from both is needed.

Definition in Social Work

In Wood and Middleman's (1989) role quadrant, the conferee role is the role
taken in the initial stages of all work, and one in which the client and worker
return to intermittently make decisions on further action. The conferee is
where pressures are translated into tasks, and alternative courses of action
and their consequences are explored. In that sense, the role becomes critical
in gaining sanctions from the client to perform in the other professional
roles.

Connaway and Gentry called this role the "clinical" role and suggested
that the demand for the role comes from the internalization of stress, and
that it focuses on "any factor or set of factors that interferes with individual
social and psychological development to impede system development and
functioning" (1988, p. 131). Conceptualization of the role here does not
preclude Connaway and Gentry's definition. Internalized stress may block

the client's ability to solve problems and may be a significant component in the problem-solving framework.

Compton and Galaway (1989, p. 510) labeled the conferee role as a "teacher" role, in which the social worker provides information that the client may need to make decisions. Both definitions are consistent with the practice demand for the worker to be the primary source of help and assistance.

More important than what the role is called is how it is carried out. Barbara Solomon (1976, p. 348) criticized the traditional configuration of social work roles and suggested that the role of conferee is too often adapted to a victim-blaming therapist stance, in which both the problem's cause and solution are seen as internal to the client. She further suggested that to avoid that disempowering kind of assistance, the role should be viewed as a sensitizer, in which the worker shares observations about the client and his or her situation. These observations may give the client insights that will work to his or her advantage. Soloman emphasized the importance of the collaborative nature of this role. The conferee role focuses on collaboration and potential resolution of problems, not on victim blaming or fixing.

The conferee role is also a point of departure to the other roles in which the clients discuss, plan, and learn. They gain support, receive validation, become more perceptive, and gain a sense of empowerment to choose and act on their own behalf to resolve their problems.

The integrated-practice model suggests that the conferee role should be defined and carried out in a specific manner. That is, it is not to be defined as a psychotherapeutic role. Rather, the conferee role is a collaborative conference on the problems at hand that deals with exploration and assessment, goal setting, planning, evaluating, and implementing the plan. This role is framed around the problem-solving process and contains a variety of problems, including what may be defined as clinical or emotional reactions to the stresses of problems, crisis intervention, and awareness raising by both the client and the worker. The role includes encouragement and support of clients in their desire and decision to seek change and help for problem situations, mutual education and decision making about alternative actions, connection with others who are experiencing the problem through referral, education resources, and development of plans to broker available services.

Although often thought of as social work activity between a single worker and a single client, the conferee role can be and is carried out between workers and families, workers and organizations, and groups of clients—wherever the worker is seen as the primary source of help in deliberating about the problem and its potential resolution.

With families, this role may take the form of family awareness and education. With groups, it may take the form of group interventions, in which the worker is the prime source of help to the system. The groups' structural model may call for the conferee role in that the critical expertise and direction comes from the worker, along with the expertise of the group members. Organizational consultants also fall into this role description because they assist the organization to define its problems and alternative solutions, choose a course of action, and plan for that action. An example illustrating this use of the conferee role is examined throughout this chapter.

Conceptualizing the Conferee Role

In Specht's (1969) continuum of roles from least- to most-disruptive tactics, conferee is best described as that collaborative activity located on the left side of the continuum that carries the least disruption. Similarly, in Wood and Middleman's (1989) principle of least to greatest contest, the conferee role is the first role taken by choice, since it creates the least amount of contest in the problem-solving situation. Theoretically, if a client or group of clients can solve a problem by collaborative consideration and decision making, then that activity poses the least disruption and contest is the first choice. It may be the least conflictual role, but it is not necessarily the first choice taken in a social problem intervention other than it often serves as an organizational beginning point. In fact, when a large number of people experience the same problem, or a trouble is seen as more of a public issue than a private trouble, then after the problem and alternative solutions are mutually defined, collaboration may not be the first choice of intervention at all, but rather perhaps class advocacy or some more disruptive strategy.

Although a social worker will assume all the roles outlined in this practice framework, he or she must decide which is the best starting point or which role best lends itself to the situation at hand. One consideration is the social justice issue. Can the decision to assume a specific role contribute to the social injustice of client systems? In considering this question, the issue of when client's problems are best described as private troubles and public issues (Mills, 1959) is important. As Wood and Middleman (1989) suggest, if a large number of clients are suffering from or experiencing the same problem or set of problems, it may be a public issue. When social workers identify public issues, they are obligated to work on the problem from a broader focus than an individual response or solution. The integrated-practice model suggests that social workers work across the victims to non-victims continuum. Which role and what size system are questions that are constantly present in role taking and are determined by the agency and the demand of the situation. The principles of the integrated-practice model guide not only the selection of roles, but how the roles are carried out. Because empowerment is both an outcome goal and a principle in practice, its components are critical to each role. This suggests that the processes of normalization of problems with clients, and the process of education and teaching skills for problem solving are critical pieces of the conferee role. Empowerment principles suggest that the client's expertise is critical and should be tapped along with the worker's expertise. The problem-solving process should become more of a mutual partnership and a more collaborative process than the psychotherapeutic version of this role might suggest.

FRAMEWORKS AND APPROACHES IN THE CONFEREE ROLE

The framework for assuming the conferee role with clients comes from a general problem-solving model. It is a mutual collaboration between the client and the worker on a problem-solving approach. It includes exploration and definition of the problem, assessment of linkages and forces that are inherent in the problem, setting of goals for reducing the stresses, generation of alternative action strategies, selection of strategies, evaluation of the results, implementation of the strategies, and termination of the contract. The framework suggested here is behaviorally based and task oriented. This process sets the stage for all subsequent work with the client and with other targets of change on behalf of the client. This broad framework lends itself to the use of a variety of conceptual screens. The concepts suggested for use here come from the theoretical screens of the integrated-practice model.

CASE STUDY: *Ms. Napier* ♦

Ms. Napier came to the attention of the Head Start social worker, Ms. Black, through the teachers who suggested that she needed help and support in parenting her twin boys. Ms. Black approached Ms. Napier and asked if she'd like to set up a time to chat about her situation. She was extremely shy and seemingly embarrassed by the approach. A meeting was set up at her home.

Presenting Information and Problems

During the first meeting, Ms. Black proceeded very gently, spending most of the time getting acquainted with Ms. Napier. She was tall and thin, had only a few teeth, was embarrassed about her appearance, covered her mouth when she smiled, and was generally nervous about interacting with Ms. Black. Pictures on the wall provided some points of discussion about her family and her background. The social worker learned that she was from a rural, economically deprived area, deep in the Appalachian Mountains; had not completed elementary school beyond the third grade; was illiterate; had rarely been out of her home when growing up, except to work in the fields; and had had only one encounter with a man when she was 19, during which she became pregnant. Giving birth to the twin boys had alienated her parents who felt shamed and rejected her. The father of the children gave her money to leave the area and establish herself in the West. She was living in a housing project where most of the residents were African American or Hispanic. She was alienated from the people in the community and lived a very closed, isolated life. Her boys were shy but appeared to be of average intelligence and abilities. They did not associate with other children in the neighborhood beyond the Head Start experience. Ms. Napier had assumed a devalued label, "unwed mother," from her parents, and another label, "strange, different, illiterate, unworthy," from her current environmental interactions. She felt powerless and unworthy of more than she had.

Work with Ms. Napier required patience and slow process. Her trust level was very low, but she had a positive feeling for the Head Start teachers and the program that gave Ms. Black an entry into her life. Since the teachers' observation was that the family, including the children, seemed isolated from the community and from everyone, Ms. Black approached her about friends and socialization for her and the boys. She revealed an isolated lifestyle, with minimum interaction with her neighbors, local organizations, family, peers, and the world in general. She sometimes went to the local church, to the doctor, and to the social services office. Beyond that, she lived in her apartment with her television and her sons. Her greatest source of embarrassment was her illiteracy, and she avoided any situation where that fact might come out and cause her to be vulnerable. Later, it was revealed that she was shy and afraid in her neighborhood. Due to her isolative behavior and appearance, she was even the object of ridicule in her neighborhood. Her negative self-valuation was deeply ingrained.

Exploration and Assessment

It is often said that the questions asked will determine the answers received. That simplistic statement is critical to the social workers' use of conceptual models. Exploration of the problem requires workers to ask questions that are pertinent to the situation at hand. Whatever theory or concept the worker thinks is important will guide the questions he or she asks, therefore constructing the reality from which practice is perceived. Integrated practice guides the nature of the questions and those concepts considered central to problem analysis and the action taken.

Social Problem Focus and Social System Linkage.   In integrated practice, client problems are viewed as component parts of larger social problems. Individual clients are seen as victims or carriers of the problem. They have their individual sets of coping behaviors, needs, and stresses based on the problem. Because social system linkages are a critical part of assessment, it is important to ask questions about the system dynamics related to the problem being presented. The critical societal systems include economic, political, the media, educational, health, legal, peer, and family. The examination includes looking at power differentials based on ethnic, cultural, social class, and gender issues. Power differentials in system linkages are often keys to understanding the client's degree of power or powerlessness (real or perceived) in the situation. The more internalized powerlessness a client has experienced, the more empowerment-based practice is necessary.

CASE STUDY: *Ms. Napier* ♦

In the exploration and assessment phase, it was clear that Ms. Napier's situation represented many social problem dynamics: poverty, lack of opportunity in the economic system, lack of contact and linkage with the education system, lack of adequate dental care, lack of access to local resources, lack of transportation, lack of involvement with peers, and the local neighborhood. She had been socialized in an extremely poor, uneducated family in an economically deprived area. That cultural experience had created a feeling of being backward, ignorant, and ashamed of who she was. Her parents' rejection added to her self-perception that she was not a person who could cope, change, and adapt to her world. Very few people in her life had believed in her or had seen her as a capable person. As a shy, illiterate, poor, isolated, single-parent, unemployed female, Ms. Napier carried all the stigma and labels of being devalued and unable to cope. She has experienced a high degree of internalized powerlessness and self-devaluation based on the devalued labels her situation represented.

♦

Client Definition of the Problem.   Acceptance of client definition of the problem is critical, along with the worker's expertise regarding the general nature of such problems. Both inputs are added to the pool of knowledge for exploration and assessment. Often, client problems are defined by someone other than the client. While the various definitions of the problem are important, none is more critical than the client's definition of the problem. Indeed, this is the beginning of the empowerment process; that is, validation of the client's view of his or her situation. In human services the person who is able to define the problem to be addressed is often the one with the most power. Thus, it is even more important that the client has a critical say in the problem definition. The worker or agency may have a different definition of the problem, which can be added to the problem-definition process, but if it is to be a mutual partnership, the client's definition of the problem is paramount. Through education, discussion, and awareness, the client's definition of the problem may change, but it is essential to begin work with the client where he or she sees the problem.

CASE STUDY: *Ms. Napier* ◆

Ms. Napier's definition of the problem centered mostly on concern and worry about her two children. She worried about them being accepted and liked, being beaten up by other kids as they grew older, not having a father in their lives, not being able to provide for them properly, about not being able to read and write and how that inhibited her from doing for them what they needed. She was basically scared that she was not an adequate parent and could not provide the right or a good environment for her children. Ms. Napier worried they might be removed from her since she saw herself as perceived as inadequate by others.

◆

Client Strengths and Weaknesses.   Clients have both strengths for and barriers to coping with a problem, and this is a necessary part of the exploration and assessment stage. Often clients bring strengths for coping with problems that we as workers could not have thought existed. Competency *assessment* involves looking at those strengths in relation to the impinging stress from the environment. How has the client coped with the problem before? What have the consequences of such coping been? Clients also bring their views of the restraining and perpetuating forces that effect their situations. The clients' perspective of their capacity for addressing a problem is an important part of assessment. The degree of learned helplessness in the face of impinging systems is a powerful dynamic and may be the key to the selection of relevant goals and strategies.

Normalization.   The screen of normalization implies viewing the client's problem in terms of its environmental context, cultural conventions and values, and the purposefulness of behavior. Often the helping process is debilitating. Clients are seen through their deficits and inadequacies by workers, agencies, and by themselves. By viewing clients as engaging in troublesome behavior such as dropping out of school, workers tend to be diverted from using deficit models. Competency assessment and normalization guides the worker/client assessment to a more positive strength-based approach. For example, a social worker interviewed an isolated, elderly person who was afraid to walk from his apartment to the bank. Before the worker was tempted to diagnose paranoia, she probed, with the client, the reasons behind his fear and found adequate cause. A gang of youths had been preying on the older residents on the days they received their Social Security checks. In addition, the traffic lights changed so quickly that the elders were unable to cross the street safely. The social worker understood the man's fear of leaving his room once she examined the environmental context and purpose of his behavior.

Resource Assessment.   Assessing resources is a necessary part of any social work assessment. Social workers are the helping professional most concerned with access to resources. The worker must have a good working knowledge of the resources available for any given problem. The client also is often aware of available resources. Developing an inventory of the resources available, as well as those not available, is necessary to begin the problem-solving process. Resources are the key to solving many problems. In the case of the elderly person, there's a good chance that neither the timing of the traffic light nor the gang behavior could be solved quickly. Resources for mitigating the problem are necessary.

Education.   Education is implied in this process. The worker and client both bring knowledge to the problem situation. The worker must educate and learn from the client. Clients may not have the specific information regarding accessibility of services that the worker probably has from dealing with similar problems. Sharing this information helps the client become better able to handle similar situations in the future for herself or for others. In this process, the worker learns about barriers to services and to coping and is able to use this information to collaborate on other problems.

Social system context and social problem focus help us view problems in a larger environmental context. Resource assessment, normalization, and competency-based assessment help focus on the client's strengths.

CASE STUDY: *Ms. Napier* ♦

Ms. Black's assessment of Ms. Napier's strengths and weaknesses revealed major power differentials in her linkages to the major systems that impinged on her life. She saw herself as helpless to make a difference in how she was treated by the environment and basically tried to stay out of people's way. Ms. Napier's strengths included a soft, loving disposition, a great deal of caring about her children, and a sense of adequate mothering and of her sons' needs. Other strengths included a thrift-conscious approach to living on AFDC grants of a very small amount. She knew how to survive, feed her children, clothe herself and her children, and get by on very little. Although illiterate, she was intelligent and had learned how to cope with the lack of such basic skills as reading and writing.

The *normalization* process with Ms. Napier involved Ms. Black's reflecting and interpreting to her her own internalized self-devaluation. Ms. Black helped Ms. Napier see that given her set of environmental circumstances, it was understandable, even predictable, that she would shy away from people and avoid situations where it would be revealed that she could not write her name. She knew how to survive alone, did not trust her environment, and therefore had become isolated. Ms. Black suggested that her coping pattern was a useful one that was understandable and seemingly worked for her. In terms of *prevention,* it appeared to Ms. Black that because of Ms. Napier's concern for her children's welfare, her linkages to her most immediate environment could be enhanced, thereby increasing her coping patterns. Two areas seemed obvious for increasing her self-esteem: getting dentures, and learning how to sign her name. These two things alone, it seemed, would enhance her ability to extend herself to others and create an opportunity for her to feel more adequate as a parent.

The resource assessment included the formal and informal local service network. Literacy classes, funds for dentures, possible networks in the neighborhood, children's programs at the community center, church activities in which she might become involved, possible child support from the father of her children—all these resources were assessed by Ms. Black, so that she could begin to show Ms. Napier what was available if she wanted to seek out assistance.

♦

Goal Setting and Planning for Action

Goal setting requires us to ask what changes are needed or indicated and what changes are realistic for the client, for the agency in other target systems than the client.

Mutuality.   Clearly, if this is a mutual process, the client's desired goals are the starting place for this phase of work. Again, the agency may have goals for the client or client group that are presented for deliberation. One person setting goals for another is often futile. We cannot overstate the necessity of a mutual partnership. At this point, the worker begins to weigh other targets for intervention. He or she looks at nonvictim targets and activities that may or may not include the client. While client-presented goals are paramount, social work practice must go beyond intervention with the client if it is to impact social problems.

Habilitation.   Principles of *habilitation* versus rehabilitation are important in goal setting. How the social worker relates to and views the client may make an enormous difference in how the client sees the helping relationship and potential for change. The worker's expectations of risks and responsibility, recognition of client strengths and capacities, a view of client behavior as troubling create the tone of the helping environment and may determine how the client responds. Holding positive expectations for clients in their problem-solving behavior is often the key to behavioral change. Many times, clients are beaten down by the system and do not hold out hope for problem resolution. Viewing the clients' situations as troubling to them or perhaps to others, but not as deficits, is a useful principle. It is very difficult to help another person move or change a situation by focusing on their deficits.

CASE STUDY: *Ms. Napier* ♦

Clearly, Ms. Black's movement with Ms. Napier had to be slow and cautious. She was distrustful and easily overwhelmed. As stated earlier, it is critical to start with the client's stated goals. Ms. Napier voiced hope for some resources for her children. She wanted them to have friends and places to play. She was interested in the boys' having opportunities. Head Start provided that to some extent.

One of Head Start's goals was to involve parents in the center and their children's educational development. Ms. Napier was reluctant to come to the center for meetings because of her embarrassment. She was also afraid to accept a volunteer job at Head Start because of her illiteracy. Ms. Black and the teachers worked out a plan for her to help prepare late-afternoon snacks for the children. They promised her that she would not have to interact with the other children. She was also asked if she would be willing to help clean the center in the afternoons. She was glad to participate in a job that she thought she could accomplish.

Through these initial goals, Ms. Napier and Ms. Black began to work out a plan of action. Verbal agreement around goals, strategies, and outcomes was used to form a contract and a plan for work.

♦

Empowerment.   Empowerment is a cornerstone of integrated practice. As presented earlier, it guides the thinking process of resolution to problems. It suggests that validation of the clients' experience and feelings and cognitive explanations of their problems are necessary for "helping" to occur. Empowerment guides the worker in choosing types of goals and strategies in the helping process. The worker is forced to create goals and strategies that are educational for the client and leave coping strategies, knowledge, and skills for problem solving that were not in place or were not at the awareness level when the helping process began.

Mutuality in goal setting using principles of habilitation and facilitating the empowerment process help guide planning.

CASE STUDY: *Ms. Napier* ◆

The principles of *empowerment* were important with Ms. Napier. She perceived herself to be quite powerless and dared not ask much from her situation. Ms. Black had to both recognize and accept that attribute, while working to change it. The *habilitative* principle of positive expectations and the right to risk, to take responsibility, and to fail were critical in how Ms. Black interacted with Ms. Napier. Ms. Black approached her as if there was no doubt that she was capable of doing numerous things for herself and for her children, given the right information, the right support, and a mutual and trusting relationship with Ms. Black.

The principles of empowerment and habilitation help the worker and the client decide what to do. Because of Ms. Napier's high degree of learned helplessness, Ms. Black had to bargain and coax her to persuade her to take actions and risks. Ms. Black observed that often Ms. Napier would avoid situations in which she had to sign in at a meeting or sign her boys in at the center. Ms. Black pointed out to Ms. Napier that learning to write her name and address and her children's names, ages, and grades could make her life much easier. This was offered as a goal, instead of teaching her to read and write, which was not something she could readily see herself doing. Ms. Napier was doubtful about how she would go about learning to write her name and address and her children's names. Ms. Black offered to teach her at least to write her name and address. Although this offer embarrassed Ms. Napier, she was willing to do it because there was only a small risk of embarrassment involved.

Ms. Black agreed to find some opportunities for the boys if Ms. Napier would come to the center every day and help with the snacks and cleaning. So, her goals and the agency's goals were both addressed. Ms. Black explored programs at the community center. The boys were enrolled in a recreation activity after school, but this meant Ms. Napier had to walk to the center with them. She was reluctant to do so, but the worker arranged for her to walk with another mother whose children were also going to the activity. This pairing of Ms. Napier with another mother in the community provided an opportunity for her to begin to establish a support system and create opportunities for her children to play with others in the neighborhood.

Next Ms. Black raised the subject of dentures. Ms. Napier's lack of teeth not only embarrassed her but also appeared to contribute to nutritional problems. Ms. Black believed that dentures would be a source of self-esteem. Again, although embarrassed by this issue, Ms. Napier agreed to allow Ms. Black to explore some resources.

Deciding What to Do and Doing It

Goal setting gives direction to pursuing the agreed-on changes. Which strategies to choose in order to carry out these goals is another decision.

Selection of Strategies.   Selection of strategies depends on what is feasible within the coping skills, expertise, and availability of resources. It constitutes the contract between the worker and client. It creates the plan of action. Within that plan, the worker may plan interventions with systems other than the client. The client may make interventions outside the relationship with the worker. To accomplish their goals, the worker and client must decide on which tasks to undertake. Accomplishing the agreed-on tasks will create new information, new goals, and new ideas for proceeding. So, the setting of goals and tasks is an ongoing, dynamic process, not a one-shot deal. This doing takes place across the continuum from victim to nonvictim intervention.

Prevention as an Alternative.   The potential for *prevention* and the appropriate level must be explored. Prevention refers to primary, secondary, and tertiary prevention. The formulation presented earlier regarding stress, organic factors, coping skills, and self-esteem is an appropriate framework for looking at the potential for prevention.

CASE STUDY: *Ms. Napier* ◆

During this process, the need for interventions in other systems became apparent to Ms. Black and the agency. While the conferee role had provided initial work on the most-significant goals, Ms. Black, through practice with Ms. Napier and other clients with similar needs, became aware of many needs in the community as a whole.

An assessment of resources at the community center revealed major problems at the center. The director was suspected of dealing drugs and a group of rough, older boys were dominating the center, making it an unwelcome place for younger children. An organized effort by Ms. Black and Head Start parents resulted in the director's dismissal. He was replaced with a director who was very cooperative with parents in the community. In her role as an enabler, Ms. Black helped the parents organize and advocate for improved operation of the center.

In the same neighborhood, there were several Hispanic women who couldn't write English. A basic English writing course was needed in the community. Work with the local minister, interagency council, city development representative, and adult education branch of the public school system brought about a basic writing class, which evolved into an English as a Second Language class. Ms. Black assumed the broker-advocate role through collaboration with a number of local city and state agencies to bring this needed service to the community.

Need for child care during these classes created a need for a child care co-op. One of Ms. Napier's strengths, not previously tapped, was her gentle, patient way with children. She became a child care provider for other women, in exchange for child care while she attended the basic writing course. She was also hired at the local church to provide child care while classes were going on. Ms. Napier was eventually viewed as an appropriate child care resource by many people in the community. In this activity, Ms. Black acted as a broker and enabler in helping Ms. Napier arrange a job and enabling her to work with others in the community to meet a mutual need.

Many older people in the community shared Ms. Napier's need for dentures, but there was not a readily available source for them. Ms. Black networked with the local Neighborhood Health Center and approached the State University Dental School about contributing dentures to local residents at a minimal fee. Dentures were eventually secured for Ms. Napier. They increased her self-confidence and willingness to reach out and be a part of the neighborhood. This willingness helped her achieve the goal of her children having more opportunity and contact in the neighborhood. Ms. Black acting as a broker/advocate provided a resource for Ms. Napier and set up a resource for other residents in the neighborhood.

Ms. Black began a woman's support and discussion group in the neighborhood and invited Ms. Napier to join. In part due to her increasing trust in the worker, Ms. Napier reluctantly agreed to try it, claiming that she wouldn't have much to say. She joined the group, and although she was silent for some time, she eventually began to share some things about herself. The group supported each other in their single-parent roles around issues of child discipline, neighborhood relationships (that is, conflicts), a low-income budget, and so on. The group raised many issues of common concern to the women in the neighborhood, eventually becoming an advocate group for social change in the community.

None of Ms. Black's roles was taken solely on behalf of Ms. Napier, but they were taken on behalf of the social problems that impinged on her and shaped her life. They represented interventions on behalf of many clients who shared the same problems. The interventions were made partially with residents who suffered directly and immediately from the problems and partially by the formal service delivery system's agents. This array of interventions represents the continuum from victims to nonvictims alluded to earlier and illustrates how the initial work may often begin in the conferee role but expand to other roles necessary for intervention into the problems identified.

♦

Evaluation. Evaluation of the intervention's effectiveness is an integral part of social work practice in all roles and in the conferee role as well. Were the intended tasks completed? Were desired outcomes achieved and did those outcomes have an impact on the goals set? There are many evaluative strategies and tools available for evaluating practice. In Chapter 6, goal attainment scaling was discussed as a tool for measuring outcomes in role taking. The client is asked to describe the desirable outcomes of the intervention. In keeping with the mutuality and partnership nature of the conferee role, a tool such as goal attainment scaling is sufficiently client centered and client determined but can still satisfy the agency's need for evaluative procedures.

CASE STUDY: *Ms. Napier* ♦

The agreements mentioned earlier became the initial working plan and contract between Ms. Black and Ms. Napier. Goal attainment scaling was used informally to help the client see small accomplishments and small steps toward reaching the goals. Ms. Black also used action research strategies to discern, with the client, alternative strategies and decide on action hypotheses.

During the four years Ms. Black was with Head Start, Ms. Napier became much less isolated in her environment and increasingly active in the neighborhood. She participated in a woman's group for three years and eventually learned to talk about her life and its frustrations, her desires and her alternatives. She became a regular babysitter for many women in the neighborhood. She was supportive to many young mothers, both Hispanic and African American. As her children grew older, she struggled with control and discipline, but she had learned how to voice her concerns, begin to get her needs met, access systems, and ask for help. Ms. Napier never became literate, but she acquired enough capacity to fill out a basic form, catch a bus, and attend church without embarrassment. Ms. Black used informal verbal goal attainment scaling and action-research strategies as evaluative tools.

♦

The conferee role established a basis for goal setting and action taking with Ms. Napier that went beyond the role itself. This is often the function of the conferee role: to begin problem assessment and set the stage for further work.

SKILLS NECESSARY FOR THE CONFEREE ROLE

The skills needed in the conferee role are the generic skills needed in social work. Listening, probing, reflecting, partializing problems into solvable pieces, summarizing, clarifying, validating, supporting, confronting, joining with clients, confirming, and normalizing are all skills necessary in this problem-solving process. To engage in mutual problem solving, the social worker must be skilled in helping the client decide what problems are most amenable for work, and which coping strategies are the most workable. The worker must also be able to support the client's right and responsibility to risk and fail and try again.

As in all social work practice, this role calls for the worker to find a balance between task and process in the helping relationship. Although the worker must empathize with the client or clients, he or she must also view the larger systems picture and the linkages between. The role calls on the worker to have a dual perspective of what the client can do to cope and of what the environmental context of the problem suggests about to resolution. Another balance that must be achieved is between what the client wants and sees as an adequate solution, and what needs to be done in the larger systems represented. This requires the worker to accept the client's present situation, while sensitizing, educating, and even politicizing him or her to the environmental impingements on the problem being examined. Whereas the example of Ms. Napier represents the conferee role as the beginning point in work with an individual, the following example illustrates the conferee role taken with an organization.

CASE STUDY: *Grand Valley School District* ♦

Dr. Doric Buchanan, Superintendent of Schools in Grand Valley District Seven, asked Mr. Timothy James and Ms. Carol Kreig, social work consultants at the State Department of Education, to meet with her regarding personnel and community relations problems in the district.

Exploration and Assessment

In the meeting, Dr. Buchanan briefed Mr. James and Ms. Kreig on a series of problems:

1. Parents of many high school students were concerned about specific aspects of the program (that is, access to library resources, responsiveness of the school's principal to these parent concerns, and the teaching abilities of several of the faculty).
2. Poor communication among administrators in the district.
3. Apparent morale problems among high school teachers.

After lengthy discussions with Dr. Buchanan, Mr. James and Ms. Kreig proposed conducting a survey of the organization's health. This involved using a variety of survey instruments and conducting selected interviews with key staff.

They further proposed conducting a series of open community forums in all of the district's schools in order to listen to concerned parties and form a collaborative assessment based on the competencies and perceived concerns of the constituencies.

The workers held seven forums over a three-month period. The forums were open to anyone in the community. A total of 77 people made statements, all of which were recorded. Mr. James and Ms. Kreig heard and validated their concerns. Participants were given an opportunity to see that their concerns were shared by others. The workers used normalization principles to suggest that such problems within a school system are understandable and are exclusive of deficits in any group. Next, they analyzed and summarized the proceedings, giving an executive copy to every teacher and administrator in the district.

During the same three months, a series of meetings were also convened with school personnel to explain the reasons for the survey and respond to questions about the instruments and other aspects of the study. Ms. Kreig and Mr. James told the staff that the survey instruments would be completed anonymously and the data would be presented to the staff later in a series of organizational meetings.

After the community forums were completed, Ms. Kreig and Mr. James conducted the survey. They color-coded the survey instruments by the school and number-coded them by department. They also interviewed selected staff and then shared the survey results through a series of meetings within the schools.

The survey revealed many problems in the system between parents and teachers, between teachers and administrators, and between administrators. There were serious morale problems among high school teachers. This was most evident among women teachers who felt that their concerns regarding pay discrepancies, maternity leave, and many other issues had not been acknowledged partially because of their status as women. Additionally, the survey verified the original concerns about poor communication among administrators regarding goal clarity, priorities, and the role of both teachers and parents in administrative decision making.

Goal Setting and Planning

Goal setting and strategy selection was a collaborative problem as well. At each meeting, Mr. James and Ms. Kreig provided opportunities for brainstorming in small groups. Each meeting produced a number of specific action proposals. The brainstorming proposals were ultimately shared with Superintendent Buchanan, the high school principal, and the several administrators. This group screened the proposals through three criteria:

1. Resources (time, money, staff)
2. Values (laws and ethical considerations)
3. Political factors (feasibility, popularity)

As a result of the screening, a plan was developed for implementing the following actions:

◆ Team building among administrators
◆ Development of an ad hoc task force (including teachers) to develop a plan to address teacher's grievances
◆ Development of a public information plan to better communicate with parents

Deciding What to Do and Doing It

Dr. Buchanan and the administrators asked Mr. James to conduct team-building sessions. He agreed to do so but reminded them this involved a commitment from them for biweekly team-building sessions for a period of up to a year. They agreed to make the commitment. The team-building effort would increase knowledge and skills regarding team approaches and problem-solving strategies. Through instrumentation and interviews, data were gathered on the team members individually and as a working group. The data were used to set action hypotheses.

Ms. Kreig convened the ad hoc task force and served as a consultant. This group analyzed teacher grievances and developed a plan to address them. The plan was then taken to teacher groups for their approval.

Mr. James and Ms. Kreig acted as consultants to the administration in developing a public information program to communicate with parents. They interviewed each of the parents about their complaints in the presence of their child and used the data to develop a more complete picture of parent concerns. This information helped generate action hypotheses regarding the new design for faculty evaluations.

Termination and Evaluation

Social work consultants James and Kreig terminated their contract with the school district after an 18-month period during which parent complaints were reduced by 75%. Most teacher concerns were also eventually resolved. A new faculty evaluation procedure was indirectly responsible for the nonrenewal of five teacher's contracts. The high school principal resigned and was replaced.

As a result of the team building, communication among administrators improved. They evolved into an administrative team that employed consensus decision making.

This case is an example of the conferee role taken with an organization, where the workers were the primary resource. The workers in this case were outside the agency. Had they been working for the organization, the role may have provided the basis for further role taking with and on behalf of the client.

Both assessment and intervention phases were geared toward the use of collectivity. Mutual aid, mutual problem definition, and collaborative agreement on solutions represented the development of empowerment by all the parties involved. The intervention left increased skills for problem solving in the hands of the participants and created an experience of collective action taking from which all participants learned how to handle such problems in the future. An action research approach was used to generate action hypotheses and to confirm or reject such hypotheses.

♦

SUMMARY

This chapter defined and presented a framework for the conferee role. Illustration with an individual and a large system, an organization, suggested the use of this role as a beginning in work with clients and confirms the practice demand in which the worker is the primary source of help. The framework for the conferee role uses the problem-solving process. The emphasis is on social problems, social system linkage, client definition, client systems strengths and weaknesses, competency assessment, normalization, resource assessment, and mutual education. In the goal-setting and planning phases, mutuality, habilitation, empowerment, and prevention are used in deciding what to do. These principles guide strategy selection. Finally, evaluation of outcome is necessary to answer questions of process, outcome, and impact. The case of Ms. Napier demonstrates the conferee role as the anchor of work with the client and the basis for viewing social problems and assuming a variety of roles. The Grand Valley School District case illustrates the conferee role in an outside consultant basis in a time-limited intervention.

STUDY QUESTIONS

1. How does integrated-practice philosophy guide the exploration and assessment phases of the conferee role?

2. How does the integrated-practice philosophy guide goal setting, planning, strategy selection, and implementation in the conferee role?

3. What is the difference between the conferee role in integrated practice and a more traditional clinical role?

4. How did the worker counter Ms. Napier's high degree of internalized powerlessness?

5. In what ways were the components of empowerment-based practice present in Ms. Napier's case?

6. In what ways were the components of empowerment-based practice present in the Grand Valley School District case?

REFERENCES

Compton, B., & Galaway, B. (1989). *Social work processes* (4th ed.). Pacific Grove, CA: Brooks/Cole.

Connaway, R. S., & Gentry, M. E. (1988). *Social work practice.* Englewood Cliffs, NJ: Prentice-Hall.

Mills, C. W. (1959). *The sociological imagination.* New York: Oxford University Press.

Solomon, B. B. (1976). *Black empowerment: Social work in oppressed communities.* New York: Columbia University Press.

Specht, H. (1969). Disruptive tactics. *Social Work, 14*(2), pp. 5–15.

Webster's New World Dictionary. (1982, 2nd College Ed.). New York: World.

Wood-Goldberg, G., & Middleman, R. (1989). *The structural approach to direct practice in social work.* New York: Columbia University Press.

Chapter 8

◆

The Enabler Role

This chapter defines and conceptualizes the enabler role in social work practice. A framework for the role is provided through an illustration of the enabler role with a neighborhood task group.

The enabler role is, to some extent, the idealized version of social work practice because it implies that social workers facilitate the capacities and task accomplishments of others. A facilitative role, rather than "doing for" someone, is highly valued in our society. The enabler role implies helping others to help themselves, and that is perhaps the vision of social work practice that many students bring with them into the field.

However, the term *enabler*, as used in the field of alcohol and drug counseling, means a dysfunctional role in which codependent personalities support each other in unhealthy patterns in relationships. So, the term is often viewed as negative and is avoided by social workers and others in the human services field. We use "enabler" here to describe a central role in the integrated-practice model of social work. This role is not disabling and dysfunctional; rather it is at the heart of the integrated model with its emphasis on empowerment, habilitation, and prevention.

DEFINING THE ENABLER ROLE

Webster's New World Dictionary (1968) defines the term *enable* as "to make able; provide with means, opportunity, make possible or effective." The traditional role of enabler in social work implies education, facilitation, and promotion of interaction and action. In social work, it means

> the responsibility to help the client become capable of coping with situational or transitional stress. Specific skills used in achieving this objective include conveying hope, reducing resistance and ambivalence, recognizing and managing feelings, identifying and supporting personal strengths and social assets, breaking down problems into parts that can be solved more readily, and maintaining a focus on goals and the means for achieving them. [Barker, 1987, p. 49]

Overlap with the Conferee Role

This definition sounds a great deal like the conferee role process described in Chapter 7, and indeed there is a blurred division between the two functions. They are often referred to as a role cluster because activities in these two roles so frequently overlap. Some social work authors label what is described as the conferee role in this text as the enabler role. Compton and Galaway described the enabler role as consisting of intervention activities that are "directed toward assisting clients to find the coping strengths and resources within themselves to produce changes necessary for accomplishing objectives of the service contract'' (1989, p. 509). They further distinguished the role from others by saying that "change occurs because of client's efforts, and the role of the worker is to facilitate or enable the client's accomplishment of a defined change." Connaway and Gentry used the "educator role" to describe activities in which social workers "teach specific skill, give needed information, and facilitate client's abilities to function in their social roles" (1988, pp. 112–115). Barbara Solomon (1976) described the function of the enabler as a trainer-teacher and suggested that it is a primary role for empowerment-based social work.

The enabler role is assumed when the practice demand is for the social worker to structure, arrange, and manipulate events, interactions, and other environmental factors to facilitate and enhance system functioning. Although more formal approaches to education and training are encompassed in the enabler role, taking the role implies getting underneath the structure of a system and supporting, strengthening, and building it in an effort to increase its strength and capacity to care for and maintain itself. Much of the role's activity is done in a small-group method (Connaway & Gentry, 1988), although its functions are also relevant to individuals, families, organizations, and communities. None of the roles in generalist practice excludes the other roles. In fact, the roles represent functions of social work, and generalist practice is multirole and multifunctional. Working as an enabler with client groups often leads to work in another of the six roles. The example in this chapter illustrates this concept.

The Enabler Role and Empowerment

The earlier discussion of the empowerment process noted that the primary strategies relevant to empowerment include self-help groups, support groups, network building, education groups, and social action groups. These strategies provide opportunity for the dialogue necessary to develop critical thinking, knowledge, skill building, validation, and support. These activities are key strategies in social problem intervention all along the continuum from victim to nonvictim and are therefore at the heart of integrated practice. The enabler role is essential to empowerment-based practice because it is the essence of creating skill, knowledge, critical thinking, and willingness to act in client systems. The enabler helps clients develop empowerment at the personal, interpersonal, and political levels.

The Enabler Role Across Systems

Social workers often assume the enabler role in organizations when attempting to assist human service agencies to function better and more efficiently in order to achieve their goals. Social workers often lead teams, direct programs, and manage services. Therefore, workers need skills to deal with colleagues and co-workers in ways that facilitate their capacities to do their work. In human service agencies, the role encompasses educating, facilitating communication, decision making, and leading task and process.

We are using the case study of a worker who leads a community interagency group to describe the enabler role. The worker organizes community residents, human service agency practitioners, community leaders, planners, and politicians in order to define need, create access to services, create services, and impact policy and social change efforts. The women's group example described in the empowerment discussion is also a good example of the enabler role. The enabler function is relevant to varied-sized client systems for many purposes. In these settings, the role calls for a generic set of skills and strategies, which is discussed in the following section.

FRAMEWORK FOR THE ENABLER ROLE

In a general sense, the approaches used in the enabler role are inherent in small-group leadership. The role includes facilitating and strengthening system functioning, regardless of the size of system. Facilitating any system's functioning includes the following processes:

♦ Defining membership or who is involved in action taking
♦ Defining the purpose of involvement
♦ Promoting communication and relationship; validating experience and valuing diversity
♦ Facilitating cohesion and synergistic qualities in the system: finding commonality and differences
♦ Facilitating education: building knowledge and skills
♦ Modeling and facilitating collaborative problem solving: promoting collective action
♦ Identifying problems for work
♦ Facilitating goal setting
♦ Generating alternative solutions
♦ Promoting task accomplishment
♦ Maintaining the system's relationship
♦ Resolving conflict

These processes are discussed and illustrated in the following case example of a public housing interagency council, led by a social worker based in a community agency.

CASE STUDY: *The Interagency Council* ◆————————————

Within the public housing project where the worker was employed by Head Start, an interagency council was established. The council was composed of Head Start representatives and employees from the local mental health center, health clinic, Department of Social Services, the school, community recreation center, and the local church. When the council began to meet, its loosely defined purpose was to coordinate the agency's work with specific families, individuals, groups of boys and, to a lesser extent, look at community-wide problems. The agency-based social worker joined that group to learn about community problems and to educate others.

————————————————————————————————◆

Defining Membership

The enabler is also responsible for helping the members of the system clarify its boundaries or membership. "Who are we?" and "What constitutes membership of this system?" are questions that lead to discussion of identity and establishment of the boundaries necessary for building cohesion and developing a healthy system.

CASE STUDY: *The Interagency Council* ◆————————————

When the worker joined the interagency council, there was discussion about community residents attending the meetings. The worker had already encouraged the women's group members (described in the discussion of empowerment) to join the council and therefore supported the effort to get community residents involved in the group. When the residents began to attend the council, turmoil and conflict arose over who had the power and the right to define problems. Eight to ten agency representatives attended the group, and approximately six or eight community residents also began to attend. Two of the residents were very vocal and somewhat angry. They immediately questioned the group's right and ability to accurately assess problems that impacted community residents, since the agency representatives were outsiders who only "thought they knew" what the community's problems were. At that point, the council chairperson perceived that the process was unproductive and destructive, became uncomfortable with the ongoing arguments and conflicts, and resigned. Agency personnel were reluctant to assume the leadership role, so the social worker volunteered to become chairperson and facilitate the council's goals and activities.

————————————————————————————————◆

Defining the Purpose

The members of a system must clarify its purpose in relation to its external environment. Enabling system functioning requires helping the system define its purpose for existence. Lack of clarity of purpose in any group or system leads to disparity in effort and perceptions of performance and often to destructive conflicts within the system. A worker in the enabler role with a group or organization must help the members of the system find their commonality; that is, their most-common thread or tie. Seeking to clarify purpose is a part of that function.

CASE STUDY: *The Interagency Council* ◆───────────

The worker distributed a flyer to residents and agencies and then made phone calls to get agency representatives and residents to attend. She called the meeting to order and asked people to introduce themselves. The worker began the meeting by thanking those in attendance and suggested that in view of past events, the group should spend some time talking about what it wants to do—its purpose.

One agency representative said, "The group has been in existence for a long time and has been clear about its purpose: to coordinate services in the community."

A resident angrily responded, "Yeah, the group has been meeting, but it hasn't done anything for the community and the residents, it's a gab session—all you do in here is talk. What does that accomplish?"

Another agency representative disagreed. "That's not entirely true. We benefit and the residents benefit from our knowing what is going on in the clinic, at the school, at Head Start, and so on."

Another resident said, "Well, you may feel as if you do your jobs better by talking, but even your jobs and the agencies ignore the real problems in this neighborhood. You may know more about what you're doing, but what you're doing is nothing compared to the problems."

The conversation continued in this vein for several more exchanges, when the worker interjected, "It sounds as if all of you are interested in a common purpose. That is, in identifying the problems of the community residents, whether they are defined by agencies or by residents, and to help one another find resources and solutions to these problems. And that is a strong and potentially powerful base—that common purpose. We may disagree about who really knows what the problems are, but if we all agree we want to define those problems and work together toward resolution, we are well on our way to something powerful for the community. Part of this group's power is the diversity of experience you each bring and the diversity of agency and community resources represented in this room. The potential for mobilizing resources and people power is tremendous. Would you agree?"

─── ◆

The first task was to help the group find some common identity and purpose. In the beginning, the group's purpose had been to coordinate services around certain clients or individuals. But when the community residents joined the group and began giving their opinions and challenging the agency personnel, the common purpose was lost. As an enabler, the social worker helped the group redefine its purpose. Each member was asked what he or she wanted to see accomplished. The worker then had to find the commonality and the themes that were voiced in their responses. Finding commonality is often done by emphasizing diversity. The group's common needs were focused on while emphasizing the members' diversity. At the same time, the question of membership was raised.

CASE STUDY: *The Social Action Council* ◆

Were all agency representatives welcome to attend? Were all residents welcomed as well? Finally, the group decided that all agency and community residents were welcomed to participate; all that was necessary for membership and attendance was an interest in doing something about problems in the community. This raised the purpose of the group again, as membership and purpose go hand-in-hand.

Community residents insisted that the group should not simply be a discussion or vehicle for communication but should be an action group. Agency representatives were more interested in the communication purpose, but residents feared that the group would talk instead of taking action. After much discussion about the group's purpose, the name of the group was changed from an interagency council to a social action council, consisting of community residents and community agency representatives. The common purpose was to identify problems and solutions within the community, including coordination of service delivery. No specific families or clients would be discussed; instead the group would focus on the general problems that agencies and residents were struggling with. This common purpose and definition of membership took much time, effort, and facilitation of communication on the worker's part. The members only had to concur before further work could proceed.

◆

Promoting Communication and Relationship

Facilitating communication is a primary function in social work practice and in the enabler role defined here as enhancing system functioning. For any system to function effectively, communication between members is the key. Members have to learn to send messages and receive them with a minimum amount of "noise" blocking the communication. The enabler should facilitate this process by role modeling and teaching effective communication, including listening, active listening, recording of pertinent information, and encouraging feedback between members and between the group and its environment. Part of this task is to raise the members' awareness of the "noise" barriers to communication. This heightened awareness will enhance the clarity of their perceptions of the issues under discussion.

CASE STUDY: *The Social Action Council* ◆

At another meeting, a resident talked about a specific agency that was mistreating a client, also a community resident. "Just because she is a Native American, you agency people think you can run over her and run her life. You don't know anything about her and you don't care, you just have your little forms to fill out."

The agency person being singled out responded, "I don't make the policies, but I have to carry them out. It's not fair of you to say we don't care. You don't have all the information."

The resident responded, "I have all the information I need. You are supposed to be helping her manage those kids and you don't help when you make the oldest one move out. She needs that oldest child and his income there to help manage. You honkies bring in your rules and regulations and you don't know what you do to Hispanic and Native American families."

The worker intervened. "So—you seem to believe that the agency's lack of understanding about culture in the family and the community becomes a problem when trying to help."

The resident responded, "Well, of course you can't help when you don't understand about the life of the family."

The worker turned to the agency representative. "And what do you think about this—is there a lack of understanding of the culture that gets in the way of your being helpful?"

◆

There were many different emotions and much miscommunication within the council's membership, which represented a diversity in age, ethnic group, race, gender, socioeconomic class, interest, and language. Residents and professionals in the group were Hispanic, African American, Native American, and white. There were subgroupings within the groups of residents and agency professionals. The miscommunication led to conflict and resentment by both residents and agency representatives. The residents accused the agency personnel of not knowing and understanding residents' problems, and the staff became defensive. Residents tended to see themselves as less powerful than the professionals. Agency representatives needed to hear of the residents' perceptions. They had to deal with their "clients" as coequals in problem definition and problem solving. Socioeconomic class, race, and educational differences were all communication barriers. The worker helped the group members share their differences and define their commonality and their need to work with one another in order to accomplish the common goals.

The diversity and differences within this group were great. The membership involved social workers, drug and alcohol counselors, therapists from a mental health center, a minister, teachers, and residents. Building commonality and mutual aid was an arduous task, requiring both agency representatives and residents to see each other as coequals, as partners in a collaborative effort. But the creation of a mutual-aid collective built a community power base, strengthened interagency, agency, and community resident relationships, and served as a vehicle for counteracting the powerlessness of both the clients and the workers.

Facilitating Cohesion and Synergism Within the System

The enabler or facilitator of a system must recognize the benefits of a cohesive relationship and work to achieve them within the system. Systems tend to work most effectively when they are more cohesive; that is, when there is a greater amount of synergy or energy in the system. Synergy may be defined as the energy created above and beyond the elements of the system through dynamic interaction between members or parts of the system. Cohesion is important in any client system such as a family or organization. The enabler function promotes and facilitates cohesion. Synergy may be thought of as cohesion or the social glue created in the system.

Often groups in social work—whether they are practitioners in agencies, client groups identified for services, or community leaders—become fragmented in their efforts to accomplish a set task. Time constraints, lack of trust, and miscommunication prohibit members from forming the kind of relationship necessary for "weathering the storm" of task accomplishment. The enabler helps the members observe and understand this fragmentation and consciously work toward keeping the system's synergism going. Facilitating cohesion is done by promoting communication, clarifying the group's purpose, and leading the group's task and process.

CASE STUDY: *The Social Action Council* ◆

A concern was raised about mistreatment of youth by the local police; that is, the police harassed the youth and provoked them into belligerent behavior, thereby creating grounds for arrest. The police sergeant in charge of the district was invited to a meeting. He brought with him the police officers who regularly worked the area. Residents began to accuse them of harassment and unfair treatment of the youth.

One resident said, "What are the statistics? How many more arrests do you make here on the weekend than in other communities of this size?"

The officers became somewhat defensive, and one replied, "Well, it is true there are always more arrests when families don't have control of their kids; when there aren't adults who really care about the kids."

The worker intervened and asked for both resident members and agency representatives to respond to that statement by giving their assessment of family concern and involvement with the children. Each member who spoke defended the families within the community. They gave specific examples of kids who had been recently arrested—and described the family life as adequately functional.

◆

As the interagency group began to identify a common purpose for its work, attention was drawn away from its internal differences and focused on outside targets. This focus forced members to join efforts and increase their interaction to work on a common purpose. Bringing in staff from the city development office and the city recreation department, school principal, and local police provided an opportunity for the council to unite against outsiders and become more cohesive. Although their internal differences were great, the group members stuck together in the face of outside influences that represented a threat because of their external power. The worker reminded the group that, at a minimum, they must present a cohesive front to the outside agencies from whom they were requesting action and change. This process created interaction and cohesion and provided a basis for building synergy within the group.

In the same manner, fragmented families can come together in the face of outside threats. Organizations often behave similarly as well. Promotion of self-maintenance, which is a primary need in all client systems, is an important part of the enabler function.

Facilitating Education

The worker in the enabler role brings relevant expertise to the system at hand. At the same time, the worker must also encourage all members to bring their expertise to the discussion of problems and solutions. A part of the communication process is to help members bring their contribution and to ensure that others hear it. Members learn to trust the efficacy of one another and to see themselves as shared experts on the problems and resolutions. They gather information and expertise from outside the system and integrate the new information into their own system.

CASE STUDY: *The Social Action Council* ♦───────────────

The social action council was discussing the possibility of securing funding for neighborhood lighting. The community development office had hinted that funds could be available but that a cohesive community effort was necessary to get a grant. The application needed to be a collaborative effort between many community components. The council members set out to become experts on lighting grants and to learn how to make their grant application viable. Tasks were assigned. Residents were to secure support for the effort from a large number of residents. Agency representatives were to find out what specific agencies would be willing to do on the grant effort. To gather more information about the issue, some members were to talk with other communities that had been successful in similar endeavors. Everyone brought back information to share.

─── ♦

Each member of the social action council brought expertise. Some agency personnel were asked to bring expertise from their own agencies and to secure information regarding other agencies and resources. Residents were asked to survey and talk to other residents and to contact other agencies within the community.

Collective problem solving and empowerment-oriented practice require mutual education. No one particular subgroup was seen as having the expertise, but instead expertise was seen as coming from the membership as a whole. Agency representatives brought some expertise, but residents brought expertise that agency people did not have. Also some information was needed that had to be obtained from outside the council. Plans were made for securing that information. This effort promoted team work and collaboration.

Modeling and Facilitating
Collaborative Problem Solving

A part of the enabler role is to teach and model collaboration in problem solving. To model such behavior, the worker first has to believe in collaboration. Having the patience to work toward a collective definition of problems and solutions is a primary skill. This skill includes facilitating communication in order to define problems and generate solutions. A leader or enabler relinquishes his or her control and power to define the problems and issues at hand and facilitates a collective definition. According to the empowerment concepts discussed earlier, collectivity and collective action are necessary if members of a group or system are to believe that they have the capacity to act on their own behalf. A worker in a fragmented family, for example, may help the family work together to solve a small problem so the members experience the feeling of successful collaboration.

In spite of the conflicts and differences within the social action council, it was critical to hold on to the theme of common interest and the contract to work together to solve problems. Collective problem solving is a very difficult way to resolve problems in a diverse group. However, it may be the only way to promote and enable the entire system to work together to achieve its purpose. The leader of collective problem solving must trust the process and promote the principle in the work undertaken. The worker in the social action council continued to identify the thread of commonality and remind the group of the problems before them, and to hold out hope that the group could work together to find solutions. In a highly conflictual family, it is easier for members to see their unique interests rather than the family's common interests. The enabler helps the family members voice their commonality and common interests.

Identifying Problems

Getting an agreement on the problems to be addressed is an important step in leading the group toward task accomplishment. In many client or practitioner groups, members may have problems they need to share. This sharing process creates a relationship and an understanding between members. It creates the opportunity for the validation that is so necessary in the empowerment process. However, eventually, the client system must decide where to focus its energy. The worker must listen as the many problems are presented and then help the members select the most pressing and the most common ones—those that seem to be the most important to the greatest number of members or to the individual. Then, with the client, the worker must clarify the problems selected.

CASE STUDY: *The Social Action Council* ◆————————

The social action council members voiced many problems, all of which needed attention. Some of the problems identified included:

♦ Drugs and drug dealing at the community recreation center
♦ Lack of lighting in the common areas of the projects, making the neighborhood unsafe at night
♦ Unfair dealing with residents by the housing project management
♦ Large fees charged by the local grocery store to cash welfare checks
♦ Old, broken playground equipment
♦ Lack of gym facilities and equipment for the entire neighborhood
♦ Mistrust and fights among residents in the neighborhood
♦ Ill-repair of the housing project units
♦ Unfair treatment of neighborhood youth by the police
♦ Lack of resources in the local schools

Although these problems were real and important, the council had to decide where to focus its energy, so that its efforts were not so scattered as to be futile. Subgroups were formed to check into the various problems and then report back to the group for further decision making. One principle at work here is that leadership for task accomplishment cannot stay in the worker's hands; it must be parceled out to members so that the commitment and ownership of the problem-solving effort is widespread. A worker in an enabler role helps the family decide which problems should receive primary attention. While that may be difficult for a highly dysfunctional family to decide, the process of deciding enables the family to work together, even on a small task.

Facilitating Goal Setting

Reaching an agreement on goals for work is a critical step in the enabling process. Once the problems have been agreed on, the next logical step is to begin identifying desired directions for change. Again, the role of the social worker in the enabler role is to help members of the system voice their goals and mesh them with the goals of other members. In any system, the leader must help each member get his or her needs met from within the system, while helping each member help other members to meet their needs. The worker must promote mutuality among members for goal accomplishment.

Generating Alternative Solutions

When goals for change are agreed on, the next process is to facilitate generation of alternative solutions. There are as many alternative solutions to problems as there are members in a system. The worker in the enabler role has to facilitate the process of getting all possible solutions out on the table for discussion. Each member of the client system must have his or her solution heard. Solutions usually come from a member's perceptions of why the identified problems exist. It is particularly important for all participants to be heard if conflict exists. Generating many alternatives provides options for action.

Choosing from Alternative Solutions

Many factors determine what solutions are actually chosen for action. The feasibility of a solution may make it viable. A specific solution may represent the group's most common view and is therefore the most compelling course of action. The worker has to help the group decide where to focus its energy. Facilitating decision making from alternatives is a step and a skill used in all social work practice. In this process, the worker reminds members of their goals, their tendencies in behavior, and their time lines and helps them sort out the pros and cons of certain alternatives.

CASE STUDY: *The Social Action Council* ◆────────────

As the various subgroups brought back information to the interagency group, goals and alternatives for action could be determined. The group agreed on the potential and priority strategies for each of the problems identified, recognizing that not all problems can be approached simultaneously and that not all problems lend themselves to immediate action. Some of the agreed-upon action strategies included:

◆ Discussing with the city development office a grant proposal for increased lighting in the neighborhood and for playground equipment

◆ Discussing with the city recreation department the dissatisfaction with the management of the local recreation center

◆ Generating a list of complaints and concerns from residents to be taken to the housing project manager

◆ Inviting the housing project management to join the social action council

◆ Organizing a boycott of the local grocery to get the owner to lower the check-cashing fee and providing transportation for residents to another store for check cashing and grocery shopping

◆ Inviting the local police captain to a meeting of the council to answer questions about the way police relate to the neighborhood youth

◆ Organizing a campaign to create neighborhood unity, and to encourage
   residents to pull together instead of fighting (for example, organizing celebra-
   tions, Easter egg hunts for the kids, community-wide bake sales as fund-raisers,
   and so on)

Promoting Task Accomplishment

Once action steps are decided on, and perhaps subunits or task groups are
formed to work toward achievement of the goals, the worker assists the
system in carrying out the tasks. This action involves monitoring, coordinating, following up on subgroups, creating time frames, and setting the
agenda for reports and checks. The worker supports others in their problem-
solving efforts, gives relevant information when available, promotes communication between one subgroup and another, and keeps the goals in front
of the group to keep it on track.

Maintaining the System's Relationship

The enabler promotes the maintenance of the system; that is, the process,
the relationship, the cohesion, the esprit de corps (the spirit), the feeling
of oneness among members. This activity helps the energy level for work
stay high. The worker recognizes and praises effort and identifies, examines,
and refocuses the failures. He or she promotes widespread participation and
the awareness of effort by the entire membership. Collaborative effort and
successes are celebrated. For example, a simple facilitation technique could
be "Let's review some of our recent efforts that have been successful. What
is going well?"

CASE STUDY: *The Social Action Council* ◆

While the work of the social action council proceeded, there were highs and
lows in the group functioning. Some members followed through better than others;
some became discouraged in the face of defeat; some dropped out due to lack
of time, lack of activity, and lack of interest. The worker promoted the relationship aspects of the council. She helped the group recognize its successes and
reframe its defeats into part of the process of work. She also addressed conflicts
and apathy in order to promote the group's relationship.

   The group met with some success and some defeat. The city development
office was extremely cooperative and two grants were developed for lighting and

playground equipment. The group had to choose between them, finally selecting the playground equipment.

Lighting was sought from the housing project. A community representative was appointed to work in the housing project office, thereby improving the communication between the management and the residents. The housing project manager solicited the council's help in putting pressure on the city housing department for improvements in their projects.

As a result of the boycott, the grocery store owner reduced the fees charged for check cashing. The owner also became more interested in and responsive to the neighborhood.

◆

Resolving the Conflict

Resolving conflict is another part of the enabler role. Conflict is an inherent part of change, arising from the disparate views of the problem, the goals, and the solution; from perceived conflict of interests; from power battle; and from tension around leadership. Conflict comes from ineffective communication between members, from stereotypes, and from lack of understanding. The social worker must recognize conflict, identify it, and bring it out in the open for resolution, either by talking to individual participants or by bringing it before all the participants.

While conflict is a healthy, inherent part of all systems and of all social change, unresolved destructive conflict can destroy a system's energy and focus, splintering it into fragments and destroying its cohesiveness. Social workers must be comfortable enough with conflict and assertive enough to see the conflict through to resolution.

Many conflicts were present in the social action council. Members represented great diversity in background, values, and perceptions. Conflict resolution was key to the group's success. The fear of conflict is often a barrier to a family's ability to attempt collaborative problem solving. If the worker can help the family experience even small success with handling conflict, trust among the members will increase.

The empowerment process has specific components: a focus on competency, strengths, and power assessments; collective action for mutual aid, support, validation, and action; and education for critical thinking, acquiring knowledge and skills, and taking action. Anderson (1992) summarized the literature on empowerment as a sociopolitical process and suggested that a development stage pattern of movement exists in the transformation of mutual aid into political movements: from (Riessman, 1986) interdependence built through mutual aid, to critical consciousness and awareness of external influences resulting in an advocacy stance, to the development of interdependent coalitions, to increased opportunities for political action and change. Anderson summarized by suggesting that the empowerment process "links individual strengths and competencies, natural mutual aid systems and pre-active behaviors to social action, social policy, social change and community development" (1992, p. 7).

CASE STUDY: *The Social Action Council* ♦———————————

The group's work brought the members together and created cohesion and energy for the members and for the mutual-aid system as a whole. Both successes and defeats reinforced the group's commonality and purpose, and perpetuated its efforts toward collective problem solving. The establishment of a strong neighborhood action council represented to residents and to agency workers the possibility of resolving existing problems. Over time, many new problems were brought to the council and many new people joined. It was important to put this structure in place for future work, to establish something strong and lasting through which collective problem solving could occur, thereby increasing the process of empowerment for both residents and agency representatives. All of these activities were facilitated through the assumption of the enabler role.

———————————————————————————————————————♦

SKILLS IN THE ENABLER ROLE

In a general sense, assuming the enabler role means creating a healthy system that has the capacity to meet its members' needs and assist them in working toward the maintenance of a healthy system. Shulman (1992) has identified this function as the role of the social group worker in creating healthy groups.

William Schwartz (1971) described the role of group leadership as having a mediating function between the group and its environment. Asserting that environments are most difficult for clients to negotiate, he identified the group as a microcosm of society in which the mediation of that environment became a reality. Leading client and nonclient systems in the negotiation and mediation of their environments is the role of the enabler in social work practice.

Henry (1991) has suggested that the appropriate role of the group worker is the dynamic position of leadership taken in response to the group's stage of development. This paradigm of group leadership is appropriate to the enabler role, in that strong leadership is necessary to enable a system to move and change. However, too much leadership or dominance of leadership may destroy the system's potential to lead itself. So, the leader must assume a dynamic role that facilitates the system's functioning to the point that it can take charge of its own facilitation. This is a delicate skill because it requires the worker to be sensitive not only to his or her own needs to lead and be in the central position, but also to recognize the needs of the system and respond accordingly.

The specific skills inherent in this framework are much the same as those called for in all social work practice: listening, reflecting, summarizing, clarifying, focusing tasks, monitoring tasks, promoting communication and relationship, and supporting growth and development. Assisting others in their task completion, educating, modeling collaborative effort, and leading the balance between task and process are also critical skills in this role. Moving in and out when needed as leader is also a necessary skill. Finally, assertive conflict resolution strategies are a requisite for building the capacity of systems.

The enabler role may be assumed with client groups and nonclient groups, with individuals and families. In all client systems, it requires skills in facilitating the development of systems so that they are better able to solve their problems both with and without the worker. To set the process in place requires support, encouragement, sensitivity, hope, and a strong task and process leadership.

SUMMARY

This chapter defined and provided a framework for the enabler role as a primary strategy for facilitating the empowerment process. The role is one of strengthening and facilitating the functioning of any client system. Facilitating system functioning includes defining membership and purpose; promoting and facilitating communication, relationship cohesion, and synergy; educating; modeling; teaching; assisting in identification of problems for work; goal setting; generating alternative solutions; promoting task accomplishment; maintaining the system's relationship; and resolving conflict.

These activities are illustrated through a worker's leadership in a social action council in a housing project. Many group leadership skills are relevant to the enabler role; however, the enabling function in social work is applicable to many client and nonclient systems in social work.

STUDY QUESTIONS

1. What is the relationship between defining membership and defining purpose?

2. Identify the components of empowerment suggested in the social action council.

3. What is the connection between promoting communication among members and building a relationship between members?

4. What behavior on the part of the worker helped turn differences into collaborative work?

5. The worker in this group was very active and involved. Can heavy involvement by a worker promote the process of empowerment? Is there a contradiction in this? Why or why not?

REFERENCES

Anderson, J. (1992). Between individual and community: Small group practice in a generalist perspective. Paper presented at Annual Program Meeting, Council on Social Work Education, Kansas City, KS.

Barker, R. L. (1987). *The social work dictionary.* Silver Spring, MD: National Association of Social Workers.

Compton, B. R., & Galaway, B. (1989). *Social work processes* (4th ed.). Pacific Grove, CA: Brooks/Cole.

Connaway, R. S., & Gentry, M. E. (1988). *Social work practice.* Englewood Cliffs, NJ: Prentice-Hall.

Henry, S. H. (1991). *Group skills in social work* (2nd ed.). Pacific Grove, CA: Brooks/Cole.

Riessman, F. (1986). The new populism and the empowerment ethos. In H. C. Boyte & F. Riessman (Eds.), *The new populism: The politics of empowerment* (pp. 53–63). Philadelphia: Temple University Press.

Schwartz, W. (1971). On the use of groups in social work practice. In W. Schwartz & S. R. Zalba (Eds.), *The practice of group work.* New York: Columbia University Press.

Shulman, L. (1992). *The skills of helping* (3rd ed.). Itasca, IL: F. E. Peacock.

Solomon, B. B. (1976). *Black empowerment: Social work in oppressed communities.* New York: Columbia University Press.

Webster's New World Dictionary. (1968, 2nd College Ed.). New York: World.

Chapter 9

◆

The Advocate Role

---

requently, social workers must intervene with political systems in order to secure needed services or resources for their clients and to accomplish intervention goals. When those services or resources are inaccessible due to resistance from systems and inadequate social policies, workers must assume the advocate role. In this chapter, we discuss political activity as a part of social work practice, define advocacy, discuss types of advocacy, and present the role's theoretical underpinnings, along with the dilemmas inherent in the advocate role. We also propose frameworks for advocacy and discuss the skills necessary to assume the role.

DEFINING THE ADVOCATE ROLE

The advocate role involves securing services or resources on behalf of clients in the face of identified resistance or developing resources or services when they are inadequate or nonexistent (Hernández et al., 1985; Lurie, 1982). In a broader sense, advocacy is also the act or process of defending or promoting a cause and the subsequent pleading of that cause (Panitch, 1974).

Advocacy takes many forms. The advocate role can be seen in the activities of a worker who represents a client who has been denied benefits in an appeal hearing, a community worker who makes a presentation before the local city council for more playgrounds for the city's youth, the social activist who makes a plea for more programs to house the homeless, and the agency worker who calls for a change in eligibility criteria so that a larger number of clients might be served.

Each of these examples illustrates one of two types of social work advocacy: case or cause. *Case advocacy* occurs when a social worker advocates on behalf of an individual client or consumer. *Cause advocacy* occurs when the effort is intended to promote an issue or act on behalf of a population, or class, of individuals. Cause advocacy is also referred to as class or issue advocacy.

In case advocacy, an identified client system is the beneficiary of the action taken; however, in cause advocacy, there may not be an immediately identified client system. Cause advocacy is generally characterized as indirect practice and occurs in a macroarena such as advocating for policy or program change. Regardless of the type, advocacy's fundamental basis is the protection of client rights and entitlements. (Ford, 1988; Reisch, 1986)

The principles of empowerment suggest that workers not just "stand up on behalf of" their clients or populations, but also enable and facilitate them to stand up for themselves. Solomon (1976) cautioned us about taking the place of clients who are able to stand on their own. Advocacy can lead to empowerment of clients if the components of empowerment are taken into account.

THE THEORETICAL
UNDERPINNINGS OF ADVOCACY

To apply the concept of advocacy in practice, social workers must be clear about the kind of advocacy they are considering and the level of social work responsibility at which it is applied. Levy (1974) identified three levels of advocacy through which workers may be able to direct their efforts toward social work responsibility. These three levels involve either conceptions of justice, distributive justice, or corrective justice.

Justice includes efforts to ensure equal opportunities and protections to all persons within the framework of formal and informal institutions and practices. *Distributive justice* is an extension of the concept of justice in that it refers to the manner in which opportunities and protections are distributed within society. *Corrective justice* involves the selective consideration of the needs of deprived groups and the institution of differential provisions for them in light of their present condition and past deprivations.

As such, corrective justice is related to conceptions of social compensation, or compensatory justice. Similarly, redistributive and integrative advocacy are consistent with the concepts of corrective and distributive justice (Lauffer, 1978). Redistributive advocacy is based on the assumption that some members of society have been unfairly deprived of access to needed services. The advocate's duty then is to strengthen the position of the deprived population vis-à-vis those social institutions that provide or distribute human services. The underlying assumption is that a conflict of interests must necessarily lead to a redistribution of resources among competing parties. Affirmative action policy is an example of redistributive justice. Veterans' benefits are another; they suggest reparation, a concept also compatible with redistributive advocacy.

Regarding integrative advocacy, Lauffer (1978) maintained that a difference in interests does not necessarily lead to conflict. These advocacy activities are generally directed at securing those rights and services that are mandated under existing law or policy but are denied in actual practice. The denial may not be intentional. It may stem from ignorance or lack of skill on the part of service providers, or ill will and inappropriate attitudes on the part of some staff members of a human services agency. Or perhaps the denial may be the result of the use of administrative methods or service approaches that are inappropriate to specific client populations. Integrative advocacy thus attempts to integrate clients into the mainstream of the service delivery system by allowing them access that had heretofore been denied them. For example, if a law that provides health care for everyone unintentionally discriminates against certain groups, the advocate would work for equal treatment under the law. The discussion in Chapter 10 on the broker role suggests that removing barriers to service may require the advocate role.

Even though integrative advocacy does not necessarily lead to conflict, advocacy still basically involves the distribution of power, authority, and/or resources. A system may feel a vested interest in maintaining business as usual, in which case a conflictual relationship would be quite likely to exist. Furthermore, the distinctions between the two strategies are often not clear in practice. As an example, Lauffer (1978) cited that grievance machinery may be used to correct systemic flaws and right individual grievances, or it may be used to redistribute decision-making power within an agency. Many times, both strategies are used either simultaneously or sequentially.

DILEMMAS OF ADVOCACY

The advocacy approach, whether case or cause, operates within a general stance of bargaining or conflictual relationships with respect to the target system (Pincus & Minahan, 1973). Because of this, workers are often confronted with several dilemmas when they assume the advocate role.

Pratt (1972) underscored the notion of advocacy as being generally conflictual; focusing around power, authority, and resources; and seeking to benefit a disenfranchised group. This description highlights some potential dilemmas of advocacy practice. For example, the practice of advocacy involves the distribution of power, authority, and resources—none of which people give up willingly. Because of this, advocacy generally requires a conflict strategy in which gain for one faction means loss for another. However, effective use of advocacy tactics may lead to negotiation and mediation where win/win outcomes are more likely.

Client Risks

Advocacy on behalf of others involves more risk than mediating differences. These risks often have more consequences for the client than for the worker. After all, the client has to live with the consequences of an unsuccessful advocacy effort. Because of the risks involved and in order to preserve client self-determination, the social worker–advocate must involve clients to the maximum extent possible at all stages of the effort.

Worker Risks

Advocacy also involves risks to the worker. If a worker must advocate for a client within his or her own agency, there is the risk of alienation from co-workers and the administration. If a worker takes on an issue that has little likelihood of success, he or she may lose credibility. There is the risk of retaliation from an irate adversary. Finally, a worker may alienate individuals or systems that might be future allies. For many of these reasons, advocacy requires a degree of autonomy for the social worker. In addition, following the principle of least contest, the social worker as advocate should escalate conflict incrementally and only to the degree necessary.

Other dilemmas involve a concern over ethical considerations of advocacy (Levy, 1974), possible violations of client self-determination (Gilbert & Specht, 1977), and client empowerment (Solomon, 1976). Richan (1973) described three additional dilemmas faced by the social worker in carrying out the advocacy function: competing loyalties, paternalism, and redress versus reform.

Competing Loyalties

The first dilemma, competing loyalties, concerns the conflicting claims of different interests for the advocate's support. Competing loyalties between the agency and the clientele is a basic example. This frequently occurs when a worker has to advocate for a client within his or her agency. Although the formal position of the social work profession favors the client, there are times when a worker may believe that other claims take precedence. For example, when agency policies may be seen as serving a "greater good" even though they may disadvantage a particular client (Ashford, Macht & Mylym, 1987). Such instances often occur when resources are scarce and eligibility criteria for services become more stringent in order to give priority to clients determined to be most in need.

What then does a worker do for a client who is clearly in need but is not quite needy enough? Securing services for this client would exhaust resources that might go to other clients and diminish the agency's ability to serve. In such a case, advocacy efforts might be better directed at securing additional resources for the agency rather than advocating on behalf of an individual client even though the client may be disadvantaged in the short run. Gilbert and Specht (1977) and Davidoff (1974) broadened this dilemma as a situation in which advocacy on behalf of an individual is incompatible with advocacy on behalf of class interests and institutional change.

Paternalism

The second dilemma, paternalism, concerns the eager advocate who may take too much responsibility and become paternalistic, perhaps doing for clients what they can learn to do for themselves. Because advocacy involves actions on behalf of a client system, it can become counterproductive to client empowerment if not used carefully. For this reason, Solomon (1976) saw advocacy as the least empowering of the social work roles. This tendency needs to be countered. Clients should be involved to the greatest extent possible to preserve self-determination and foster empowerment. Group advocacy derived from the formation of a mutual-aid system that increases its members' awareness of their rights is a form of advocacy that facilitates empowerment in clients and in workers.

Redress Versus Reform

The third dilemma, individual *redress versus reform*, concerns the risk that case action to alleviate individual stress will act as a palliative and divert energies from the fundamental reform of social institutions. An advocate who is successful in redressing the plight of an individual client may feel that once the primary responsibility to the client has been met, there is no need to sustain the advocacy effort. This position loses sight of the fact that others may be similarly affected and that the need for advocacy may lie in some institutionalized policy or practice that needs to be changed. Such a dilemma also arises because the process of reforming institutions happens incrementally over time, whereas the need for individual redress is often immediate. Workers often perceive themselves as having to choose between meeting the immediate needs of individuals or working toward social reform. Such a dichotomy is false since it is possible to do both simultaneously (Longres, 1981).

CASE OR CAUSE: WHICH STRATEGY IS APPROPRIATE?

The dilemma around individual redress versus social reform underscores one of the most fundamental issues facing worker-advocates. That is, the question of when it is appropriate to advocate on behalf of an individual (case advocacy) and when it is appropriate to advocate on behalf of a class of individuals (cause or issue advocacy).

In this profession, workers are socialized to value the uniqueness of the individual and to view the client as our primary responsibility and source of sanction. Therefore, social workers are predisposed to advocate for individual clients in an attempt to respond to their immediate needs rather than see that for every client in need of advocacy, there are many more in similar circumstances. If, however, we as social workers see clients as victims of broader social problems and if we see the proper role of social work as solving those problems, then it would follow that we would see every instance of need for individual advocacy as representing the potential for institutional change. Cause advocacy would then become an appropriate strategy.

While we maintain that class advocacy is preferable to case advocacy because it offers redress for a greater number of individuals, such a perspective needs to be tempered by practical considerations. The process of deciding whether to engage in case or cause advocacy needs to consider several factors: (1) the number of people or prevalence affected; (2) the immediacy of their need; (3) the ability to identify and have access to a target for change; (4) the level and magnitude of change necessary; (5) the resources available to the advocate; and (6) the amenability of the target system to change. Most important is the issue of mobilizing clients or groups of clients to take a self-advocacy stance that lasts beyond the presence of the worker.

Advocacy and Social Reform

The issue of fundamental reform of social institutions begins to form the bridge between individual advocacy and social actionism. Social action includes those aspects of social work and agency activity that promote change in the clients's situation rather than in the client system itself (Shelton, Chalmers, & Dunster, 1978). Social reform involves, in part, a mixture of social action and social planning (Rothman, 1974). Social reform generally involves action by a group or coalition of interests that acts vigorously on behalf of some outside client group (community segment), which is at risk or disadvantaged. Organizational activity and goal determination take place within the entities that act on behalf of others, not within the client group itself. Historically, many social work reform efforts have followed this pattern.

Advocacy practice recognizes the need for restructuring the nature of the decision-making process within systems (Albert, 1983). It assumes that the established decision centers will not readily relinquish power and control over the resources for decision-making and that decision makers working out of these agencies are constrained by the notion of public interest. Recognizing that society relies primarily on resources from established institutions, the advocacy process places a major emphasis on impacting the outcome of such decision making.

Social Problems and Social Policy

In practice, social problem intervention requires a holistic focus that integrates advocacy and policy development. Social policies are in some measure society's response to social problems. Responsive policy cannot be developed and implemented without the determined and consistent involvement of advocates who represent the disadvantaged groups in the political process (Dluhy, 1981). To be successful, the advocate must take a proactive stance toward policy and the political process on a regular, on-going basis.

From the integrated-practice perspective, social problems are seen as rooted in the societal structures that comprise a person's macroenvironment. This perspective is consistent with Middleman and Goldberg's (1974) structural approach, which proposes that practice should adjust the environment to the needs of individuals rather than help individuals adjust to their situations.

A structural approach maintains that the proper focus of social work is to intervene in society's social structures. This approach is built on two central assumptions. First, individuals' problems are manifestations of social disorganization and dysfunctional structures, not of individual pathology. Second, the response of the social work profession to the need for social change is the obligation of social workers wherever they may be.

> Social change is not separated from social work, not relegated to specialists within the social work profession; rather it is pursued at every level of assignment, every working day by all social workers, and especially by those who must face the clients directly. [Middleman & Goldberg, 1974, p. 13]

The preceding discussion needs to be understood within a broader model of advocacy. If policy making is a part of professional practice, we need a model of practice that helps practitioners adopt a frame of reference that can strengthen their policy consciousness. Such a model helps them identify policy in their practice arena and develop the ability to move from practice issues, to knowledge of policy making and policy makers, to carrying out and influencing the development of social policy. In short, social workers must be able to integrate practice and policy (Pierce, 1984).

There are various points of view on the relationship between policy and direct practice. Dolgoff and Gordon (1981) discussed three such perspectives. One perspective suggests that policy and practice support each other. The second perspective finds that policy is enacted in practice and controls the way practice is implemented. The third perspective holds that direct practitioners make policy; they are not merely controlled by it. Integrated practice contains policy change and policy making as a level of practice that directly involves social and political action.

SOCIAL WORK AND POLITICAL ACTIVITY

Social problem solving and social change aimed at alleviating the plight of disadvantaged groups on a long-term basis necessitates political activity for influencing the nature of social policies. Social problem solving is a political process conducted in the public arena. Not only is the definition of social problems political but societal responses to social problems are themselves politically determined (York, 1982). Social policies, at one level, can be seen as societal responses to social problems and are themselves developed within a political and economic context (DiNitto & Dye, 1987).

A professional commitment to social change requires disregarding myths and stereotypes about political activity. Myths and stereotypes that portray political activity as being a waste of time, unprofessional, and dirty need to be reexamined (Dluhy, 1981). Social workers are often reluctant to engage in politics and strategies for political intervention and often have not been educated to do so. This lack of attention to political advocacy within the education and practice experience of social workers has led some research-ers to conclude that "a commitment to social change without the means to achieve it is futile in any profession" (Haynes & Mickelson, 1986, p. x).

Social Work's Unique Position for Political Advocacy

By virtue of their training, value base, and orientation to social purpose, social workers are in a unique position to impact and direct the nature of social policy. However, much needs to be done to develop policy con-sciousness (Pierce, 1984). For many social workers, the profession's early emphasis on political activity and social reform has been lost due to a variety of influences (Reeser & Epstein, 1987). Increasing professionalization of social work and the rise of specialization, for example, have contributed to the development of a problem-solving arena in which both problems and solutions are narrowly viewed as technical or individual in nature, rather than as structural or political. However, social workers engaged in clinical relationships with clients are in a uniquely powerful position to gather data and knowledge about social problems and probable solutions (Walz & Groze, 1991).

Haynes and Mickelson (1986) and Pierce (1984), for example, maintained that practitioners can have tremendous impact on policy decision making simply by using their practice knowledge and data. They would not nec-essarily need to add additional tasks to their role or learn new skills, because the actions involved consist primarily of information dissemination and client-empowerment strategies. Haynes and Mickelson (1986) delineated the range of activities and roles for practitioners in the policy arena as providing documentation of needs, giving testimony, serving as expert witnesses, offering written communication, serving as a client enabler or advocate, serving as an evaluator or consultant, lobbying, participating in voter regis-tration drives, becoming active with professional or advocacy groups and organizations, endorsing and supporting candidates, monitoring the bureau-cracy, and running for political office. Each of these activities presents op-portunities to apply social work knowledge and skill.

Whatever activities are employed, promotion of social policy, will be conducted in a political arena with both proponents and opponents. Social problem solving is first and foremost a process of social exchange. It involves
reciprocity; namely, a give-and-take that results in compromise.

This social exchange involves balancing the people's needs against the
political popularity of meeting those needs. It involves weighing the demands on a service agency by its clientele against its budget constraints.
For the worker, it means considering his or her actions in the light of professional expectations, values, and ethics as well as of the practice demands
of consumers. And finally, the politics of social problem solving demands
that a practitioner be cognizant of future ramifications of his or her actions.

Attributes for Political Activity

Often social workers interested in direct practice do not see themselves as
having the attributes and skills for political activity. However, many of these
attributes are the same as those needed for direct practice; for example, networking and linking skills, tolerance for conflict, tolerance for ambiguity,
optimism, and an empowerment philosophy.

Networking

Social problems are unlikely to be solved by any one discipline or institution. Thus, it behooves the social problem–based practitioner to become
proficient in interorganizational networking (Rossi, Gilmartin, & Dayton,
1982). Interorganizational cooperation is not necessarily easy to achieve,
given the reality of interagency competition and the resulting territorial
issues. Nevertheless, the notion of consortiums of human services agencies acting in concert is attractive, and the potential payoff is enough to
make networking a worthwhile goal. If health and welfare agencies can find
their ecological niche within a total community response to social problems,
they are less likely to be adversarial and competitive and more likely to see
the merit in cooperation.

Networking is to be encouraged at another level as well: the level of self-
help and mutual aid. People who have been victimized by special circumstances are most likely to find the empowerment to proceed with their
lives when they can rely on informal support networks to energize them.
These networks are also capable of becoming forces for both case and cause
advocacy, a necessary ingredient in social action. Unless the large numbers
of people who are most vulnerable are activated to make their legitimate
claims on society, social problem resolution will remain one step short of
realization. Without worker assertiveness, social problems are likely to remain entrenched.

Tolerance for Conflict

In that social problems are political in nature, they are thus embedded in conflicting values. Under such conditions, social work practice will be surrounded by conflict. To deal with this conflict, practitioners will have to be able to tolerate conflict, realizing that it can be a positive as well as a negative force.

As we know, conflict does not always take a positive turn. When people are polarized to the point that the conflict itself becomes more important than the issues, a potentially destructive win/lose dichotomy develops. Often forgotten in the heat of battle is the fact that conflict theory includes the process of conflict resolution; that is, the basis for joining contending parties. An alternative to negative conflict occurs when the conflict is normalized and presented as a natural process in which issues are clarified, thus creating opportunities for public education. Such creative conflict doesn't happen easily. It requires workers who are comfortable in managing conflict and in communicating through it.

Tolerance for Ambiguity

Just as the social problem–focused worker must learn to tolerate conflict, he or she must also develop a tolerance for ambiguity.

Dealing with social problem intervention is not a predictable activity. The political nature of problems makes their environment fluid and uncertain. Some workers refer to social problems as ''moving targets.'' There are often no clear-cut answers. What seemed right yesterday may not be appropriate today. Instead of absolutes, there are more likely to be continuums.

Under such conditions, it is not always apparent what direction to take, and decision making becomes more complex. Actions create reactions and interventions result in unintended consequences.

Yet the worker must proceed and it will be more feasible to do so if he or she can internalize his or her own guidelines and reference points.

Optimism

Setting the agenda for social problem solving dictates that the problem be defined in a manner that describes its nature as well as how it will look when it is reduced or solved. In short, the parameters of both the problem and the solution must be defined. The problem can then be conceptualized as the distance or difference between the current condition and what is believed to be possible future improvement. This creates a sense of optimism. In many respects, how a worker views the future dictates the degree of optimism he or she brings to designing programs that prevent breakdown and promote ideal conditions. The optimist believes that the future is yet to be invented, while the pessimist views the future as a predetermined straight line from the past.

A new perspective brings a sense of hope, renewal, and optimism, not necessarily the naive optimism associated with the "harmonic convergence" of the New Age philosophy (although that is not unimportant), but the optimism associated with the belief that problems can be confronted and diminished. Weick (1984) spoke of optimism as a duty:

> Optimism is also not naive if we can deny the relevance of hopelessness for the spirit of optimism. We justify what we do, not by belief in its efficacy but by an acceptance of its necessity. [p. 48]

Empowerment

Empowerment is one of the most subtle concepts to understand and the most difficult to employ. There are two reasons for this.

First, when people are suffering, workers naturally want to do things for them rather than with them. Because of their degree of need, it seems reasonable to alleviate that need as soon as possible by acting unilaterally on behalf of at-risk groups.

Second, disempowered, powerless people are not necessarily ready to be empowered. Having lost their power and replaced it with learned helplessness, they are not necessarily ready to take it back.

Empowering, then, is facilitating a process in which people make decisions and take actions that promote some degree of mastery in their lives. Social planners who plan without citizen involvement disempower the citizens for whom they plan. When people are positioned to advocate for themselves, they become a force, not only for implementing change but for making these changes more permanent. When consumers are capable of negotiating, bargaining, and dictating their needs, they are much less likely to be powerless and more likely to feel empowered. Finally, empowered people are less likely to become the victims or carriers of social problems and more likely to become active political entities who are involved in setting the direction of their own future. The advocacy framework employed in integrated practice promotes the empowerment process for clients.

FRAMEWORK FOR THE ADVOCATE ROLE

Successful advocacy needs to involve various parties in the resolution of a problem. Key figures and groups need to assume a role in the process. Advocacy should involve those people who are crucial for legitimation, implementation, and support of the effort. Thus the advocate system and the action system need to coincide. A case study of the Washington family and the housing authority is used to discuss the advocacy framework.

CASE STUDY: *The Housing Authority* ◆————————————————

Ms. Roberts, who was employed as a social worker in an urban housing authority, was faced with a dilemma that depicts assumption of the advocate role. The
Washington family had requested a transfer from the Regis Park housing complex to the Crestwood Homes projects. Living in Crestwood Homes would place
them in a school district with better special education resources for their disabled son. Since the housing authority had never responded to their request,
the Washingtons requested help from Ms. Roberts.

In conference with the Deputy Director of Housing, Ms. Roberts learned that
the director's office was "sitting" on several transfer requests. The unofficial position was that the housing authority was not to accommodate requests based on
special needs. "We are a housing authority and transfers should be considered
within the context of housing needs rather than other social needs," said the
director.

Ms. Roberts found this position at odds with the housing authority charter.
The mission statement clearly spelled out the authority's responsibility to "use
the total resources of the agency to enhance the quality of life of the families
living within housing authority units."

After further investigation, Ms. Roberts learned that the director's office had
also failed to act on at least 30 other transfer requests. These requests were based
on such factors as proximity to extended family members who could provide
child care, access to public transportation, and proximity to employment, health
stations, and more appropriate educational facilities.

——◆

Clearly, the Washington family was not the only family being ignored.
The question that arose centered around the political implications of involving the other families. The case of the Washingtons was obviously a
"cause." Should all 30 families be contacted? How many of them felt
strongly enough about their requests to sanction advocacy by the worker?
What would the repercussions be if the transfer requests became an issue?
What were the ethical issues here?

Pluralistic Advocacy

Advocacy tends to be pluralistic. It recognizes the multiplicity of special
interests, each with limited power, each having to adapt to other systems.
Advocacy is flexible and emergent rather than rigid and discrete and is
characterized by "serial analysis and evaluation" (Warren, 1971). From this
perspective, advocacy is oriented toward a conscious assessment of values,
situations, objectives, methods, implementation, and acceptance in their

relation to one another and to an aggregate outcome that is the optimum combination of these components.

Rothblatt (1978) presented an example of this approach. He identified his approach as a multiple advocacy model. As presented by Rothblatt, the crucial components of such an approach include systematic provisions for the following:

◆ Openness—allowing various points of view to be heard

◆ Broad representation—representing all actors having an interest in the decision: professional/lay, affluent/poor, and so on

◆ Fairness—having a system of equity whereby opposing positions can be comparatively assessed

◆ Hostility reduction—developing a decision environment that helps de-escalate hostility and alienation

◆ Information—presenting each view together with supporting documentation and analysis

◆ Encouragement of broad-range participation

◆ Responsiveness—inducing decision-makers to really listen, consider, and be responsive to the concerns and positions of others

Though presented here in a somewhat general fashion, each of these components is further defined and developed in accordance with the problem's particular demands and the characteristics of the actors involved. Through such a pluralistic process, the advocacy effort moves from coalition to independence, with participating parties acting as either cooperating or conflicting adversaries.

CASE STUDY: *The Housing Authority* ◆————————————

Ms. Roberts identified four of the families whose requests the housing office had ignored. She arranged a meeting between the families and two representatives from the housing authority. Each person aired his or her concerns and issues. Opposing positions were heard and the hostility was reduced.

——◆

The concept of pluralistic advocacy presents some interesting possibilities. Certainly, the advocate's expertise and skill in having previously disenfranchised interest groups advocate on their own behalf could be quite advantageous and potentially effective. It is not, however, without its obstacles. Effective intervention commonly depends on the following factors:

◆ The need to establish legitimacy for the effort

◆ The need to establish appropriate action systems that incorporate, as broadly as possible, representation from the pluralistic interest groups likely to be impacted by the decision

◆ The development and use of substantive expertise

◆ The appropriate and effective use of conflict resolution as a cohesion-inducing process

◆ The need to choose a strategy based on careful analysis of how decision makers will react to the change goals proposed and the types of power (coercion, referents, expertise, legitimacy, and value) that are available and can be mobilized

◆ The sensitive use of interpersonal skills

◆ The maximum possible involvement of those affected by the advocacy effort

◆ The maximization of client self-determination

◆ The ability to teach clients to plead their own cases to diminish dependency on the advocate

◆ The need to work toward social reform and system change to effect change for a class of people rather than on a case-by-case basis

Teaching such skills to client groups is necessary to create new knowledge and skills for future use.

CASE STUDY: *The Housing Authority* ◆——————————————

Ms. Roberts believed that the overriding issue was that the housing authority's actions were not congruent with its mission statement. She helped the family members write a memorandum to the director with a copy to the deputy director, citing that the mission statement was being misunderstood, ignored, or circumvented. The memorandum proposed that the authority's policy be reflected in responding to the transfer requests and in fact offered Ms. Roberts's assistance in processing the requests. The family memo also suggested that if it was not the intent of the agency to live up to its mission statement, the mission statement should be modified by the board of directors of the housing authority. Ms. Roberts also offered to testify before the board in the event the administration sought such modification.

The problem was ultimately resolved. Ms. Roberts was appointed to the review committee for transfer requests and a set of guidelines were drawn up for agency transfer decisions. These guidelines were developed with input from the resident advisory committees. Three families who had met with Ms. Roberts and the Housing authority became members of the resident advisory committees.

——————————————————————————————————◆

Demonstrating Need

As advocates make their case, they are frequently called on to demonstrate as clearly as possible their client's needs. They must be clear and concise and, whenever possible, document the need with statistics, research, case records, surveys, and so on. This documentation must be presented in the form that best reflects the target group, offers comparisons with other groups to demonstrate level of need, and is most understandable to the audience. Ms. Roberts collected as much data as possible on the 30 families who had requested a move. The families present at the meeting also gave detailed information.

In representing client groups, the language the workers uses to refer to them is critical because it may raise the audience's fears or touch their hearts. Words represent values, and social workers must consider whether their words affirm or reinforce acceptable and widely shared values, new (but positive) values, or negative or deviant values. Advocates must identify the most effective way of referring to the group they represent. In the case of Ms. Roberts, the families she could locate and identify were named as examples of the need she attempted to promote.

Importance of Values

Values become particularly important when framing the issue. One of the advocate's most difficult tasks is to make sure that the issues are clearly stated and presented in a way that other participants understand. The task of issue framing is critical to the overall advocacy debate. Successful advocates need to develop skills in framing issues in a common language. This involves clarifying and understanding the value systems or ideologies of the participants in the decision-making process.

Organizational Support

An additional element in advocacy, particularly at a system level, involves building organizational support (Dluhy, 1981). Advocates may have the proper value appeal, the right statistics on their side, and the appropriate policy design and still fail because they lack an adequate support base. Successful advocates constantly struggle to create, build, and maintain organizations and coalitions that will effectively support their positions. Dluhy noted that organizations are more powerful if they (1) have large memberships, (2) have distinctive ideologies and clear value positions, (3) are easy to mobilize in advocacy debates, (4) have large amounts of tangible resources at their disposal, (5) possess leadership that represents the organization's position in debates, and (6) are stable over time (1981, p. 23). The social worker must recognize the pluralistic interests contained in the advocate role. Demonstration of need and the value system in which the issue is framed are crucial.

CASE STUDY: *The Housing Authority* ◆——————————

In the case of Ms. Roberts, case advocacy evolved into cause advocacy without the direct sanction of the 30 other families. The overriding factor was the agency's negligence in not living up to its rules. By calling attention to the agency's inconsistency, Ms. Roberts was on firm ground. Need was demonstrated by the number of cases on file with the housing authority. Ms. Roberts clearly articulated the values by identifying the value and commitment to service stated in the authority's mission statement. The mission statement also gave implicit organizational support to the change goal she identified. She also strengthened her case by offering to assist in solving the problem. By involving residents (consumers) in developing transfer guidelines, Ms. Roberts utilized an empowerment strategy.

——◆

SUMMARY

The advocate role is taken when identified resistance exists and the need for defending or promoting a cause is present. The role may be taken on behalf of a client (case advocacy) or of a group or population (cause advocacy).

Levels of advocacy are conceptualized as justice, distributive justice, or corrective justice, or redistributive and integrative advocacy. All advocacy is related to power distribution and is usually conflictual. The advocate role creates conflictual dilemmas for the practitioner in that redistribution of power involves involuntary movement by some social systems. Therefore, risks to the client (or clients) and to the worker are always present. Such dilemmas include evaluation of client self-determination, client empowerment principles, competing loyalties, paternalism, and redress versus reform. Advocacy tends to be pluralistic in knowledge, skills, values, and decision making. Appropriate strategies include demonstrating need, articulating values, obtaining organizational support, and helping clients act as their own advocates.

STUDY QUESTIONS

1. What is the difference between case advocacy and cause advocacy? Cite an example of each.

2. What are the differences between justice, distributive justice, and corrective justice? How are they related to redistributive and integrative advocacy?
3. What are some types of ethical dilemmas that are likely to emerge in assuming the advocate role? Give an example of one of these dilemmas.
4. Solomon (1976) believed that advocacy is the least empowering of the social work roles. Why is this so?
5. How is social policy formulation related to advocacy? Give an example.
6. How is social action related to advocacy? Give an example.
7. How does the principle of least contest relate to advocacy?

REFERENCES

Albert, R. (1983). Social work advocacy in the regulatory process. *Social Casework,* 64(8), pp. 473–481.

Ashford, J. B., Macht, M. W., & Mylym, M. (1987). Advocacy by social workers in the public defender's office. *Social Work, 32*(3), pp. 199–203.

Davidoff, P. (1974). Advocacy and pluralism in planning. In N. Gilbert & H. Specht, *Planning for social welfare: Issues, models, and tasks.* Englewood Cliffs, NJ: Prentice-Hall.

DiNitto, D. M., & Dye, T. R. (1987). *Social welfare: Politics and public policy.* Englewood Cliffs, NJ: Prentice-Hall.

Dluhy, M. J. (1981). *Changing the system: Political advocacy for disadvantaged groups.* Beverly Hills, CA: Sage.

Dolgoff, R., & Gordon, M. (1981). Educating for policy making at the direct and local levels. *Journal of Education for Social Work, 17*(2), pp. 98–105.

Ford, J. (1988). Negotiation (counselling and advocacy): A response to Bill Jordan. *British Journal of Social Work, 18*(1), pp. 57–61.

Gilbert, N., & Specht, H. (1977). *Planning for social welfare: Issues, models, and tasks.* Englewood Cliffs, NJ: Prentice-Hall.

Haynes, K. S., & Mickelson, J. S. (1986). *Affecting change: Social workers in the political arena.* New York: Longman.

Hernández, S., Jorgensen, J., Judd, P., Gould, M., & Parsons, R. (1985). Integrated practice: Preparing the social problem specialist through a generalist curriculum. *Journal of Social Work Education.*

Lauffer, A. (1978). *Social planning at the community level.* Englewood Cliffs, NJ: Prentice-Hall.

Levy, C. S. (1974). *Social work ethics.* New York: Human Services Books.

Longres, J. F. (1981). Reactions to working statement on purpose. *Social Work, 26*(1), pp. 85–87.

Lurie, A. (1982). The social work advocacy role in discharge planning. *Social Work in Health Care, 8*(2), pp. 75–85.

Middleman, R. R., & Goldberg, G. (1974). *Social service delivery: A structural approach to social work practice.* New York: Columbia University Press.

Panitch, A. (1974). Advocacy in practice. *Social Work, 19*(3), pp. 326–332.

Pierce, D. (1984). *Policy for the social work practitioner.* New York: Longman.

Pincus, A., & Minahan, A. (1973). *Social work practice: Model and method.* Itasca, IL: F. E. Peacock.

Pratt, M. (1972). Partisan of the disadvantaged. *Social Work, 17*(4), pp. 66–72.

Reeser, L. C., & Epstein, I. (1987). Social workers' attitudes toward poverty and social action: 1968–1984. *Social Service Review, 61*(4), pp. 610–622.

Reisch, M. (1986). From cause to case and back again: The reemergence of advocacy in social work. *Urban and Social Change Review, 19* (Winter/Summer), pp. 20–24.

Richan, W. C. (1973). Dilemmas of the social work advocate. *Child Welfare, 52*(4), pp. 220–226.

Rossi, R., Gilmartin, K., & Dayton, C. (1982). *Agencies working together: A guide to coordination and planning.* Beverly Hills, CA: Sage.

Rothblatt, D. N. (1978). Multiple advocacy: An approach to metropolitan planning. *Journal of the American Institute of Planners, 44*(2), pp. 193–199.

Rothman, J. (1974). *Planning and organizing for social change.* New York: Columbia University Press.

Shelton, P., Chambers, J., & Dunster, R. (1978). Social work and social action. *Social Work Today, 10*(1), pp. 15–16.

Solomon, B. (1976). *Black empowerment: Social work in oppressed communities.* New York: Columbia University Press.

Walz, T., & Groze, V. (1991). The mission of social work revisited: An agenda for the 1990s. *Social Work, 36*(6), pp. 500–504.

Warren, R. L. (1971). *Truth, love, and social change.* Chicago: Rand McNally.

Weick, K. E. (1984). Small wins: Redefining the scale of social problems. *American Psychologist, 37.*

York, R. O. (1982). *Human service planning: Concepts, tools, and methods.* Chapel Hill: University of North Carolina Press.

◆

The Broker Role

In the traditional sense, a broker buys and sells stocks and bonds for clients in the commercial market. The broker attempts to maximize the gains from these transactions so that the client can realize the greatest possible profit. When clients hire a broker, they seek his or her expert knowledge of the stock market, a knowledge developed through day-to-day experience.

As conceptualized in social work, brokerage is not altogether dissimilar from stock brokerage. As in the stock market, there is the client or consumer. The social worker–broker, however, transacts in another market—the social services network. As with the stock broker, the social service broker's understanding of the relative quality of social services is critical to promoting his or her client's welfare.

The broker role is central to minimizing the impact of social problems. Meeting human need can make the difference between an individual's becoming at risk or being protected from risk. Meeting need may provide the margin between remaining a victim of negative social conditions and escaping them. To be connected with preventive health services may mean the difference between being hospitalized or not, with all the social cost that implies. To be linked to job retraining may well provide the distinction between employment, underemployment, and unemployment. Referral to a shelter for battered women may mean the difference between life and death.

DEFINING THE BROKER ROLE

Anderson has referred to brokerage as having three stages: "locating appropriate community resources; consistency of connecting the consumer to the resource; and evaluating the effectiveness of the resource in relation to the consumer's needs" (1981, p. 42). This is consistent with the way we have defined the term. The broker role is assumed when the practice demand is for the social worker to link the client with existing goods and services and control the quality of these goods and services. The key terms in this definition are *link*, *goods and services*, and *quality control*. It would be helpful, perhaps, if we examined each of these terms more closely.

Linking is a process of connecting people with agencies and other entities that are in control of needed resources. It involves substantially more than merely referring people to a resource, although that may be one small part of the process. Linking may require that the resource agency be referred to the client. Thus, true linkage may include referral, follow-up, delivery of the client to a resource, mutual introduction of the client and the resource agency, follow-up and follow through with either or both parties, and verification that goods or services were received. It may require interorganizational linking as well.

Goods involve such tangibles as food, food stamps, money, clothing, housing, medicines, and so on, while *services* are the agency service outputs designed to enhance a client's life. They may include emergency care, education, training, counseling, day care, and so on.

Quality control is a process of ensuring that the products of resource agencies match their promises. The goods and services that a client consumes should be of a qualitatively high standard and certainly at the level of the quality advertised. Controlling for quality requires the broker to continually monitor agencies within the service network to assess the ongoing quality of their product. Just as stocks and bonds vary in quality, there are also differences among social services.

Thus the broker's work is an ongoing process of assessing the "parts" or agencies within the service network as well as the network itself. The broker must be vigilant for gaps, overlaps, breakdowns, lapses, interruptions, and inconsistencies within the system and be prepared to call them to the attention of the appropriate source. Of even more importance, the broker must be cognizant of the degree of need that exists in the community. The ultimate matching of community resources with community needs characterizes this role. This necessitates that the broker be involved in designing and conducting community needs assessments.

COMMUNITY NEEDS ASSESSMENT

A community needs assessment is the initial step in responding to human need (York, 1982). It serves as a community planning tool and is usually conducted through the combined efforts of several organizations. It provides valid information to decision makers regarding (1) the degree and types of need, (2) the distribution of need, (3) the demand for services, (4) service utilization patterns, and (5) barriers to service utilization. Indirectly, a community needs assessment also provides data regarding the cost of meeting these needs.

Degree and Types of Need

Need can be categorized into four types: normative need, felt need, expressed need, and comparative need (Bradshaw, 1977). Each type of need presents quite a different picture.

Normative needs are those needs, as defined by experts in various fields, that are based on selected standards. Examples might include dietary standards, physical space, quality of clean air, number of bathrooms, and so on. Normative needs are generally easy to measure although they are often quite value laden and thus arbitrary.

Felt need, as the name implies, is reflected by what people say they want or need. Felt need is usually determined through a survey. Since survey respondents aren't necessarily aware of what they need, this method has been criticized as a meaningful measure of need. A person's frame of reference may result in minimizing the need for education or law enforcement or clean air, even though such needs may be urgent. People who have been devalued and feel disempowered may conclude that they shouldn't feel the need for things that others consider a necessity.

Expressed need is reflected by a request or a demand for something. It goes beyond felt need in that people actively seek out a service. A waiting list or a backlog of applications for food baskets are examples of expressed need.

As a measure of need, expressed need is not necessarily an accurate indicator either. Lack of knowledge regarding the availability of a service or misconceptions about an agency may deter clients from expressing their needs through applications for help.

Comparative need is a measurement of the differences between levels of need in various neighborhoods and communities, weighted to account for differences in population characteristics. In other words, a demographic picture of need is developed. A young African American urban population, for example, would have a greater need for employment than an elderly community of retired whites, even though both populations reside in Miami. A neighborhood with a rising population of single parents may have a higher need for day care than two-parent households located in that same neighborhood.

Distribution of Need

In the final analysis, a needs assessment must pinpoint need distribution patterns. It must answer the question "Where?" Where do the people in need live? What neighborhoods are affected? Which parts of the county suffer the most? Distribution of need may reflect the problem of demand outrunning supply, or it may reflect lack of access on the part of those in need.

Lack of medical care, for example, may be a result of the patients' inability to pay, or it may be a function of the absence of physicians and nurses in a remote county. In the first instance, the supply of health caregivers is adequate and the need for health care is evident, but the ability to afford the care is restricted. In the second instance, the ability to pay is sufficient, but the supply of caregivers is inadequate or unavailable. In the first instance, the need may be met through subsidized medical care, while the second problem may be solved through improved transportation or mobile clinics.

Demand for Services

A needs assessment attempts to establish that a need for a service exists and that the service will be used once it is developed.

Communities can err in this respect. If delinquency is believed to be the result of a lack of good recreational programs, it would be logical to build recreation centers. However, this does not ensure that the recreation centers would be used. One community embarked on an extensive program of youth recreation centers only to find that most of the youth preferred the local pool halls. A pilot recreational program might have helped pinpoint this reality before substantial community resources were invested.

Service Utilization Patterns

Determining how the existing social service network is being used is also within the scope of a community needs assessment. Of particular significance is why some programs are used extensively by some groups and avoided by others. Answers to these questions can result in services being relocated, modified, or even dismantled.

For example, a Colorado regional mental health center's records showed a disproportionate use by Anglos and only negligible use by Hispanics, even though the two populations were equally represented within the center's catchment area. A thorough study was done only after this pattern came under public scrutiny. The result was that mental health services were redefined and restructured to be less intimidating to Hispanic mental health consumers. Subsequently, use of the center by Hispanics showed a marked increase.

Barriers to Service Utilization

Finally, community needs assessments help determine what restraining forces may be preventing consumers from using social services. Such forces may appear as high levels of ignorance regarding the existence of a service or personal bias toward using a "welfare" agency. Language and cultural barriers may also present impediments. The location of an agency may be a barrier to its utilization. Lum's (1992) discussion of barriers to ethnic minority populations was discussed earlier.

The above barriers point to the need for using community needs assessments as important feedback loops. Such feedback may suggest the need for better public education about agencies, multilingual staff, outreach, or decentralization to remove obstacles to agency use.

APPROACHES TO COMMUNITY
NEEDS ASSESSMENT

There are five basic approaches to assessing community needs. They are often used in combination, depending on the availability of resources. Each approach has its liabilities and its attributes. These five approaches are the key informant approach, the community forum approach, the rates-under-treatment approach, the social indicators approach, and the field survey approach (Warheit, Bell, & Schwab, 1974).

Key Informant Approach

A key informant is knowledgeable about how the community works in terms of its day-to-day problems, political and economic operations, resources, and needs. Because they are considered to be "in the know" in terms of their sphere of operations, key informants are sought out for surveys or interviews. Their detailed knowledge of a specific population enables them to provide a narrow focus of inquiry around which some of the other approaches can be designed (Lewis, Lewis, & Souflee, 1991).

Key informants include public officials, administrators of human services agencies, professional caregivers, and, in some instances, even informal caregivers such as barbers, beauticians, and bartenders.

The key informant approach, while relatively simple, has some limitations in terms of reliability. The views expressed, while valuable enough, are exactly that—personal opinions. They may be biased or self-serving and certainly can be misleading if they become the sole basis for planning social services. This approach can provide a basis for determining the extent of normative need, however, if used in conjunction with other approaches.

Community Forum Approach

Community forums, or public hearings as they are sometimes called, directly involve the total community in assessing need. In that respect, they have some political value. They are not forums for experts only; they are also open to average citizens who choose to attend.

The format involves giving public notice of place and time and inviting anyone who is interested to testify. Hearings are usually sponsored by some official planning body. A number of key informants are generally invited to be on the program.

As might be surmised, community forums can be loaded with opponents or proponents, so that representative involvement is difficult to ensure. There is always the possibility that the forums may do more to incite or polarize a community than to help it. Critics of this approach feel that forums may tend to raise community expectations beyond realistic levels. Many such meetings have ended in stand-offs or become repositories for complaints, thus preventing any meaningful planning input. The forums also provide ready-made photo opportunities for the media; comments can easily be taken out of context and distorted.

Rates-Under-Treatment Approach

Another method of assessing community need is to examine the characteristics of the users or consumers of services. This is known as the rates-under-treatment approach. By studying profiles of samples of people who have received services over time, social workers can infer the amount of expressed need in a community. An additional indicator of need might be drawn from the lists of those waiting for the services.

Although the rates-under-treatment approach has the potential to provide useful data and can focus in on user trends, it should by no means be used as the sole source of data. Its limits are fairly obvious. There are some built-in problems in assuming that those who have used a service and those who want to use it present an accurate picture of those who may need it. Because of lack of awareness or confidence in a particular agency, many needy people may never show up on its doorstep.

Social Indicators Approach

Public agencies are usually charged with the legal responsibility for projecting future needs. For planning purposes, data are collected for annual reports to legislative bodies, boards of directors, and administrators. These data are in the public domain and can be used as social indicators for a variety of social conditions.

The census, which is taken every ten years, is one of the better-known social indicators. As such, it is used to determine formulas for the allocation of federal monies.

On a smaller scale, state and county vital statistics bureaus record births, deaths, marriages, and so on. The Federal Bureau of Investigation and city and state criminal justice–planning agencies collect information on crime patterns. Health departments, labor departments, education departments, housing authorities, and economic planning bodies are all engaged in gathering data on their respective services. These data are usually readily available and presented in a form designed for planning purposes.

Social indicators approaches are particularly helpful in determining comparative need. Since data are usually collected by census tract, catchment area, or precinct, neighborhoods can be identified, studied, and targeted as unique entities.

Field Survey Approach

The most comprehensive approach to conducting a needs assessment is in the field survey approach. Distinct from the other methods, the field survey is a study of representative samples of the community at large. It is conducted like a public opinion poll. Survey instruments are mailed out, and selected interviews are held to glean the opinions of a cross section of people regarding their needs, perceptions of the social services network, and service use patterns.

While the field survey is considered a more reliable method for need assessment, it too has its limitations. On the plus side, it samples both felt and expressed need. The most significant disadvantage is that the field survey requires more time, staff, expertise, and money than any of the other approaches. Thus it may be beyond the scope of a single agency and is more likely to be conducted through the cooperative efforts of several related agencies or by a central planning body.

The Community Oriented Needs Assessment (CONA) model (Neuber, 1980) incorporates several approaches. Originating from the mental health field, CONA collects data from three sources: demographic statistical profiles, key informants, and interviews with the general public. Findings from all three sources are analyzed and shared with appropriate agencies and used as a planning tool for program planning, implementation, and evaluation.

CONSORTIUM BUILDING AND INTERORGANIZATIONAL NETWORKING

Once a community needs assessment has been completed, a major obstacle still remains to be overcome in addressing need; namely, the formation of a coherent service delivery system.

Efficient delivery of goods and services to at-risk populations is an exceedingly complex proposition. The demand for services tends to exceed supply, thus creating a scarcity; however, part of this scarcity can be attributed to the fact that while the problems of marginalized populations are interrelated, the potential sources of help are fragmented among and even within agencies.

Traditionally, social services agencies have organized their programs into highly specialized units of service. Thus, members of the same family often receive service from more than one specialist even within the same agency. No single professional takes the responsibility for coordinating services for the total family. It is ironic that to find help to alleviate their multiple problems, families must shop among the specialized agencies in the social services network, when they would be better served by "one-stop shopping." Under current conditions, this is not likely to happen. Engaged as they are in the crisis nature of the families they are serving, social workers have little time for integrating and coordinating the resources that are needed.

Communication, collaboration, and cooperation present logistical problems. The prospect of trying to overcome logistics often becomes a restraining force in interorganizational networking, creating an environment where agencies plan and operate their respective programs in isolation, thus creating the fragmentation mentioned earlier.

By its nature, the broker role mandates that clients be linked to services and that the quality of these services be maintained. To achieve these two goals, services deliverers must somehow be linked. This linkage requires a system that promotes cooperation, coordination, and social exchange. Such a cooperative arrangement results when agencies decide to formally interact and plan together.

A group of agencies that decides to collaborate in an ongoing, formal relationship is referred to as a *consortium*. To determine how they will operate with one another, the agencies regularly engage in a process of role negotiation. Such negotiations may result in case advocacy, cause advocacy, grant writing, and other forms of collaboration. Consortiums of agencies are also more likely to command the necessary resources to conduct community needs assessments, which ultimately provide the basis for program planning.

Uses of Consortiums

Consortiums have the capacity to accomplish the following:

1. Clarify individual social agency policies
2. Define the potential roles of individual agencies
3. Define the potentials and limitations of each member agency
4. Establish methods for determining individual agency participation in serving multiple-problem families
5. Develop procedures for eliminating duplication of services
6. Develop procedures for identifying and filling gaps in service

Although consortium building provides several advantages over "going it alone," it is threatening to agencies that exist in an environment of competition and turf protection. It calls for a transition from a culture of competition to one of cooperation. If such a culture can be created, the consortium sets the stage for various forms of interagency coordination.

Organizing a Consortium

Organizing a consortium is a sequential process. These steps are presented here.

Identifying Members.   The first stage in organizing a consortium of agencies is to identify the primary actors among the agencies serving a given population. They may be a small group of agencies that already communicate, either formally or informally, with one another to some degree. This communication may arise out of necessity more than desire. The necessary ingredient is that there is some cooperation and collaboration on which to build.

Inviting Representatives to an Organizing Meeting.   The next step is to invite selected representatives of these agencies to a "summit meeting." These representatives may not necessarily be executives, but they should be able to speak for their agency and to some degree make commitments of agency resources.

Managing the Summit Meeting.   Step three is to manage the summit meeting itself. Recognizing the potential for suspicion, the convener must provide an acceptable rationale for the meeting. It can be stated honestly and directly; for example, coordination and collaboration among the convened agencies will multiply their separate, independent contributions. In other words, the assumption is that the whole is greater than the sum of the parts. The attempt is to establish a nonthreatening atmosphere in which agencies can learn more about each other's policies and programs, communicate, solve problems, plan, and ultimately make more informal decisions. The convener should not take sole ownership for the consortium and may not even want to refer to it by that name.

An initial summit meeting usually begins with perception checking, a process in which each agency orients the others to its policies, procedures, and limitations. These insights help educate the total group and clarify misperceptions. This process also tends to identify program gaps and overlaps, and provide a context for reexamining existing policies and redirecting programs.

Those agencies that agree to attend future meetings will have to make several decisions:

1. Are there other agencies that should be invited to these meetings?
2. Who should be responsible for convening future meetings?
3. How often should they be held?
4. What will be the nature of interorganizational cooperation?

Cooperative Agency Arrangements

The decision on interorganizational cooperation will likely determine which cooperative arrangements agencies undertake. Rossi, Gilmartin, and Dayton (1982) have identified the following possibilities: joint intake and assessment, referral, cross-referral, case consultation, client conferences, client teams, case management, colocation, outstationing, and staff loans.

Joint intake and assessment helps clients move through the service delivery system by having agencies use a common system for screening and diagnosing client needs. A single form is used among the cooperating agencies and facilitates potential information sharing.

Referral is when one agency sends clients to another agency for the most appropriate service. Cross-referral is when agencies mutually refer clients to each other. To the degree that there is reciprocity in referrals, there is greater potential for interagency cooperation and coordination.

Case consultation is an arrangement where "staff at one agency ask advice from staff at another agency about particular clients . . . to pool the professional knowledge about the case at the two agencies and to coordinate the services that are provided" (Rossi, Gilmartin, & Dayton, p. 55).

At client conferences, "staff from two or more agencies discuss the needs of all the clients they have in common at a single meeting" (Rossi, Gilmartin, & Dayton, p. 55).

Client teams are "staff from two or more agencies who coordinate their activities to meet the needs of a number of clients through continuous and systematic interaction" (Rossi, Gilmartin, & Dayton, p. 56).

Case management, which will be discussed later in greater detail, is "a system for linking and coordinating segments of a service delivery system— to insure the most comprehensive program for meeting an individual client's need for care" (p. 58).

Colocation "involves two or more agencies having staff and separate facilities in the same location" (p. 61). It obviously facilitates "one-stop shopping" for clients.

Outstationing is when "staff from one agency are sent to work in the facilities of another" (p. 63). Because the staff are not being merged, this procedure demands definitive understanding of exactly how the arrangement will work.

Staff loans occur when "staff from one agency work under the direct supervision of another agency and on tasks assigned by that agency for a temporary period" (p. 64). Staff loans are usually undertaken to promote interagency operations or staff development or to lend one agency's resources to another.

CASE STUDY: *Lewis High School* ◆————————————

In Lewis High's dropout prevention program, described in Chapters 1 and 6, a team approach was used to work on the problem, from microsystem to macrosystem involvement. A consortium of ten agencies were identified that were involved, either directly or indirectly, in working with dropout youth. The objectives for developing the consortium were as follows:

1. To provide a network of agencies in order to share knowledge and responses

2. To increase community involvement in the dropout problem

3. To provide a collectivity of agencies for purposes of case coordination and case management

The mental health team invited the following agencies to participate in the consortium:

1. Juvenile Court (Probation Department)

2. Police, Task Force on Youth

3. Mayor's Commission on Youth

4. Social Services Adolescent Unit

5. Big Brothers/Big Sisters

6. Partners, a private program for predelinquent youth

7. Two church leaders, who are focused on gangs

8. Drop In, a nonprofit voluntary organization targeting potential dropouts

9. Street Smart, a grassroots community organization that focuses on dropouts and gang members

10. Conway Foundation, a local private foundation with a proven record of funding youth programs

The agency participants met monthly. Meetings were structured so that case consultation issues were addressed during the first hour. From these meetings, it became apparent that the dropouts were already known to several of the agencies, particularly the police and the probation office.

————————————————————————————————◆

CASE MANAGEMENT

The process of case management is discussed in greater detail here because it is at the heart of the broker role.

Aside from the broker role, case management has also been included in the advocate role and attributed to the roles of problem solver, planner, community organizer, service monitor, record keeper, evaluator, consultant, collaborator, coordinator, counselor, and expediter (Weil, Karls, and Associates, 1985). All of these functions are called for at some point in case management and are discussed in this section.

The case manager is responsible for coordinating a range of services provided by numerous resource agencies on behalf of specific clients. Because one agency is in the position of managing the services, resources, and personnel of other agencies, the process of case management is politically sensitive and must be based on sound communication and agreements. Austin (1978) cautioned that case management refers to the management of a system of services, not the management of a single person; this is an important distinction.

Case management has been defined as "client-level strategy for promoting the coordination of human services, opportunities, or benefits" (Moxley, 1989, p. 11). Rubin referred to case management as a "boundary spanning approach" (1992, p. 5). Instead of providing a direct service, it uses case managers who link the client to the maze of direct service providers. Moore (1992) noted that case management can be a means of rationing scarce resources. Netting (1992) cautioned that case management may mask the fact that the health and human services are fragmented "nonsystems."

Case management generally includes the following functions, which may be used in combination: consumer identification and outreach, intake, assessment of need, service planning, implementation of the plan, crisis management, and termination and evaluation.

Consumer Identification and Outreach

This case management function may be achieved through the intake process. If, however, intake is limited to screening only those who request agency services, it will not reach those people who for various reasons may never present themselves for service.

Outreach involves case finding. It calls for assertiveness in communicating with people who wouldn't normally seek out social services and in making certain that they are made aware of these services. Outreach is community based rather than agency based. Agency representatives go to the places where potential users of services congregate and communicate. Those in need of basic shelter, for example, may be found living under bridges or loading docks. People who need home health care may be found in social services waiting rooms.

Intake

Intake is a twofold process. On the one hand, individuals and families seek help and are screened into a service network based on the appropriateness of the match between their needs and the agency's resources. Where there is no match, intake links the clients to alternative sources of assistance.

As noted in discussing the rates-under-treatment approach to community needs assessment, people going through the intake process provide an important gauge of the degree of need in a given community. In light of this, all requests for services should be recorded. This should be done in a manner that allows for periodic retrieval, because these requests provide important program planning data. Changes in patterns of requests for services may be an indicator of changing need. Unless such changes are monitored, an agency might stray from its mission.

Unfortunately, intake is often perceived and even experienced as a barrier or hurdle rather than as a screening and referral process. Individuals seeking help may encounter economic, cultural, language, and professional barriers.

Economic Barriers.   Economic barriers may be raised due to lack of income on the part of the consumer. An attitude of "those who can't pay, don't get" may be the de facto rule if not the stated policy.

Cultural Barriers.   Cultural barriers are possible in cases where an agency is viewed as a middle-class agency by the poor or when middle-class people refuse to use an agency they perceive to be a "welfare" agency. Such barriers highlight the need for outreach, case finding, and public education, either as separate functions of case management or as functions within intake itself.

Language Barriers.   Language barriers may emerge in intake, particularly when a large segment of the consumer population does not speak English. Fear that their inability to converse will embarrass them may be enough to discourage some people from seeking assistance. This points up the necessity of having multilingual as well as multicultural staff.

Information Barriers.   Information barriers are natural outgrowths of the absence of public education programs. At a minimum, potential consumers need to be aware of an agency's existence and its purpose. The users of a social services agency are numerous and varied but all share the need for ongoing information about its goals.

Professional Barriers. Clients may experience professional barriers when social service agencies are insensitive to threatening cues within the agency environment. Our language as well as our symbolic communication, even though professionally appropriate, may nevertheless be seen as threatening. An appointment book, for example, while functional for a worker scheduling appointments, may be viewed by clients as a time barrier standing between them and a needed resource.

Provision of Open Access

To the extent possible, intake procedures should ensure open access. By open access, we mean that the reason for denial of service should be client ineligibility rather than nonservice-related factors. The following guidelines will help ensure open access.

Written Policies and Procedures. Having written policies increases the likelihood of consumers being treated equitably from one intake worker to another. Rather than leaving a disposition to the vagaries of individual intake workers, written guidelines provide more precise frameworks for action. The written word can be used to guide and interpret actions and justify decisions.

A Priority System. Requests for help can have far different levels of urgency and therefore need to be ranked in order of a priority. A waiting list is inadequate because it conveys a policy of "first come, first served." In contrast, triage, a three-level indicator for medical help, provides a rationale for determining relative need and subsequent agency action.

Consideration of All Service Requests. Keeping in mind that expressed need may not necessarily reflect actual need, the intake process should be used to explore each request carefully. Senility, psychoses, or crises may prevent people from adequately communicating their need. Secondary sources of information may need to be contacted in such cases. Service requests, even though beyond the scope of one agency, may be appropriate for referral to another and may serve to link a client to a source of help.

Intake workers must possess a combination of skills. They should be knowledgeable about their agency and other agencies in the community, they must be sensitive to the personal needs that attend various problems, and they must be people oriented and proficient in writing. The intake worker must practice active listening while securing and recording information on forms, schedules, and computers, and keeping the consumer abreast of what is being done.

Assessment of Need

In assessing need, the goal is to develop a comprehensive view of the person in terms of several factors. The following considerations are generally included in the assessment:

Abilities and Strengths.   In operating from a competency model, abilities and strengths should be considered before deficits and weaknesses. Competency is often overlooked in favor of focusing on incompetency. What a person is capable of doing represents a potential resource that can be mobilized; it is something to build on. Competency is also an important empowerment tool.

Dysfunctions and Weaknesses.   The opposite of competence is incompetence and it cannot be ignored. A person's limitations are important in establishing parameters of functioning and are thus important indicators of need.

Quality of Life.   Regardless of the population at risk, there are measures that can be taken of the quality of life along several dimensions. The more common dimensions include employment, education and training, physical and mental health, housing, financial security, family, drug and alcohol abuse, and legal issues. Where a person stands in relation to these indicators provides important baselines from which to establish goals and objectives.

Client's Perception of Need.   The measures of quality of life are very subjective and should be determined *with* the client. They should not be used as outside arbitrary measures.

Past Coping Patterns.   How an individual has managed problems in the past, while not necessarily predictive of future functioning, can nevertheless provides clues. Thus we attempt to learn from history. If known, successful past coping patterns can possibly be restored and used as empowering tools.

Support Systems.   An often overlooked resource in need assessment is the support system in which an individual lives. In fact, this resource is more likely to be utilized in a crisis (Rothman, 1992). An informal support system may consist of family and relatives, neighbors, friends and allies, work associates, or other significant individuals. The family system can be a sustaining force in an individual's life. If the worker understands this system, he or she can possibly promote or strengthen it. This is particularly important in case management with developmentally disabled children (Fiene & Taylor, 1991).

Generally, in assessing a support system, social workers look for available support people in terms of numbers (how many people in the network), frequency of contact, the importance of the relationship to the client, and the degree of perceived support.

Special Needs. As we discussed earlier, quality-of-life measures may quickly uncover special needs. For example, exploring the category of health may reveal a need for home health care. Exploring employment may suggest a need for vocational training.

Priorities. Finally, the case manager must determine with the client what is most urgent. In short, what need must be satisfied first? When ''A'' is completed, what should be done next? Such a priority scheme leads to the next function of case management: service planning.

Service Planning

A service plan can be thought of as a road map that directs the routing of services. It should do the following:

♦ Clearly describe the rationale for services.
♦ Spell out the goals of service.
♦ Specify what services will be provided and how they will be delivered.
♦ Specify when services will start.
♦ Specify the criteria for evaluation of services.
♦ Specify the criteria for termination of services.

In doing service planning, the case manager is faced with critical choices because, with the implementation of each plan, agency resources will be allocated and further diminished. It is precisely for this reason that a priority scheme must be developed to determine who gets first call on existing services. Agencies must know what budgetary resources are available, and how many people can be served at a particular level of service before they can begin service planning.

Goal Setting and Evaluation

Just as workers must arrive jointly at an assessment of need with clients, they must also determine jointly which goals to pursue. A helpful tool in this respect is goal attainment scaling (Kiresuk & Sherman, 1968), referred to in Chapter 6 on practice evaluation. GAS is a method for documenting and evaluating specified service goals.

Assuming that a goal for a chronic psychiatric patient is "to improve self-concept," and that bathing is one of the behaviors used to reflect achievement of the goal, movement away from or toward that goal might be stated and measured as follows:

-2 = The patient bathes only under direct staff supervision (most unfavorable outcome).

-1 = The patient bathes when instructed by staff to do so (less than expected level).

0 = The patient bathes every other day without staff direction (expected level of success).

+1 = The patient bathes daily without staff direction (more than the expected level).

+2 = The patient bathes voluntarily on a daily basis and after strenuous exercise (most favorable outcome).

We stress here that goal attainment scaling or whatever other measures are used to measure movement must be made in agreement *with* a client, not a measure to be applied unilaterally by a worker without client consent. In a real sense, goals are contracts with at least an implied understanding that both the agency and client have certain responsibilities in pursuing them.

Implementation of the Plan

Implementation includes all those actions that the agency carries out to assure the effective delivery of service or care. Service effectiveness has been described as (1) agency success in generating change for clients, (2) service quality (namely, how competent the agency is in utilizing methods for achieving change), and (3) client satisfaction with the outcome of agency services (Patti, 1987). Implementation includes the following steps:

◆ Selecting and assigning personnel
◆ Instructing personnel
◆ Referral and linkage
◆ Coordinating personnel
◆ Monitoring, reassessment, modification, and follow-up
◆ Ensuring quality control and reporting problems
◆ Record keeping
◆ Advocating for the consumer

Selecting and Assigning Personnel

Those agencies within the consortium best able to provide a given service are the most likely organizations to be involved in carrying out a service plan. They should be contacted and assigned. Where several agencies are delivering services concurrently, it is important to ensure that those services are complementary rather than conflicting or duplicative. They must also be accessible. Needless to say, the case manager may be faced with trade-offs. For example, the case worker may have to select a less effective service if it is the only one within the client's access. On the other hand, a service located out of a client's neighborhood may be so superior in quality that the case worker may decide to provide transportation.

Instructing Personnel

This aspect of implementation involves giving the service deliverers specific directives regarding what is to be done, by whom, and by when. Austin, Kopp, & Smith (1986) provided a helpful checklist to consult in carrying out this function.

1. A time limit has been established with each resource person.
2. Each involved resource person has agreed to pursue specific objectives within the agreed-on time frame.
3. Clear criteria are agreed on to evaluate progress.
4. Each resource person has agreed to share needed data according to an agreed-on schedule.
5. Each resource person has agreed to meet with you as necessary.
6. A written agreement between each resource person and the social worker has been formed, signed, and distributed to other involved parties (as appropriate).

Referral and Linkage

In referring clients, the worker should be guided by the principle of least-restrictive environment. That principle requires that the more informal systems of help be explored before seeking help from formal helping organizations.

We have previously mentioned informal networks as resources for support. Guided by the principles of least-restrictive environment and normalization, this source of help would be explored first. If it is deemed insufficient, mutual-aid and self-help groups should be investigated. Assignment of volunteers, if called for, might reflect a more appropriate mode of help before considering professional intervention.

Referral and linkage of clients is done under the assumption that clients may seek out additional resources on their own. The principle of client empowerment would suggest that they be encouraged to do so and to maximize such resources to the fullest.

CASE STUDY: *Lewis High School* ◆

The social workers in the Lewis High dropout prevention program designed a self-help network to focus on both parents and their children. The needs assessment revealed that 85% of the parents of the target group were single parents. In examining several research reports regarding single parents, the team quickly discovered that, as a group, single parents tend to be overextended in terms of time and energy, more likely to feel a sense of disconnectedness and isolation from their community and less likely to be fully invested in their child's education. This certainly had implications for their investment in self-help groups.

Nevertheless, the team moved ahead with the idea of a pilot self-help group. It was thought that parents would be more likely to invest in such an activity if there were provisions for child care during the meetings. The team contacted a local church group near the school. They agreed to provide child care, if it was on the same night they were already providing care for children during a regular church meeting. The group agreed to do this for free.

The three social workers and two school counselors decided their role in initiating the groups would be limited to inviting parents to the first meeting, offering financial support for group activities, providing a meeting place (at the school), and helping with the planning of the group's program. Their intent was to withdraw into a consultive role as strength mobilized and group members felt a greater sense of their own empowerment.

Each new student who was matched with a mentor was given a brochure to present to his or her parent inviting that parent to the weekly group meeting. The workers then called or contacted the parent, requesting their presence and emphasizing that child care would be provided.

The parent group began with only 7 members but grew to 15. In the beginning, the parents complained about the school. Gradually, the focus shifted to the students, with the meetings becoming a litany of dropout "horror stories." One of the more assertive parents finally asked one of the social workers if it wasn't time that they "did something." This led to planning a weekly program. The parents were asked what kind of programs they felt would be helpful. A subcommittee was formed, and with the help of a counselor they developed a "curriculum." The curriculum consisted of the following topics:

1. Family communication
2. Dealing with the school system
3. Finding, assessing, and paying for day care
4. Arranging transportation

5. Developmental issues of adolescence

6. Job hunting

7. Dating relationships

8. Assertiveness and decision making

Much of the self-help curriculum was parent oriented rather than child oriented. The group decided to set aside some time each week to address a part of the curriculum. This was done in some instances by outside presenters or by school staff who were willing to volunteer. As new members joined the group, the curriculum was repeated. Ultimately, the entire mental health team became involved in the curriculum.

Since the "horror stories" were important in the beginning, each meeting was given time for what came to be known as "war stories." Eventually, the social workers were able to use these stories as a basis for "lessons learned." The group norms ultimately demanded that each person relating a war story come back a week later to explain how he or she was dealing with the problem.

One of the most important self-help features was a telephone tree; that is, a listing of the name and telephone number of each group member. This became an important tool in communication among group members during the week, and most members used it as a means of mutual support.

The student self-help network, while not as active as the parent network, nevertheless played a significant role for many of the participants. Interestingly, many members of the school peer-counseling program showed an interest in a self-help group and, with one of the social workers, took the lead in its development.

Group meetings were held weekly at Lewis High School after the end of the school day. The group used a modified problem-solving method, in which each participant was asked to state any school-related problems. The student presented the problem in written form on a flip chart or blackboard using the following format: statement of the problem, results of the problem, effect of the problem on the student, any efforts made toward solution, a description of the desired solution, ideas developed by brainstorming, and an action plan (who does what by when).

Students were responsible for leading meetings around their problems, which elicited the technique of brainstorming. This proved to be a powerful tool in giving the students confidence in group leadership, empowering them to find solutions to their own problems, developing their own action plans.

Group members also used the telephone tree extensively. In view of the natural adolescent inclination to use the telephone, the tree provided an attractive tool for socializing as well as seeking help with school assignments and homework.

Because self-help networks were not deemed inclusive enough to impact a large number of students, the social workers designed a volunteer program. Its goal was to build student self-esteem through a positive one-on-one relationship with a mentor. In addition, the mentors acted as liaisons between the school and students. They discussed students' educational problems, thus enhancing their chances for success. Mentors agreed to the following activities to reach the goal:

1. Meet with the student once a week for a minimum of two hours.
2. Commit to working with an assigned student for at least one year.
3. Meet with an assigned member of the mental health team once a month to discuss problems, goals, progress, and issues.
4. Take students to weekly tutoring sessions if necessary.
5. Attend meetings of the mental health team if the assigned youth is a topic of discussion at the meeting.
6. When feasible, take students to their place of employment and orient students to the "world of work."
7. Communicate any crisis to the mental health team immediately.

All mentors underwent a screening process, which included a two-hour interview. They provided copies of their driver's records and proof of auto liability insurance and submitted the names of four references. They also gave permission to the school to check for any criminal record.

After the volunteers' applications were processed and approved, they were invited to an eight-hour orientation program conducted by the mental health team. This session focused on understanding the phenomenon of school dropout behavior, discussing the program in which they would be involved, including its policies and procedures, and basic training in interpersonal communication. The mentors were also familiarized with state laws regarding the reporting of child abuse. At the end of this orientation session, they were given an opportunity to leave the program, no questions asked. Those who completed the orientation were given a reminder of the importance of keeping their commitments to their charges.

To insure the smooth integration of mentors into the school, the mental health team interpreted the role of the volunteers in the dropout prevention program to both faculty and staff. The mentors were to be friends and advocates, if necessary, for the youth who dropped out. The mentors could also call on a teacher if they felt they could assist in a student's progress by doing so.

Because the goal was to make the program as open and accessible to students as possible, none of the students who applied for a mentor were denied access to the program. A shortage of mentors, however, did mean that some students did not get an immediate match during the academic year. Ultimately, students were matched with mentors on the basis of sex, race or ethnicity, proximity of residence, interests, and a subjective staff assessment of the potential match.

Within the first year of the program, 153 individuals applied to the school to become mentors. Thirty-one applications were rejected for various reasons and another 10 withdrew during or after the initial orientation. Ninety-seven actual "matches" were made.

Participant Selection

The school faculty and staff were briefed on the mentor program and were considered as sources of referral. Self-referral was also accepted.

When a faculty or staff member referred a student to the program, they were requested to meet with the student to determine if that student wished to be involved in the mentor program. If so, the staff member would make a referral to the social worker who would initiate further contact.

The mental health team held monthly meetings to match mentors with students. These meetings were open to any school staff member who could shed light on the student's needs. Once the match was tentatively made, a member of the team called the mentor to describe the student. If and when the volunteer accepted the student, the worker then called the student's parent to describe the mentor. On parental approval, a final match was made. The social worker's next step was to introduce the student and parent to the mentor, provide further role clarification, and secure permission slips.

The workers determined that a caseload of 40 matches per worker would constitute the maximum number, considering their other administrative responsibilities and the coordination of the entire program. This allowed for the management of a maximum of 120 matches, given that there were three social workers. This maximum was never reached.

♦

Coordinating Personnel

While much of the exchange of information among caregivers is achieved through the case record, other communication forms may need to be implemented. Case managers should schedule regular meetings and certainly initiate telephone contacts whenever there are questions and uncertainties.

Monitoring, Reassessment, Modification, and Follow-Up

A client's progress or lack of progress should be monitored and reassessed periodically. As the client's situations change so do their service needs. Then the case manager needs to adjust their program accordingly.

Reassessment should take place at regular intervals, but certainly whenever there is a change in status, role, or situation. If services are delivered by different disciplines, each discipline should reassess the client's situation.

There is a natural tendency in long-term service, particularly when progress is not evident, to proceed without making significant program changes. This is perhaps a built-in hazard in making long-range decisions and irrevocable commitments. Because we want a program to work, we wait for the hoped-for results, perhaps too long. Workers need skill in recognizing and admitting that the services being delivered have *not* had the desired impact on the problem.

CASE STUDY: *Lewis High School* ◆

Because the dropout program needed an efficient means of tracking the students' progress with their mentors, the workers developed monitoring procedures.

During the first meetings between the student and the social worker, the worker assessed the students' perceptions of the mentoring program and clarified any misconceptions. The worker explained the process of matching student to mentor and gave the student a pamphlet describing the program, a cover letter for the parent, an application form, and a permission slip to be completed and signed by both parent and student.

One week after the initial meeting, the parent was contacted to determine if he or she had any questions and was interested in the program. If the parent expressed interest, the social worker scheduled a home visit with the parent and student together. The purpose of this visit was to develop a short family history, explain the goals of the program, and determine if the program goals were congruent with those of the parent and student.

Every month, the social worker called the mentors, students, and parents to assess how the match was working. All calls were recorded on a contact sheet. The social worker monitored the progress of the relationship, school attendance, grades, and behavior, consulting with parent, student, or mentor, and serving as a broker of services from among the agencies in the consortium.

◆

Ensuring Quality Control

When the case management process is monitored, there is greater assurance that the quality of services will be protected.

One of the more obvious points of control is where complaints about the service are registered. While we may not like to hear negative reports about a service, it is important to investigate all complaints if for no other reason than to determine their legitimacy. Beyond that, however, is the need to correct any existing problems. Much client criticism may have no basis in fact; nevertheless, both destructive and constructive criticism need to be heard. There may be elements of legitimacy even in destructive criticism.

Once the worker investigates the complaints, they should be documented to determine if patterns emerge that can help pinpoint sources of problems. The case manager may find it helpful to learn who among the caregivers are consistently generating complaints as well as which services are being rejected. This knowledge can help the manager do preventive maintenance and thus contain minor problems before they become serious.

Record Keeping

Keeping accurate records serves several purposes. Records justify what we have done, what we are currently doing, how effectively we do it, and assist us in determining the cost of these services. When a record is examined, it should reveal a current concise picture of the individual being served, the individual's needs, the services delivered, the effects of the services, and what services are being planned.

A vital part of record keeping is documenting incident reports. In the event a lawsuit is filed against an agency, a point of protection is the agency's documentation of the incident being contested. Thus all caregivers within the case management process must understand the rationale for recording and documenting. Too often caregivers dismiss record keeping as unimportant "because no one reads it." The case manager can counter this argument by making sure records are examined while stressing the inherent protection of documentation for everyone concerned.

Recording can be costly, but in a litigious society, it is cost effective in the long run, particularly if much of the function can be located within the clerical domain.

Advocating for the Consumer

In selecting agencies to provide service to clients, the broker attempts to select those agencies that will best meet human needs, while empowering people to meet their own needs. Still, there will be instances when agencies may not fulfill their obligations to a client. Quality control and reporting of problems may uncover trouble spots where service providers are negligent. When this happens, case managers must be prepared to become advocates, particularly when clients are incapable of advocating for themselves. This may take the form of case-by-case advocacy or cause advocacy, in the event of system failure on a large scale.

Crisis Management

Case management is an operation that is more likely to be community based than office based. In view of this, the case management process must have the capacity to deal with crises as they occur. What this means in practice is that there must be some type of 24-hour contact point where emergencies and crises can be reported. An on-call pager system may satisfy this requirement or an "officer of the day" may also be appropriate.

Termination and Evaluation

Planning for termination should begin at the time of initial assessment. Termination should occur when the service goals have been achieved or when a decision is made that those goals are not achievable.

Evaluation of the service should occur throughout the several stages of case management, but certainly at the point of termination. A termination interview provides an opportunity for the case manager to evaluate both the outcome of service and the means employed in working toward that outcome.

CASE STUDY: *Lewis High School* ◆

Termination of the mentor-student dropout match normally ended after a period of one year, although it could be continued beyond that time if all parties agreed and there was a demonstrated need for continuation. Earlier terminations did occur, due to destructive match dynamics, graduation of the student, or lack of support by the parent. Expulsion or suspension was not a basis for termination, because the workers believed that the volunteers could play a constructive crisis intervention role under such circumstances and could help the youth reenter school.

◆

SUMMARY

A social worker assumes the broker role when there is a practice demand to link the client with goods and services and to control the quality of those goods and services.

The community needs assessment provides a basis for the broker role. It measures degree and types of need, distribution of need, demand for services, service utilization patterns, and barriers to service utilization. Five basic approaches to conducting a community needs assessment include the key informant, community forum, rates-under-treatment, social indicators, and field survey approaches.

Since brokerage involves interorganizational networking, developing a consortium of cooperating agencies is a necessary step in enhancing the organization field. A consortium provides opportunities for mutual collaboration in such activities as joint intake and assessment, referral and cross-referral, case consultation, client conferences, client teams, case management, colocation, outstationing, and staff loans.

Case management, the management of a system of services for the benefit of a client, is at the core of brokerage. It includes the functions of consumer identification and outreach, intake, assessment of need, service planning, implementation of the plan, crisis management, and termination and evaluation.

STUDY QUESTIONS

1. What are the four types of need? Give an example of each.

2. What are the five basic approaches to assessing community needs? What are some of the assets and limitations of each approach?

3. What is a "consortium"? What are some advantages of consortiums in delivering social services?

4. Define the term *case management*. How does it differ from "case work"?

5. List the seven functions of case management. Give an example of each of these functions in regard to a particular kind of service.

6. What are some of the limitations and problems of case management?

REFERENCES

Anderson, J. (1981). *Social work methods and processes*. Belmont, CA: Wadsworth.

Austin, M. J. (1978). *Management simulations for mental health and human service administration*. New York: Haworth Press.

Austin, M. J., Kopp, J., & Smith, P. L. (Eds.). (1986). *Delivering human services: A self-instructional approach* (2nd ed.). New York: Longman.

Bradshaw, J. (1977). The concept of social need. In N. Gilbert & H. Specht (Eds.)., *Planning for social welfare*. Englewood Cliffs, NJ: Prentice-Hall.

Fiene, J. I., & Taylor, P. A. (1991). Serving rural families of developmentally disabled children: A case management model. *Social Work*, 36(4), pp. 323–327.

Kiresuk, T. J., & Sherman, R. (1968, Dec.). Goal attainment scaling: A general method for evaluating comprehensive mental health programs. *Community Mental Health Journal*, 4, pp. 443–453.

Lewis, J. A., Lewis, M. D., & Souflee, F. (1991). *Management of human service programs* (2nd ed.). Pacific Grove, CA: Brooks/Cole.

Lum, D. (1992). *Social work practice and people of color*. Pacific Grove, CA: Brooks/Cole.

Moore, S. (1992). Case management and the integration of services: How service delivery systems shape case management. *Social Work, 37*(5), pp. 418–423.

Moxley, D. P. (1989). *The practice of case management.* Newbury Park, CA: Sage.

Netting, F. E. (1992). Case management: Service or system? *Social Work, 37*(2), pp. 160–164.

Neuber, K. A. (1980). *Needs assessment: A model for community planning.* Beverly Hills, CA: Sage.

Patti, R. J. (1987). Managing for service effectiveness in social welfare organizations. *Social Work, 32*(5), p. 377.

Rossi, R. J., Gilmartin, K. J., & Dayton, C. W. (1982). *Agencies working together: A guide to coordination and planning.* Beverly Hills, CA: Sage.

Rothman, J. (1992). *Guidelines for case management.* Itasca, IL: F. E. Peacock.

Rubin, A. (1992). Case management. In S. M. Rose (Ed.), *Case management and social work practice.* New York: Longman.

Warheit, G. J., Bell, R. A., & Schwab, J. J. (1974). Planning for change: Needs assessment approaches. NIMH Grant 15900-05 S-I.

Weil, M., Karls, J. M., & associates. (1985). *Case management in human service practice.* San Francisco: Jossey-Bass.

York, R. O. (1982). *Human service planning: Concepts, tools and methods.* Chapel Hill: University of North Carolina Press.

◆

The Mediator Role

This chapter presents the mediator role: when to assume it, its theoretical underpinnings, a definition, and a description. A four-step framework for assuming the role and a social work practice example are also included.

THE MEDIATOR FUNCTION

Within the profession, the role of social work has often been conceptualized as a mediator. William Schwartz proposed a general functional statement for the social work profession as mediating the individual social engagement (Gitterman & Shulman, 1986). Schwartz viewed the small group as a microcosm of society. He suggested the group worker represented a "third-force function" to mediate between the group members and the systems that impinge on them (Lee & Swenson, 1986). Other authors have viewed social work's role as mediating and linking systems or promoting interaction at the boundary of systems (Hearn, 1970).

Assuming the Mediator Role

Social workers assume mediating functions in many practice situations. Whether the behaviors are formally identified as mediation, this role is critical to generalist practice.

Practice Demand

The mediator role is assumed when the practice demand is for the social worker to reconcile opposite or disparate points of view and engage the disputants in unified action. Within this role, activities range from behavioral contracting, to negotiation, to third-party peace making and other forms of conflict resolution. The role is taken between clients and their impinging systems, between systems on behalf of clients, and between client groups. The mediator role is appropriate when there is perceived mutual interest; when conflict of interest is perceived, the advocacy role is more appropriate. "In mediation, the effort is to secure resolution benefits to a dispute through give-and-take on both sides; in advocacy, the effort is to win for the client or help the client win for himself or herself" (Compton & Galaway, 1989).

Overlapping Roles

While these roles are discussed separately here, in practice they are much more likely to mesh and overlap. In fact, at times, the roles are taken sequentially; that is, one role is assumed in order to get to the other. A worker may find it necessary to take the broker or advocate role to get to a mediator role. Perhaps only through the advocacy role do workers representing social systems or groups of unequal power see themselves as mutually involved in the issues being negotiated. For example, a divorcing couple in the midst of a custody conflict may need to go through the adversarial court process in order to see mediation as a better or even viable alternative.

In another example, a worker in a community center that served low-income residents became aware of a housing problem. A development company was tearing down low-income housing units and replacing them with high-income condominiums, thus reducing the availability of low-income housing in the neighborhood. The worker tried to get the development company to hear the community group's concerns, but the company was not sympathetic. The worker asked herself how she and the community group could bring pressure on the developers to negotiate. There was clearly such a power difference that the development company had little to gain by negotiating with a group of low-income community residents. So the worker engaged newspapers, television, and other media to bring public sentiment pressure on the development company. The company agreed to meet with the community group and hear their concerns. They reached a partial resolution: the developer built some of the apartments for low-income residents. In this case, it was not possible for the worker to take a mediator role without first taking an adversarial role and using pressure-bearing tactics to force negotiation (Parsons, 1991).

In practice with devalued populations, power differential is often an issue. While mediation is perceived to be most appropriate when parties have equal power, this is not often the case. When social workers intervene with oppressed, devalued populations, they often have to broker and advocate power through negotiation and mediation.

The question of when the mediator role becomes a barrier to social justice is pertinent. Can mediation bring about a resolution that is less socially just than what litigation might bring? At times, the answer is yes. What situations should and should not be mediated are significant questions that are dealt with at the end of this chapter.

The Theoretical Underpinnings of Mediation

The theoretical basis for the mediator role includes conflict theory, systems theory, and social exchange theory.

Systems Theory

While social systems theory has been used heavily as a theoretical base for the psycho-social-political context of social problems, one major criticism is that it fails to recognize power differentials. "Systems" do not mutually influence one another, and therefore, the promotion of interaction between systems such as individuals and groups, organizations, or communities does not necessarily result in mutually reciprocal interaction. Instead, the result might be further oppression from the more powerful system. In other words, functional systems thinking fails to take into account the vast power differences that exist between groups or systems. To ignore power and value differences between groups is to underestimate the role of power in human change (Gould, 1987). Systems theory is best used along with concepts that do recognize social differences.

Conflict Theory

If systems theory is utilized as a conceptual foundation for social work practice, then it must be recognized that interacting systems have power differences and value differences, and that the process of converging diverse interests and goals is inherently conflictual and confrontational. Gould suggested that the feminist perspective provides a framework that "stresses it is not always possible or desirable to strive for an adaptive balance between the person and the environment, especially when the basic goal should be to break the cycle of institutional effects on personal problems" (1987, p. 348). Drawing from Horton's work, Gould suggested that a suitable paradigm for social work is the conflict model, in which society is a "contested struggle between groups with opposed aims and perspectives," where multiple allegiances and conflicts between groups are considered part of the natural order (1987, p. 349).

How conflict is viewed, understood, and approached determines whether it serves as a positive developmental purpose or a destructive force. This expanded view of systems interaction provides the context for the mediator role. Social workers who intervene in conflictual interaction need to have adequate conflict resolution skills in order to facilitate communication in the form of negotiation, bargaining, mediation, behavioral contracting, arbitration, or litigation. At a minimum, social workers have to have a basic comfort level with conflict in order to deal with social change, which is conflictual in nature.

Social Exchange Theory

If competition, conflict, and the struggle for power are inherent in human interaction, particularly in hierarchical systems, then change-oriented intervention must take them into account. Negotiation and contracting strategies recognize power differences and seek a fair-minded exchange in behaviors. Participants need to recognize that each person needs something from the other person and negotiate a behavioral exchange. If people in systems of great power disparity can see what they need from each other, they can exchange and bargain behaviors. Teenagers and parents in conflict may be able to exchange and bargain specific behaviors from one another when they cannot listen and communicate their needs. Called *behavioral contracting*, the process is simply agreeing to exchange one behavior to get another behavior. To get teenagers to contract, parents may need help in recognizing what they each need and can get from the other.

When the power difference is so great that one system does not need anything from the other, mutual needs may be created by educational or perhaps adversarial tactics. For example, a homeless citizen led a group of other homeless citizens in a demonstration and occupation of empty Housing and Urban Development (HUD) houses to bring pressure on the agency to provide housing. The result was that the individual stood trial for breaking the trespassing law and for inciting disturbances and illegal activities. One of our students asked, "How do you get HUD to negotiate with homeless people, to see themselves as needing anything from this homeless woman and her group?" Obviously, here is a very good example of two "systems" of great power differences. Alone, the homeless groups had no way of getting HUD to negotiate their available homes with the need for housing the homeless. HUD was under no pressure to do so. To create a situation where HUD would want to negotiate, the citizens group would have to figure how to create pressure on HUD. They might do so by bringing a class action suit against HUD for failing in its mission to provide housing for the needy. Or, they might join with other groups with like interests, form a coalition, and get to their congressional representatives or to someone in the federal government with some power to exert over HUD.

The student pointed out that organizations interested in the homeless problem were often in conflict because they disagreed over the causes of homelessness. Some believe in psychological causation and solution, whereas others believe homelessness is simply a result of economic barriers and housing shortages and therefore perceive different solutions. The student pointed out that their organizations could not get together to bring joint pressure on HUD, because their different perceptions tended to keep them away from one another. The need for the mediator role is obvious. A systems boundary worker must be prepared to work between and within families, groups, or larger systems to resolve existing conflict, ameliorate problems, bring problems to the bargaining table, and find socially just resolutions to existing situations.

Defining the Mediator Role

The mediator role is taken between two or more conflicting parties to promote reconciliation, settlement, compromise, or understanding. It is a process of facilitating communication between opposing positions around mutual interests. Mediation focuses on behaviorally oriented change rather than on attitudinal change, although attitudinal change may very well follow behavioral change. The role is problem based and problem solving in nature. The desired outcome is a behavioral agreement mutually agreed on by the parties. The process assumes that the involved parties are able to isolate issues, interests, positions, alternatives, and resources to find agreed-on solutions. The tactics do not focus on personality change, attitude change, or therapeutic process of the participants. Personal changes, if they occur, are a secondary outcome. Assuming the mediator role involves creating choices for the participants that can significantly improve their quality of life (Connaway & Gentry, 1988).

Retaining Power or Giving It Away

When conflicts are solved closer to "home" or to the people with the conflict, the more power they retain. The farther away from the people a resolution is sought, the more power they give away. Conflict resolution strategy choices include negotiation, mediation, arbitration, and litigation (depicted schematically in Figures 11.1, 11.2, 11.3, and 11.4). *Negotiation* involves direct communication between two parties (Figure 11.1). If the conflicting parties cannot sit down and negotiate a solution, a third party is needed to *mediate* and promote communication and conciliation (Figure 11.2). If a third party is unable to promote negotiation between the parties, an *arbitrator* may be used. The arbitrator does not attempt to promote communication and negotiation; instead, like a judge, he or she hears both sides of the conflict situation and decides the resolution (Figure 11.3). It is obvious how much less power this process leaves with the participants than the negotiation or mediation process. Finally, if arbitration is not successful, the parties may resort to *litigation*, in which each party is represented by an attorney. If a jury is involved, the decision is made by an outside group through the intervention of attorneys and the parties in conflict do not ever have to even talk to one another (Figure 11.4). This conflict resolution strategy retains the least power for the participants.

For example, if a family in conflict over elder care or adolescent emancipation can resolve the conflict themselves, they will retain greater power. If they are unable to resolve the conflict and have to take it to a judge, jury, or even an arbitrator, they will give up power. In the same way, two community groups in conflict will retain power if they can (with the help of a facilitator or by themselves) resolve the problem or conflict. So, promoting and facilitating problem solving with people in conflict is a power-retaining intervention that also has empowering qualities.

Our society's strong litigation mind-set suggests that we are socialized to give away power to others to resolve our problems. The common retort, "So sue me," reflects our dependence on outsiders for problem solving.

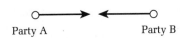

Party A   Party B

Figure 11.1 Negotiation. *Source:* Parsons, 1991.

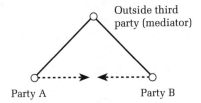

Outside third
party (mediator)

Party A   Party B

Figure 11.2 Mediation. *Source:* Parsons, 1991.

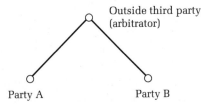

Outside third party
(arbitrator)

Party A   Party B

Figure 11.3 Arbitration. *Source:* Parsons, 1991.

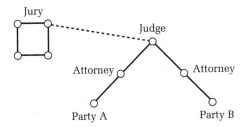

Jury

Judge

Attorney   Attorney

Party A   Party B

Figure 11.4 Litigation. *Source:* Parsons, 1991.

Two outcomes are important in relation to power retention in conflict resolution. One is that the stronger the intervention from outsiders, the more estranged the parties will be after the resolution. For families, this has serious consequences. Called *shadow of the future*, it means that the greater the presence of future relationship, the more important it is for parties to work out differences themselves instead of turning the problem over to an outsider (Parsons & Cox, 1989). And second, everyone does not have equal access to the court system. So, while the litigation process may seem to be a clean, efficient solution to conflict, social justice through the court system is more accessible to those with money and power than to those without.

Mediation for Empowerment

The mediation process has other empowering qualities that are not present in many problem-solving strategies. One such quality is its educational nature (Parsons & Cox, 1989). Participants learn to identify their needs, interests, and solutions and to present them to the other disputant. The mediator educates participants to negotiate to get their needs met. Chandler (1985) described mediation as joint advocacy, wherein the social worker promotes the interests and negotiating strengths of each participant. Another quality is the emphasis placed on each participant's responsibility for decision making and outcome. "Mediation assumes that participants have the capacity to examine facts and make rational choices with assistance of a mediator" (Connaway & Gentry, 1988, p. 147). Barbara Solomon (1976) suggested that empowerment-based practice leaves skills and knowledge with the client after the worker is gone. Successful mediation leaves the client with new skills for negotiation.

Mediation takes different forms based on its participants and the context in which it occurs. Social workers and disputants have different styles of mediating and negotiation. Weingarten and Douvan (1985) found that female mediators construct the mediator role more from a relationship-oriented process, whereas male mediators tend to be more task and outcome oriented. The approach and process may also need to be altered to fit the norms of some culture (see Lederach, 1990; LeResche, 1990, 1992; Stamato, 1992; Klugman, 1992.)

Neutrality

Neutrality is a controversial issue in the assumption of the mediator role. The mediation process suggests that to be effective, the mediator must be completely neutral. However, by its very nature, social work operates in value-laden contexts. The value base is perhaps the most strongly articulated and most common thread within the profession. Social workers intervene with a definitive set of values: the promotion of individual differences and uniqueness, and the promotion of social justice and optimal opportunity for the capacity development of all people. A social worker cannot facilitate a mutually agreed-on resolution that is not socially just. For that reason, a social worker cannot mediate physical and emotional violence, and he or she cannot mediate an illegal activity in lieu of litigation. Mediation does not take the place of litigation and adjudication when the law has been broken and when social justice is violated. A decision of what is ethical to mediate and what is not must be weighed heavily and carefully (Parsons, 1991).

As Susskind and Ozawa pointed out, "While it may be necessary for mediators to be perceived as neutral, the claim of neutrality is misleading"

(1983, p. 262). The question goes beyond whether a mediator *can* be neutral to whether he or she *should* be neutral. The social worker–mediator is not an objective, disinterested, nonbiased third-party intervenor. The role is taken to help bring problems and issues to the bargaining table and to promote communication toward resolution of problems within the profession's value base. Beyond that, when a social worker is not and cannot be neutral in a situation, she or he must state up front the set of values that guide his or her role. A social worker mediating with a family about elder care must make it clear that he will not participate in any decision that exploits the elder. If a supervisor mediates between two employees, she must state up front what boundaries or criteria must be met by the common agreement that the participants choose. Otherwise, the worker makes a mockery of a mutually empowering, educational intervention.

THE NATURE OF CONFLICT

While conflict is an everyday occurrence, we understand little about its nature. We tend to have a negative reaction to conflict although it is inherent in social system functioning. Bisno (1988) pointed out that human service organizations are not free of conflicts nor should they be. Because conflict is as natural as harmony, it is difficult to envision the attainment of social goals without it. Blake and Mouton (1985) further suggested that while organizational conflict is often attributed to the traits of the individuals involved in it, intergroup conflict is a natural dynamic of group functioning and interface in an organization.

Strengths of Conflict

One reason we are reluctant to engage in our own conflict resolution is that we are socialized to think of conflict as negative, as something to be avoided. Perhaps the negative connotation comes from an association with win/lose outcomes in competitive conflict resolution. As a society, we tend to believe that engagement in conflict resolution brings either a win or a loss, and we tend to have had negative experiences with conflict and its resolution.

Conflict can function, however, in important and positive ways. It helps set group boundaries by strengthening group cohesion; it reduces incipient tension by making issues manifest; it clarifies objectives; and it helps establish group norms (Coser, 1956). Conflict has the potential of creating both energy and a relationship where none had existed. A family or organization full of unresolved conflict becomes highly disorganized and dysfunctional. The capacity to identify conflict and work on its resolution can strengthen the system.

Definition of Conflict

Conflict has been defined as ''a clash of power in the striving of all things to be manifest'' (Rummel, 1976, p. 237); ''a situation of competition in which the parties are aware of the incompatibility of potential future positions and in which each party wishes to occupy a position which is incompatible with the wishes of the other'' (Boulding, 1962 p. 5). Or conflict may be thought of as the perceived mutual exclusivity of goals or procedures (Parsons, 1991).

Sources of Conflict

Conflict may come from several sources: *emotional*, *substantive*, and *values* (Kriesberg, 1982; Coser, 1956); see Figure 11.5.

Conflict usually surfaces around substantive issues, whether or not substance is actually the key element in the conflict. As conflicts escalate, the emotional aspect tends to obscure and take over the substantive aspect, although the conflict is attributed to substance. Substantive conflict arises when participants have different data, interpret the same data in different ways, or disagree on procedures. For example, family members may disagree on what is best for their elder member because of their different percep-tions of the person's functioning level, resources, or desires. Attempts to resolve conflicts create history and often resentment.

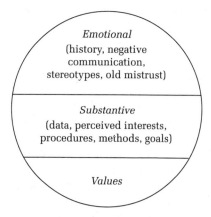

Figure 11.5 Sphere of conflict. *Source:* Adapted with permission from *The Media-tion Process* by C. W. Moore. Copyright © 1986 by Jossey-Bass Publishers.

The emotional arena of conflict grows out of mistrust created from past attempts to resolve the conflict or out of old, negative relationship components that existed before the conflict. Family members with differing perceptions may not communicate directly, or they may fall back into old negative attitudes and stereotypes of one another.

Value difference as a cause of conflict is not usually as great as the conflicting parties perceived it to be. When the conflict is broken down into understandable parts, the value differences are normally reduced to small fractions of the overall conflict. Neither values nor emotions are easily negotiable; only the substantive part of the conflict lends itself to negotiation. Therefore, in conflict resolution, the substantive aspect must be enlarged and opened up to increase potential for negotiation.

Evolution of Conflict

The evolution of conflict is illustrated in Figure 11.6. First, a set of antecedent conditions exist. In an organization or community, antecedent conditions may be competition for scarce resources, lack of role clarity, or other distancing mechanisms. Distancing mechanisms tend to create a "we/they" mind-set. Antecedent conditions may create either perceived conflict or felt conflict in the persons involved. Either conflict feeds the other as indicated by the arrows in Figure 11.6. Then a trigger issue stimulates manifest conflict. Some attempt at conflict resolution usually occurs, creating a conflict resolution aftermath, which may feed any component of the conflict or may help decrease any component of the conflict evolution.

The earlier conflict resolution occurs, the more likely it is to have positive results. For example, intervention in conflict resolution with a family around adolescent emancipation issues will be far less effective if it occurs after the adolescent has run away. By this time, both the adolescent and the family may believe that communication is impossible. If intervention occurs while the adolescent is still at home and there is still some thread of communication left, it has a better chance of being successful.

Conflict Resolution Outcomes

Deutsch (1973) suggested that conflict resolution may result in different outcomes, both destructive and constructive. Which outcomes result depends on the strategies chosen for resolution or management. The possibilities include (1) mutual loss or *lose/lose* outcomes; (2) gains for one, loss for another, or *lose/win* outcomes; or (3) mutual gain, or *win/win* outcomes.

Resolution through power and dominance strategies often creates win/lose outcomes. Other strategies that lead to win/lose are "majority rules" and

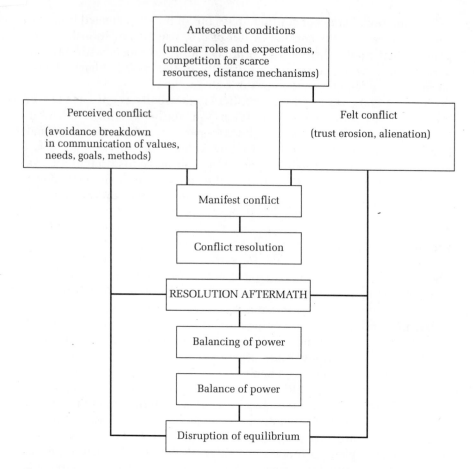

Figure 11.6 Evolution of conflict. Based on Rummel, 1976.

intimidation. In any of these strategies, one side's interests are not considered, and the other side's interests prevail. Lose/lose outcomes are associated with arbitrary solutions by a third party; neither party's interests are met usually due to bribery or bad compromises. Denial and suppression of conflict lead to either lose/lose or win/lose outcomes, depending on the nature of the conflict. Neither strategy is the optimal strategy for conflict resolution; they both delay the inevitable or push the issues underground for the time being. Denied or suppressed conflicts usually surface later with increased emotional and substantive elements. Win/win outcomes are thought to result from consensus seeking; that is, integrative problem solving, in which the interests of all parties are examined for the potential of mutual gain.

FRAMEWORK FOR THE MEDIATOR ROLE

Integrative problem solving is a process of consensus decision making that results from sharing perceptions of the problem and alternative solutions. Participants share perceptions and attitudes around the identified issues, define problems, and generate solutions that either satisfy each party's interest or are at least mutually acceptable to both parties. The strategy promotes both development of outcomes and the process of feelings attached to the conflict. Integrative problem solving is the basic problem-solving process applied to conflict resolution and therefore is a familiar framework to social workers. The process can be conceptualized by Figure 11.7. The first phase is to review and adjust relational conditions, since relationship is often the key focus of participants in a conflict, even though it is rarely the cause. This process helps in reviewing and adjusting perceptions and attitudes about the conflict. Then, a definition of the problem, a search for the solution, and other decisions can be discussed and worked on.

The techniques and steps for integrative problem solving are critical for the social worker as mediator. They will be detailed here. Integrative problem solving may be accomplished through negotiation between two parties without the intervention of a third party. If this is not possible, then the mediator role is utilized. The framework outlined here for the process of integrative problem solving is taken from Fisher, Ury, and Patton's *Getting to Yes* (1991). The framework includes four steps: separate the people from the problem, focus on interests instead of positions, create options for

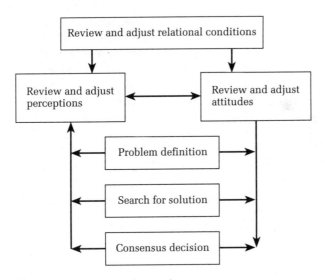

Figure 11.7 The integrative problem-solving process

mutual gain, and select criteria for choosing alternatives. These steps will be illustrated through the case of Ms. Gold.

Exploration and Assessment

CASE STUDY: *Ms. Gold** ◆—————————————————————

Ms. Gold, an 87-year-old woman, has been living with Ms. Brown, her 67-year-old daughter, for about two years. They have been living in Ms. Gold's house, which she still owns. Recently, Ms. Gold fell and fractured her left hip. This injury required surgery and a two-week hospital stay with physical therapy. The hospital social worker was in the process of establishing a discharge plan when some complications arose. Ms. Gold was taking longer to rehabilitate than expected. The physical therapist believed that she was hindered from walking by her fear of falling.

One of the doctors suggested temporary nursing home care. Ms. Brown disagreed. She argued that she could care for her mother at home whether or not she could walk as well as before. Ms. Brown, who is also physically weak, argued that she has managed her mother so far, and she can do so in the future. In conversation with Ms. Brown, the worker discovered that there were two other daughters, Ms. Ivan and Ms. Sands, who lived out of state. They were pressuring Ms. Brown to put their mother in a nursing home. The worker also learned that Ms. Ivan and Ms. Sands were coming to town to see that the nursing home placement took place.

The social worker met individually with Ms. Sands and Ms. Ivan to get their perspectives. Both women believed that a good nursing home would be the best permanent environment for their mother. They believed that their sister was too frail to care for their mother. They were also suspicious, suggesting that her main concern was their mother's Social Security check and the security of living in her home. It had been two years since either of them had seen their mother, and they were both appalled at her deteriorated condition and appearance, which made them even more adamant about a nursing home placement.

Ms. Gold wanted to return to her own home under the care of Ms. Brown. She was opposed to going to a nursing home even on a temporary basis because she feared she would never return home. She thought that she and Ms. Brown could manage very well, especially if her daughter would stop going out to play bridge with her friends so much.

Medical information on Ms. Gold and the worker's assessment of Ms. Brown suggested that Ms. Gold could not return home without some in-home services.

*Based on a case from Ledbetter-Hancock, 1987.

However, payment for the services would be a stumbling block. While Ms. Ivan and Ms. Sands were willing to contribute to the cost of a nursing home placement, they would not give any money to their sister to care for their mother. The worker also learned that there was a long-standing conflict between Ms. Ivan and Ms. Brown and that Ms. Sands had taken Ms. Ivan's side and therefore was involved in the conflict as well. The conflict was over Ms. Brown's previous husband, who had not been hospitable to either sister. No visits or communication had occurred directly between either Ms. Ivan and Ms. Brown or between Ms. Sands and Ms. Brown for eight years. Neither Ms. Ivan nor Ms. Sands contributed to their mother's expenses. Both Ms. Gold and Ms. Brown lived on modest Social Security payments. By pooling their resources, they were able to make expenses.

♦

Value differences, differences in perceptions, and emotional components can be seen in this family dispute. Family history created a set of antecedent conditions and an erosion of trust. The current crisis created a manifest conflict. All parties perceive a win/lose outcome, which increased their emotional anxiety around the conflict.

Getting Disputants to the Table

CASE STUDY: *Ms. Gold* ♦

The worker talked to each sister separately and to Ms. Gold and asked if they would be willing to sit down with her and discuss the situation. After getting their permission, she arranged a meeting time at the hospital. She began the meeting by saying that she understood that the sisters all had good intentions toward their mother, and that was the common ground from which they could work. The worker explained that she would present the medical information from the hospital and that her interest would be to formulate a plan that suited Ms. Gold's needs. Other than that, she would remain neutral in the situation. The worker also explained that as a mediator, she would help them express their perceptions and desires, come to an agreement that was mutually acceptable, and then carry out that agreement.

♦

Separating the People from the Problem

As pointed out earlier, while conflict usually begins around some substantive issue, the emotional arena grows rapidly as the conflict progresses. By the time a serious attempt at resolution is sought, the emotional aspect has taken over and the substantive issues are lost. In the minds of the participants, the problem is the other person or persons involved. There is no separation between the persons and the problem. This perception can prevent one-to-one negotiation.

The first step in mediation then becomes to separate the people from the problem. The mediator facilitates this by asking each participant to describe the problem and to state his or her feelings about the problem. The mediator's skills are to help clarify perceptions, to reframe the problem presented in the interests of the participants present, and to validate each participant by using reflective listening techniques.

Each participant needs to feel heard by the mediator, if not by the other participant. The mediator promotes listening by modeling good listening behavior and by asking participants to repeat in their own words what they hear the other party saying. Each party is encouraged to use "I" statements instead of "you" statements.

These techniques promote communication between the participants. By hearing each other, the participants are able to begin to define the problem as separate from the person. The mediator works to get the problems, and each participant's perception of the problems, out on the table and then to build an agenda for work. The issues need to be separated into entities that are small enough to deal with.

CASE STUDY: *Ms. Gold* ♦

The worker began by asking Ms. Ivan to state how she saw the situation and her feelings about it. Having been angry at Ms. Brown for a long time, Ms. Ivan took this opportunity to get rid of some of her anger. She accused Ms. Brown of using her mother for her own support and of not being able to give her the care she needed. Ms. Ivan saw Ms. Brown as her mother's favorite child and resented her for that. Ms. Ivan took this opportunity to get back at both Ms. Brown and Ms. Gold by insisting that the current arrangement would no longer work. The worker reflected Ms. Ivan's feelings of resentment at being shut out by Ms. Brown's husband, by Ms. Brown, and by her own mother. The worker empathized with Ms. Ivan's feelings and asked her if there were any other related issues she wanted to raise. Ms. Ivan said that she was willing to help her mother with expenses, but she would not give any money to her mother's household as long as her sister was in charge. She wanted her mother in a nursing home where she could receive the care she needed.

The worker then asked Ms. Sands to state her perception and feelings about the situation. While Ms. Sands was not as angry at Ms. Brown as Ms. Ivan was, she basically took the position that her mother had to go into a nursing home and could no longer stay at home with Ms. Brown's inadequate care. Ms. Sands blamed her sister for being careless about the house and held her responsible for her mother's fall. When the social worker asked her why she insisted that her mother go to a nursing home, Ms. Sands stated that she had to feel good about the care her mother was receiving in order to live with herself.

Next, it was Ms. Brown's turn to talk. She was adamant that her mother not go to a nursing home as long as she was able to care for her. She reminded her sisters that she had given their mother care for three years and could continue to do so if they were willing to help with some of the extra medical expenses that would occur as a result of her fall. She also reminded them that they had been basically uninterested in the situation, and now they seemed to have all the answers. Furthermore, she reminded them that Ms. Gold did not want to go into a nursing home, was not crazy, and could make that decision for herself. The worker reflected Ms. Brown's feelings of anger and resentment and reflected and praised her concern for her mother.

Then the worker asked Ms. Gold to talk about the situation. She was shy about stating her position and did not want to aggravate the already uncomfortable conflict among her daughters. She did say that she didn't want to go to a nursing home unless there was no other choice. She said she wanted her daughters to bury old problems and get along, if they could.

The worker then related the medical information important to the situation. Ms. Gold would need intense physical therapy for a while because she was not yet walking. Wherever she went after being discharged from the hospital had to have wheelchair accessibility because she was going to be in a wheelchair until she was able to get around on a walker. She would also need either special transportation to physical therapy or in-home physical rehabilitation.

With the problems out on the table, the worker could begin to identify interests.

♦

Focusing on Interests Instead of Positions

As the problems are presented, the mediator listens for the interests behind the positions. Positions are what the participants may ''want,'' as opposed to what they need. Positions are often the predetermined solutions that a participant brings to the table. Interests, on the other hand, are those common human needs reflected by the position taken. A position of ''My mother will not (or will) go to a nursing home'' may reflect an underlying interest of ''I need to feel that my mother is getting the best care available'' or ''I need to not feel guilty about this plan of care for my mother.'' The key to interest-based problem solving is to find the common interests of the parties or at least the compatible individual interests.

A mediator can facilitate the location of interests in a conflict by asking the parties what the impact of their positions is on the other party. Another helpful question is to ask what the participants need out of this problem-solving process to feel good about their participation. If the participants can see that their needs are not terribly different, they may be able to negotiate out of interests instead of positions. Often the mediator must point out areas of common interest because they are hidden behind the emotions.

CASE STUDY: *Ms. Gold* ◆

At this point, the social worker had gotten the perceptions and feelings out on the table and had attempted to reframe each party's concerns into a commonality. She had framed each of their concerns into their common concern for their mother's care and praised them for that. By doing that, she had begun to separate the people from the problem and the positions expressed from the interests behind them. Now, she could begin to build an agenda for work. She suggested that they list the problems and issues for discussion during their work together. As each person began to reiterate her concerns, the worker reframed those concerns into problems for work.

1. Where will Ms. Gold go after her discharge from the hospital?
2. Who is to pay for the needed care wherever she goes?
3. What were Ms. Gold's Social Security checks used for in the past? What will they be used for in the future?
4. What are the long-term plans for Ms. Gold's care? .
5. What will be done with Ms. Gold's house?

After getting everyone to agree that these were the issues that must be decided, the worker made an informal contract with the participants to agree to work together to generate solutions and to abide by them if everyone agreed.

◆

Creating Options that Satisfy Mutual Gain

During this process, many options that provide mutual satisfaction of interests are generated and explored. The mediator helps each participant see that there are options beyond his or her position. There should be at least one more option on the floor than there are participants. If the mediator has expertise in the substantive area of the conflict—such as aging, divorce, or mental health services—he or she can make substantive suggestions for resolution, but it is not the mediator's task to come up with alternatives from which solutions may be chosen. Of course, the generation of many options increases the possibilities for problem resolution. Brainstorming techniques are also helpful for generating alternatives. Suggesting frivolous alternatives helps participants become less rigid in their brainstorming.

CASE STUDY: *Ms. Gold* ◆

The worker began with the expenditures of Ms. Gold's check because she thought this was a less emotional subject. She knew from conversations with Ms. Brown that none of the money had been spent irresponsibly; the sisters were simply not informed and therefore were suspicious. The worker asked Ms. Brown and Ms. Gold for information regarding monthly expenses and expenditures, so that Ms. Ivan and Ms. Sands could see that their mother's checks were indeed spent on their mother's expenses and not used irresponsibly by Ms. Brown.

When that subject was discussed to everyone's satisfaction, the worker decided to take up the problem of where Ms. Gold would go after she left the hospital. The worker began by asking the group to brainstorm solutions even if they were not feasible, just to get everyone's creative thinking out on the table. Ms. Gold's returning to her home under Ms. Brown's care was obviously an option. Going into a nursing home was another. Because these two options represented the two positions brought by the disputants, the worker wanted to get other alternatives out for consideration. Remembering that there should always be one more solution than positions taken by disputants, the worker suggested that Ms. Gold could go back home with either Ms. Ivan or Ms. Sands. Ms. Ivan said that they could pool financial resources and hire a third party to take Ms. Gold into his or her home, which was wheelchair accessible. Ms. Sands suggested that they spend the money to make Ms. Gold's home accessible to wheelchairs.

◆

Selecting Criteria for Choosing Alternatives

When a number of solutions have been generated, alternatives can be selected. The mediator helps the participants decide how the alternatives will be selected; that is, according to what criterion or what objective standard. In elder-care decision making, the objective criteria are likely to be based on economic feasibility or shared economic responsibility combined with quality of care. If a family can agree to select alternative solutions using an acceptable set of criteria, the resolution is practically done. Once alternatives are chosen, they are spelled out procedurally, written down, and distributed to everyone. Then plans are made to carry them out. This is also a time to decide about follow-up meetings or check-in procedures.

Fisher, Ury, and Patton (1991) suggested that negotiation produces a wise agreement; that is, one that satisfies the interests of all participants. Choosing options based on objective criteria helps produce a wise agreement.

CASE STUDY: *Ms. Gold* ◆

After a number of alternatives had been generated, the worker asked how they would select a solution from the alternatives. On what basis would one solution be considered better than another? One criterion everyone decided on was that the solution had to fit the worker's perception of meeting Ms. Gold's needs, based on the medical information. Another criterion was that the solution had to be financially feasible. Although both Ms. Brown and Ms. Gold wanted her to go back to her house, it became apparent that this solution was not possible for two reasons: the house was not wheelchair accessible and Ms. Brown could not lift her mother. Thus, everyone agreed that a temporary nursing home placement would be necessary until Ms. Gold could walk again.

Because they had been able to discuss temporary care plans for Ms. Gold, the worker thought they could probably take on the question of long-term care. Because the other two problems on the list were both financial, the worker thought they went together. She asked the group to brainstorm ideas for long-term care for Ms. Gold. The group suggested, of course, long-term nursing home placement and returning Ms. Gold to her own house under Ms. Brown's care. Again, these alternatives represented the positions taken by the disputants. The worker had to enlarge the "option pie" by helping them generate more solutions than positions. She encouraged them to brainstorm much as they had before, suggesting that either Ms. Sand or Ms. Ivan provide a care setting for their mother.

Other suggestions included some form of assisted living arrangements where Ms. Gold would have partial care, but not skilled nursing care. It was time to choose an option to the key issue. Again, the worker asked how this solution would be chosen. What criteria would be used? Again, they agreed that the plan must be appropriate for what the medical staff projected as Ms. Gold's long-term functioning level. The worker told them that it was difficult to predict the outcome of hip breaks for a person of Ms. Gold's age, but she should regain her ability to walk within a few months.

Through the process, each person's hard-line position had softened. By helping the participants separate the people from the problem and interests from positions, the social worker had helped the sisters look more objectively at the problem, having brought in their common goal of making decisions that would work for their mother. Although Ms. Brown had the most to lose by negotiating, she knew that without her sisters' cooperation, she could not provide the needed care for her mother and would likely lose her place to live. So she was willing to negotiate because her BATNA (best alternative to a negotiated agreement) was not good. After holding a caucus with each participant, the worker was able to reach an agreement. Ms. Gold would return to her own home under Ms. Brown's care, but with some additional home health care and some respite care built in for Ms. Brown. It had become evident in the discussion that caring for Ms. Gold could be very stressful if there were no built-in relief for the caregiver. Because the worker was an expert in her field, she knew of available resources to meet Ms. Gold's and Ms. Brown's needs.

The last two problems were financial: who would pay for the care and what would happen to Ms. Gold's house? As is so often the case, families trying to give care to an elder are faced with scarce resources. Without using the equity in the house, there was not enough of a financial base among them to meet the anticipated expenses. The worker again asked them to brainstorm options. She was able to add to the list of options the idea of selling the house and placing the equity in some type of interest-bearing savings account. Then the money would be available to help with expenses incurred by Ms. Gold's care. She was further able to direct both Ms. Gold and Ms. Brown to housing resources, such as rent subsidies. This is a typical move for many families in this situation: all is sacrificed to meet the medical expenses. After brainstorming and selecting options, this was the option chosen. The house would be sold and the equity put in an interest-bearing savings account to be used to augment the care expenses. The account would be monitored by an accountant and each sister would receive an accounting of all expenditures.

Having reached solutions for their stated problems, each participant felt as if her needs had been heard and considered and that she had an opportunity to participate in the decision making. The arrangements met their interests if not their positions. The worker was then able to get the agreements in writing, including steps and procedures for carrying them out. The conflict within the family was not completely resolved, but the issues were settled in a manner all family members could accept. This type of problem solving created a much more tolerable "shadow of the future" for this family than would a lawsuit or some other coercive form of conflict resolution.

◆

Relationship or Outcome

Common questions about this process include "How can you get to the task or problems for resolution when the emotions run so high?" "Don't you have to deal with the feelings before people can deal with the task?" Mediation techniques differ in their emphasis on task and process. Some strategies are task oriented and others are more process oriented. As in all social work intervention, mediation is a fine balance between task and process. When the shadow of the future is critical, the relational component of the mediation becomes more important. If the shadow of the future is not great, the outcome can take precedence over the relationship. Emotions in a conflict must be heard, listened to, and reflected on. They must be dealt with to the extent that they get in the way of problem resolution. Emotions should neither be discounted nor should they become the focus. Emotional change and attitude change is a by-product in mediation, not a goal. The goal is to create workable solutions that promote mutual gain or at least decrease destructive conflict.

Caucus

The caucus is used in mediation to stop the process and talk individually with the parties about either highly emotional issues or to help them sort out information that is overwhelming them. It is used to bolster up a less empowered disputant so that the person does not give up or give in due to intimidation or pressure. The caucus is not used to manipulate parties in the dispute, but to facilitate the communication process between the disputants.

Information obtained and discussed in an individual caucus is best shared later in the presence of all participants, but it may be kept between the mediator and the individual participant if he or she does not want it shared. The mediator must be sure to ask whether such information can be shared.

The worker may use the caucus at any time in the process. However, it is more commonly used in the early phases to elicit information and deal with the emotions surrounding the information. During the problem discussion phase, the caucus is most likely to be used to clarify interests or positions regarding problems being discussed and to negotiate on solutions.

Techniques and Skills

According to Compton and Galaway, the techniques used in mediation include the following:

♦ Bring about convergence of the perceived values of both parties to the conflict.

♦ Help each party recognize the legitimacy of the others' interests.

♦ Assist the parties in identifying common interest in a successful outcome.

♦ Avoid a situation in which issues of winning and losing are paramount.

♦ Attempt to localize the conflict to specific issues, times, and places.

♦ Break the conflict down to separate issues.

♦ Help parties identify that they have more at stake in a continuing relationship than the issue of the specific conflict.

♦ Facilitate communication by encouraging them to talk to one another.

♦ Use persuasion procedures. [1989, p. 511]

The specific skills needed by the mediator include the following:

1. Attentive and reflective listening to both perceptions of problems and feelings attached to those perceptions

2. Reframing partisan, persuasive, and emotionally laden statements into less toxic, more interests-based language

3. Encouraging the clear expression of ideas

4. Promoting each participant's listening by reflecting and asking each participant to reflect back what he or she heard

5. Asking participants to state problems from a mutual framework

6. Using a nonemotional tone of voice

7. Moderating so that one person does not dominate the conversation or does not dominate the other party

8. Giving feedback to participants, clarifying confusing points, confronting inconsistencies

9. Keeping the conversation focused on the problem at hand, and on the present aspects of the problem, not the past

10. Staying in control of the situation so that participants see the process as safe and trustworthy

11. Maintaining as much neutrality as is possible within the social work value base

12. Being clear with participants on what the limitations of neutrality are

Settings for the Mediator Role

There are many potential roles in this case study for other mediating and conflict resolution strategies. There could be conflicts between service providers in the community that affect the service delivery to Ms. Gold. To broker the needed service delivery to Ms. Gold, the worker may have had to resolve a conflict between service providers. Other conflicts could be internal to the hospital staff regarding conflicting opinions or procedures on behalf of Ms. Gold, between Ms. Gold and the potential nursing home, or in negotiating the financial reimbursement policy between Ms. Gold and her insurance company. Unresolved conflicts between these parties would undermine the service goals and the worker's efforts in implementing the goals with the client. The potential need for conflict resolution between and among the various systems impinging on this case reflects the diverse roles of the mediator.

The mediator role has been used in many social work interventions in many settings. It is often used in children and family service agencies with couples who are separated and in the process of divorce; with adolescents and parents, particularly in runaway problems; in hospital discharge planning between family members and between medical staff and families; in schools and residential treatment facilities between youth and between teachers and youth; in schools between parents and teachers and administrators; in organizations between staff, between management and staff, between staff and community consumers; between communities and neighborhood groups; in coalitions and between citizens and large or small organizations. This role is necessary in human service delivery and one in which social workers need basic skills.

MEDIATOR ROLE TAKING: CAUTIONS AND CONSTRAINTS

An important question is "When should the mediator role be assumed rather than other social work roles?" For a situation to be mediable, there must be more than one way to settle or negotiate the issue. If there are no choices in the settlement, mediation is not suggested. For example, if an executive director of an organization is not willing to abide by the decisions made by the participants, there is no point in an integrative problem-solving process.

Participants must be competent to negotiate. Drug- and alcohol-dependent persons are not considered appropriate participants, neither are mentally incompetent persons for they may not be able to follow through with a behavioral contract to resolve problems. Obviously, life-threatening situations are not amenable to mediation intervention; instead, they must be handled in a more direct, expedient manner.

Chandler (1985) compared mediation and other social work interventive strategies, particularly problem-solving casework. She suggested that mediation is most successful when there is an ongoing personal interaction between disputants, when all parties are willing to express personal wants and needs, and when there is a relatively egalitarian relationship between the disputants. Even when the parties do not have an egalitarian relationship, mediation serves as joint advocacy and tends to equalize status differentials among parties.

Mediation may not be an appropriate strategy when social justice is at stake. It is not a substitute for social justice. Domestic violence should not be mediated; it should be prosecuted. Prejudicial treatment, discrimination, and denial of equality of rights are not appropriate issues for mediation. These problems should be handled in the courts in the litigation process because they violate the law. When rights are denied, the advocacy role is more appropriate until the parties see that they need to negotiate with a client or with one another to settle the rights issue.

A third-party mediator should not be chosen over a client or a number of clients negotiating for themselves. Mediation should be chosen when the conferee role or broker role will not suffice. It is not a role intended to secure resources nor to alter the way a system works internally. Mediation can be used for power brokerage in that it can change the balance of power in a given situation. It is desirable when the future of the relationship is a critical factor, but the relationship is at an impasse.

SUMMARY

This chapter has discussed the context of the mediator role and the assumptions in taking that role. Theoretical underpinnings for the mediator role include systems theory, conflict theory, and social exchange theory. Conflict resolution strategy choices include negotiation, mediation, arbitration, and litigation. Negotiation and mediation are more empowering strategies because of the educational attributes.

Neutrality is considered necessary for effective mediation, but the mediator role in social work is taken under the rubric of professional values. Although conflict is usually perceived as negative, it has many positive aspects. Conflict arises from emotional, substantive, and value differences. It begins with antecedent conditions and proceeds to perceived conflict, full conflict, manifest conflict, attempts at resolution that create an aftermath, some balance of power, and subsequent disruption. Outcomes in conflict resolution can be thought of as lose/lose, lose/win, and win/win. Integrative problem solving, the process reflected in mediation, is directed toward win/win.

The mediation process includes four steps: separate the people from the problem, focus on interests instead of positions, create options for mutual gain, and select criteria for choosing alternatives. While both the relationship of disputants and the outcome of resolution are important in the mediation process, the outcome is the goal and the relationship is a by-product. This emphasis may vary, depending on the shadow of the future of the participants.

The mediator role is to be assumed carefully, not as a substitute for social justice. The role is more appropriate when the shadow of the future of the participants is great.

STUDY QUESTIONS

1. When is the mediator function most appropriate in solving social problems, as contrasted with the conferee, enabler, or advocate role?
2. Is worker neutrality attainable in the social work mediator role?
3. Identify the sources of conflict and their relationship to one another.
4. What are the positive attributes of conflict in a system?
5. Take a conflict example from your practice and trace it through the evolutionary stages of conflict.
6. Identify how the worker was able to separate the people from the problem in the case study of Ms. Gold.
7. What are the skills involved in the process of focusing on interests instead of positions?

REFERENCES

Bisno, H. (1988). Managing conflict. Newbury Park, CA: Sage.
Blake, R., & Mouton, J. (1985). Solving costly organizational conflicts. San Francisco: Jossey-Bass.
Boulding, K. (1962). Conflict and defense: A general theory. New York: Harper & Row.
Chandler, S. M. (1985). Mediation: Conjoint problem solving. Social Work, 30, pp. 347–349.
Compton, B., & Galaway, B. (1989). Social work processes (4th ed.). Pacific Grove, CA: Brooks/Cole.
Connaway, R. S., & Gentry, M. E. (1988). Social work practice. Englewood Cliffs, NJ: Prentice-Hall.
Coser, L. (1956). The functions of social conflict. New York: Free Press.
Deutsch, M. (1973). The resolution of conflict. New Haven, CT: Yale University Press.
Fisher, R., Ury, W., & Patton, B. (1991). Getting to yes: Negotiating agreement without giving in (2nd ed.). New York: Penguin Books.
Gitterman, A., & Shulman, L. (Eds.). (1986). Mutual aid groups and the life cycle. Itasca, IL: F. E. Peacock.
Gould, K. H. (1987). Life model versus conflict model: A feminist perspective. Social Work, 32(4), pp. 346–351.
Hearn, G. (1970, April). Social work as boundary work. Paper presented at the Third Annual Institute on Services to Families and Children, School of Social Work, University of Iowa, Iowa City.
Klugman, J. (1992). Negotiating agreements and resolving disputes across cultures. Mediation Quarterly, 9(4), pp. 387–390.
Kriesberg, L. (1982). Social conflicts (2nd ed.). Englewood Cliffs, NJ: Prentice-Hall.
Ledbetter-Hancock, B. (1987). Social work with older people. Englewood Cliffs, NJ: Prentice-Hall.

Lederach, J. P. (1990). Training on culture: Four approaches. *Mennonite Concilia-tion Service Mediation Quarterly, 9*(1), p. 11.

Lee, J., & Swenson, C. (1986). The concept of mutual aid. In A. Gitterman & L. Shulman (Eds.), *Mutual aid and the life cycle.* Itasca, IL: F. E. Peacock.

LeResche, D. (1990). Suggested outline for training on culture. *Mennonite Concilia-tion Service Mediation Quarterly, 9*(1), p. 11.

LeResche, D. (1992). Comparison of the American mediation process with the Korean-American harmony restoration process. *Mennonite Conciliation Service Media-tion Quarterly, 9*(4), pp. 323–340.

Moore, C. W. (1986). *The mediation process.* San Francisco, CA: Jossey-Bass.

Parsons, R. J. (1991). The mediator role in social work. *Social Work, 36*(6), pp. 483–487.

Parsons, R. J., & Cox, E. O. (1989). Family mediation in elder care decisions: An empowerment intervention. *Social Work, 34*(2), pp. 122–127.

Rummel, R. J. (1976). *Understanding conflict and war, 1–2.* New York: Wiley.

Solomon, B. (1976). *Black empowerment: Work with oppressed populations.* New York: Columbia University Press.

Stamato, L. (1992). Voice, place and process: Research on gender negotiation and conflict resolution. *Mediation Quarterly, 9*(4), pp. 375–386.

Susskind, T., & Ozawa, C. (Eds.). (1983). Mediated negotiation in the public sector. *American Behavioral Scientist, 27*, pp. 255–279.

Weingarten, H., & Douvan, E. (1985). Male and female visions of mediation. *Negotia-tion Journal, 4*, pp. 349–358.

The Guardian Role

The responsibility of the social work profession to the community is often defined by law. These laws empower social workers with sanctions and the authority to serve as protectors of vulnerable people. In carrying out this protector role, social workers act in the interest of victims, potential victims, self-destructive individuals, and other endangered people. When the community sanctions social workers to serve people by protecting them, it follows that the worker may not necessarily have a contract with the benefactor of the service. On the contrary, the implicit contract may be with the community itself. In this sense, the social worker may be charged with protecting the community. This chapter presents the context of the guardian role in social work. The nature of social control, power, and authority in social work is examined. Values, ethics, and skills in the guardian role are also discussed.

DEFINITION AND PRACTICE DEMAND

Certainly a social problem–focused profession has a responsibility to serve as well as protect at-risk populations. Such protection necessitates the application of power, influence, authority, and social control. Under such circumstances, a unique role is created—the guardian role. This role is assumed when there is a practice demand for the social worker to perform in a social control function and act on behalf of clients (consumers) whose competency level is determined to be below minimal standards.

Social Control and Social Work

Authority and power, two central ingredients of social control, have been difficult concepts for social workers to apply (Compton & Galaway, 1989). Thus social control is controversial and there is considerable disagreement within the profession whether it should be a part of the social worker's repertoire. A major point of contention is whether social control is properly within the realm of social work. For many, the word *control* has a pejorative meaning. Adding the word *social* to it only expands the negative connotation into the broadest possible sphere. Chess and Norlin define social control as:

> . . . the means utilized by a system to secure compliance to its rules (normative expectations). Conceptually compliance is sought through socialization measures. When these measures are unsuccessful, they are, so to speak, backed up by social control measures. [1988, p. 381]

While social workers are quite comfortable with the socialization aspect of social control, the back-up measures are often considered negative and somehow inconsistent with social work values.

Part of the issue is that control is often equated with corrupt application of power. With the recent history of power abuse among members of Congress, other high government officials, and Wall Street insiders fresh in our minds, wariness regarding possible misapplication of power is probably well founded. Watergate, the Iran-Contra scandals, and influence peddling in both the public and private sectors give credence to the adage "Power corrupts, and absolute power corrupts absolutely." It is thus tempting for social work practitioners to disclaim their power and operate solely on a voluntary partnership basis with their clients.

Yet this is hardly possible. Our profession is a response to societal norms and values as they are played out in the community. Freedburg confronts the dilemma:

> To deliver necessary services to the community, the agency (an instrument of that community) and its agents (social workers) must maintain control of the services and to that extent also maintain control of the clients. The unresolved tensions in the ideological, political, and practice-oriented concept of self-determination reflect the social worker's contradictory position within democratic society. Social workers thus strive for a balance between responsibility to the community and responsibility to the self-determination of the individual client system. [1989, p. 33]

Settings for Assuming the Guardian Role

It is ironic that this role, while subject to so much debate, is highly institutionalized in practice. When serving individuals who are unable to protect themselves or act in their own behalf, social workers routinely act in their interest; for example, petitioning courts on behalf of abused and neglected children, placing children for adoption, and reporting the failure of parents to provide medical care.

When one person's rights are threatened by another, social workers are empowered to seek protection for that person. Thus workers may be found preventing financial exploitation of senile nursing home patients by seeking a conservator for their estate.

When an individual becomes a danger to self or others, workers control and protect them. This may take the form of initiating a mental health hold or hospitalizing someone who is making lethal suicidal gestures.

Although social workers recognize and promote competence in those they serve, they are also cognizant of the many factors that render people incompetent. Individuals who are developmentally disabled, brain injured, senile, or victimized by chronic mental illness or Alzheimer's disease may require the protection of guardianship in many areas of their lives. This protection has been and remains well within the scope of professional social work.

Finally, social workers are employed in psychiatric hospitals, courts, probation and parole departments, and prisons. They intervene in the lives of involuntary clients who have lost many of their rights of self-determination as a result of civil or criminal court proceedings. Forensic social workers evaluate defendants in terms of their dangerousness and treatability and advise the court of their findings in order to help prevent future violent acts. Private mental health clinics accept patients who are ordered into treatment by court and paroling authorities for sexual offenses. They are obliged to report the patient's progress or lack thereof to the referring authority and to notify them if the patient discontinues treatment. Violent and dangerous people will continue to exist in an imperfect society, and many who have given up hope of ever mattering will remain dangerous, undeterred, and unchanged.

THE NATURE OF SOCIAL CONTROL

Even if the social work profession were to abandon these social control functions, the controls would still have to be performed. They would very likely be administered by policing agencies that are less sensitive to possible abuses of power and perhaps less bound by a strong code of ethics. Our support for the legitimacy of social control as a social work function is that it is already a necessary reality of practice. Further, we believe that a democratic society is better served by social controls that are applied by a humanistic profession than by social control agents who are guided by coercive, autocratic values.

Social Control and Socialization

As previously mentioned, social control is not necessarily a negative restraining force. It can be a cohesive driving force that holds society together. Communities are not inherently unified. Where unity is present, there is an element of social exchange based on reciprocity and mutuality. This type of control comprises the threads that form a community's social fabric. Since social work's emphasis is social, it can hardly avoid its share of responsibility for social control.

Chess and Norlin link social control to socialization:

> It is useful to think of social control as a backup to the socialization system, "the enforcers." It could be argued that if every member of society was

perfectly socialized, and therefore acted in ways that were fully in accord with the prevailing cultural standards, there would be no need for a social control subsystem. In other words, socialization pertains to the development of internalized controls that result in behavioral compliance with established norms, while social control pertains to external forms of control aimed at securing compliance with these norms. [1988, p. 366]

Social controls, then, can be seen as the embodiment of both driving and restraining forces. As restraining forces, they provide the outside parameters for the ultimate social contract that a community forms with its individuals. These outside parameters limit what people are allowed to do to each other. Such limits provide a framework for spelling out the duties and responsibilities of individuals *toward* one another. It is what people recognize as their points of interdependence that provides the ultimate social control. This is the basis of community.

Power

As previously noted, social control involves the exercise of power. In exploring power self-perceptions of social work students, Feld (1987) discussed seven bases of power: coercive, reward, expert, connection, referent, informational, and legitimate. We will discuss each of them separately as they pertain to the guardian role.

Coercive Power

The power to coerce behavior is repugnant to most social work practitioners. It runs counter to their need to be liked. Coercive power is rooted in the potential to punish, and punishment is also alien to social work values.

Yet coercion is a reality. It should not be surprising that social agency policies and action are frequently viewed as coercive and punishing. For example, court actions initiated on behalf of children may be viewed by the beneficiaries of the action as punishments. Forced alcohol treatment may be ordered by a court in the spirit of rehabilitation. To the captive patient, the treatment may be considered a form of punishment.

Social workers placed in situations where their actions might be considered punitive need to acknowledge these concerns with clients (Hutchinson, 1987). Doing so may provide the critical ingredient in constructing a working relationship. Murdach (1980) proposed that workers negotiate and bargain with nonvoluntary clients as a means of overcoming conflict.

Reward Power

Just as social workers have the power (intentionally or unintentionally) to punish, they also have the power to reward. Whether these rewards are tangible or symbolic, they constitute an important incentive for initiating and maintaining social exchange. Professional as well as personal relationships are based on social exchange. Successful social exchange requires that each participant in the transaction receives enough rewards from the other participants to make the relationship endure. It follows then that awareness of how we reward others corresponds with an increased sense of power. For example, a social worker's testimony in court as to the positive attributes of a parent is a reward if that testimony leads to the parent's receiving custody of his or her child.

Expert Power

Knowledge, expertise, and skills are central to a social worker's power. Expert power may include knowledge of policy and rules as well as ability to apply various technologies. What a social worker knows and is able to do represent potential outputs. To the extent these outputs are required as inputs to another system, the worker's power is increased. It is important in this regard to examine a worker's willingness to master areas that are avoided by others. In so doing, it is possible to become one of an elite few who are in command of that expertise.

Connection Power

The more central a worker is to an operation, the more he or she will likely possess connection power. Communicating with power actors and other influentials opens up access to resources, information, and other rewards. Such connections also pave the way for membership in alliances and coalitions. In numbers, there is strength and there is also the potential for increased power.

Referent Power

This form of power lies in the degree of a person's personal attractiveness and charisma as perceived by others. It may be uncomfortable to consciously take stock of one's positive attributes; however, these attributes cause others to either like or dislike an individual. Being liked and admired provides a base for personal power. In the absence of other power sources, it may constitute the core of a person's power. As we now know, respect, empathy, and genuineness are traits long associated with helping, and they are all a part of referent power (Carkhuff, 1983).

Informational Power

We noted earlier that expertise gives power. The same is true for information. Being in control, or at the hub of the information flow, gives the holder of that information power over those who need it.

Legitimate Power

When a person has the right to make decisions and take action, it is considered having authority. Authority is a form of legitimate power. Palmer (1983) discussed five levels of authority: legally constituted, institutionally constituted, inherent in a position, constituted by expertise, and inherent in the person. These levels of authority are necessary in the performance of all roles, but they are particularly pertinent to carrying out the guardian role since it is not necessarily endorsed with a contract from the person being served. On the contrary, the worker's contract may be an implied agreement with the public at large.

Legally constituted authority carries the highest level of strength in terms of what it allows the worker to do and, more important, what it mandates that the worker must do.

Reporting child abuse is one example. In most jurisdictions, reporting this phenomenon is a legal requirement. Failure to do so places a social worker (as well as other professionals) in legal jeopardy. Reporting suspected abuse has serious implications for any future professional relationship with the child's parents. However, that relationship is secondary to the first priority that a worker has to the endangered child. Child welfare workers, medical social workers, and school social workers all face the dilemma of the personal conflict inherent in the guardian role, but legal requirements establish clear expectations as to what the worker must do. As such, these legal requirements are empowering.

Authority

Authority may come from three sources: institutional, positional, and expert. Social workers derive authority from all three sources.

Institutional Authority

Authority that is institutionally constituted flows from the functions a service agency performs. A public assistance agency is a case in point. It is governed by eligibility rules and regulations. The worker's authority is thus embodied in the interpretations of those guidelines and the resulting decisions that may affect a client either positively or negatively.

A more subtle form is the authority inherent in a position. Decisions made from the unique position of social workers are shaped by the code of ethics that regulates the professional, the authority that is spelled out by the position's job description, and the discretion that the worker exercises in making practice decisions.

Positional Authority

Positional authority is exemplified in the following situation. A child protection worker took custody of an abused child through a voluntary release from the parents. The child was placed in a temporary foster home. The child's aunt and uncle requested that the worker place the child with them, explaining that God had instructed them to take the child. On the basis of several interviews with the couple, the worker made a professional judgment that the couple was emotionally unstable and refused their request. In this case, he was clearly within the appropriate decisional boundaries of the position of child protection worker. The worker made a "judgment call," based on the job description, which gave him the power to "make day-to-day decisions regarding the welfare of children placed in the custody of the agency."

Expert Authority

Expert authority, like expert power, is the result of technical knowledge and skills that are particular to a worker. The demand for that knowledge and skill establishes authority for the holder.

One of the best examples of this is when the social worker is certified as an expert witness (Gothard, 1987). This certification establishes the expert as one of an elite few who can lay claim to unique knowledge. Workers who conduct or are conversant with research in selected areas or who work in technically specific areas are established as experts. Their possession of knowledge establishes them as resource people who are sought out for consultation.

Inherent authority is intrinsic in the worker/client transaction. To the degree that clients confide and trust in a worker, that trust and confidence ultimately translates into the amount of authority that worker is granted. In other words, the authority lies not within the worker, but rather within the client's acceptance of the worker's ability to render help.

AUTHORITY ACTIONS

Ultimately the social worker–guardian is faced with carrying out authority actions. Authority actions are taken to protect someone or because they are inherent in an agency's function or mandated by law. The following list contains 25 typical authority actions. Note that these actions are sanctioned by someone other than the client. Yet, they are common expectations of behavior in the guardian role.

1. Initiating a petition to remove a child from a sexually abusive parent
2. Initiating a petition to remove a child from a physically abusive parent

3. Accepting relinquishment of custody of a child by a parent
4. Reporting suspected physical abuse to the appropriate agency
5. Reporting suspected sexual abuse to the appropriate agency
6. Conducting coerced treatment (or providing an unrequested social service)
7. Initiating a legal action for the termination of parental rights
8. Initiating guardianship proceedings to protect a mental patient
9. Initiating guardianship proceedings to protect a senile client
10. Acting in behalf of a child in the role of guardian ad litem
11. Testifying in court against a client
12. Testifying as to the competence of a defendant to stand trial
13. Assessing and reporting on a client's potential for dangerousness
14. Supervising and imposing limits on offenders who are placed on probation or parole
15. Submitting a pre-sentence (or parole) recommendation
16. Instituting a mental health hold
17. Revoking an offender's probation or parole
18. Reporting welfare fraud
19. Making life decisions for a developmentally disabled client
20. Petitioning the court to enforce medical treatment for a child whose parents refuse to provide it
21. Enforcing school attendance laws
22. Disapproving an adoptive home for adoptive placement
23. Placing a child for adoption
24. As a private practitioner, referring an uncooperative patient back to the court for further disposition
25. Using physical force to control a child's actions.

Authority Actions and Social Work Values

Some of these actions may be seen as more objectionable than others, but all of them challenge the practice values that guide the social worker's decisions (NASW, 1980). The values are as follows:

1. Commitment to the primary importance of the individual in society
2. Commitment to social change to meet socially recognized needs
3. Commitment to social justice and the economic physical and mental well-being of all in society

4. Respect and appreciation for individual and group differences
5. Commitment to develop clients' ability to help themselves
6. Willingness to transmit knowledge and skills to others
7. Willingness to keep personal feelings and needs separate from professional relationships
8. Respect for the confidentiality of relationships with clients
9. Willingness to persist in efforts on behalf of clients despite frustration
10. Commitment to a high standard of personal and professional conduct

Principles of the Guardian Role

Three principles pertain to carrying out the guardian role in a way that is congruent with social work values: (1) determining who the primary client is, (2) ensuring that actions are taken with the protection of due process, and (3) communicating with all parties impacted by the action as to the rationale for such action and the legal and ethical responsibilities under which the worker is operating.

In such drastic actions as petitioning the court for the removal of a child from physically or sexually abusive parents or from parents who are neglectful, the primary client is the child. The authority action is thus an expression of the first social work practice value of "commitment to the primary importance of the individual in society"; the third, "commitment to social justice and the economic, physical, and mental well-being of all in society"; the seventh, "willingness to keep personal feelings and needs separate from professional relationships"; and the ninth, "willingness to persist in efforts on behalf of clients despite frustration."

Authority actions are unlikely to please all parties. The U.S. Constitution guarantees "pursuit of happiness," not happiness itself. Expressed unhappiness may well challenge personal feelings and needs. If a person's need is for consensus, conflict will certainly not meet that need. Separating personal needs, whatever they may be, from professional relationships provides a clearer picture of the professional responsibility that shapes workers' actions. Because authority actions may challenge the rights of individuals who are impacted by them, they should be undertaken with the proper attention to due process. This may include such procedures as administrative review, judicial review, appeals, the right to legal counsel, and other protections.

For example, if physical force is to be used to control a client's actions, there should be written policies and procedures in place that define the necessity for such actions. Such policies and procedures protect the client by setting limits and prescriptions for any physical actions.

Because authority actions can be arbitrary and thus contentious, there is a special need for the client or others bearing the consequence of the action to be informed of the rationale for them. Ethical and legal obligations may commit a worker to a course of action which, unpleasant as it may be, is still required. Thus letting all parties know what is being done and why is a courtesy in keeping with social work practice values.

Authority Actions and Social Work Ethics

Within the Social Work Code of Ethics (NASW, 1980, Section II), "The Social Worker's Ethical Responsibility to Clients," special attention is given to rights and prerogatives of clients (Part G): "The social worker should make every effort to foster maximum self-determination on the part of clients." This is spelled out in greater detail:

1. When the social worker must act on behalf of a client who has been adjudged legally incompetent, the social worker should safeguard the interests and rights of that client.

2. When another individual has been legally authorized to act in behalf of a client, the social worker should deal with that person always with the client's best interest in mind.

3. The social worker should not engage in any action that violates or diminishes the civil or legal rights of clients. [NASW, 1980, Section II, Part G]

In terms of guiding and regulating practice behavior, this section of the Code of Ethics is notable in setting forth the reality of incompetence and the resulting need to act in a client's interest. It also gives attention to the legal reality of acting on behalf of clients while recognizing that rights that still pertain should be preserved.

The code of ethics also speaks to the social worker's ethical responsibility to society (Section VI), stating:

The social worker should promote the general welfare of society. . . . The social worker should act to prevent and eliminate discrimination against any person or group on the basis of race, color, sex, sexual orientation, age, religion, national origin, marital status, political belief, mental or physical handicap, or any other preference or personal characteristic, condition or status. [NASW, 1980, Section VI]

While these actions might be more consistent with the advocate role, it is conceivable that authority actions might be taken for people with mental or physical handicaps or age limitations, which would be sanctioned by this section of the Code of Ethics.

Authority Actions and Social Work Skills

Exercising authority requires recognizing the difference between authoritativeness and authoritarianism. Authoritativeness assumes that authority is based on competence and proper sanctions, whereas authoritarianism is an autocratic exercise of power based on dominance. The guardian role requires a clear understanding that authority must be rooted in legitimacy. This helps establish boundaries around the authority and limits to its application. Knowing one's limits promotes self-restraint.

Recognizing the limits of one's authority, it follows that these limits be spelled out to the parties affected. If the authority is derived from law, this law should be explained, particularly as to how it defines or limits one's role. It is then incumbent on the guardian to act in a way that is consistent with the laws, policies, and procedures that constrain the action. In practice, this means that actions should be fair and equitable and that the worker should be honest and aboveboard in communicating with the affected parties.

Because authority actions may be experienced as aversive, the guardian will need to express awareness and understanding of this negative impact as well as concern for the possible inconvenience the action may cause. The guardian role need not be devoid of warmth and compassion; in fact, these qualities can defuse some of the natural anger that results from an experience that is perceived as punitive.

Authority actions are also not necessarily disempowering. Even if clients disagree with a worker's course of action, they can still be asked to join with the worker in achieving a goal.

An example of joining and empowering is presented in the case of a child protective worker who petitioned the court for the removal of a four-year-old boy from the home of abusive parents. Because the parents were deemed unsuitable as parents and the child needed a permanent home, permanent custody was granted to the child placement agency. The worker asked the parents if they would join with him in helping the child terminate, pointing out their need to express in their own words their inability to care for him as a way of helping him release himself from them. As the parents found the appropriate words to explain their situation to the child, the worker was able to support their behavior and empower them in their decision. They ultimately thanked the worker for "helping us do what had to be done."

CASE STUDY: Ms. Dora Alias ♦

The case of Dora Alias, an 18-year-old female misdemeanant, illustrates the application of the guardian role. The setting is a misdemeanant probation department, which employs graduate social workers as probation officers.

Exploration

Dora was arrested at approximately 2:40 P.M., April 13, 1990, at Republic Drugs, 1600 Albion. She was attempting to fill a stolen and forged prescription for Methedrine. At the time of her apprehension, Dora was found to possess several hypodermic needles and other implements for drug use. She entered a not guilty plea and trial was set for June 27, 1990. Dora remained in jail for three days until family friends posted the cash bond. At her court appearance, she entered a guilty plea to the implement charge. Dora readily admits the use of various drugs and hallucinogenics and states that the needles and other implements were for this purpose. She admits knowing that the prescription she was attempting to fill had been stolen and was forged, but she would not reveal any information regarding its origin other than that it came from a friend. There were no previous offenses.

Assessment

Family.   Dora was born March 1, 1972, in Denver, Colorado, the second of three children born to Mr. and Mrs. Alias. At the time of her birth, her father was in the Air Force and assigned to Lowry Air Force Base. Throughout the interview, she was confused about time, but it is believed the family remained in Denver for about nine years. Then her father left the Air Force and the family moved to Tennessee, where they remained until returning to the Denver area in 1979. Mr. Alias entered a Baptist seminary in April 1988 in Denver. Before this, he had been employed as a watchmaker. The father is an overly rigid, strict man who views his daughter as a sinner beyond hope of change. The mother, on the contrary, is an overly permissive, passive woman who has been totally dominated by her husband. Dora has had serious conflicts with her father since she was 9 years old, and she has engaged in a long period of rebellion against him. Dora's 20-year-old brother, John, is a music student at a local university and continues to live in the parental home.

Living in the rented home at 8915 S. LaVeta Ct., in addition to Mr. and Mrs. Alias and John, is Dora's 16-year-old brother, Bob. Dora has been influential in involving Bob in the use of drugs, and their father is particularly concerned about Bob's future behavior should this close relationship with Dora continue. This, in part, is one reason the father approves of Dora's being out of the home.

Dora has been using assorted forms of drugs and narcotics for at least two years. From time to time, to temporarily stop drug usage, her father has had her committed, through the family physician, to Mt. Airy Mental Hospital in Denver. During the past two years, she has depended primarily on friends for her basic needs. As a result, she has moved around a lot in the Denver area. At the time of her arrest, Dora was staying at 96 Sherman; but at the time of this report, she lives with a group of male and female friends on South Clayton. She has no desire to return to her parents' home, even during the absence of her father. Shortly after being released from jail on May 1, 1990, Dora went to San Francisco, remaining approximately one month. She voluntarily returned to Denver a few days before her scheduled court appearance on this charge.

Employment.   None

Education.   Dora last attended school at Central High School in January 1988. Her academic achievement was very poor as was her attendance. She failed the 10th grade and was repeating these classes at the time of her last enrollment. She was not involved in any extracurricular activities.

Health.   Dora does not report any serious illnesses or injuries, but it is apparent from observation that she is seriously underweight as a result of poor eating habits and the effects of drugs. The interview was quite difficult, because she does not appear to have completely recovered from recent drug usage. Her speech was slurred and occasionally incoherent. She made inappropriate gestures and burst into laughter. She complained numerous times that her speech could not keep up with her mind, attributing this on one occasion to using "speed."

In February 1988, Dora was committed to Mt. Airy Mental Hospital by the family physician and then was placed on a 90-day hold-and-treat order at Fort Logan Mental Health Center. An interview with her psychiatric social worker, Miss M., disclosed much of the above social information. Dora is on outpatient treatment. She is supposed to be attending weekly sessions, but has failed to do so since her arrest. However, before the arrest, she kept appointments regularly, obtaining transportation through friends or using public transportation.

During her commitment at Fort Logan, Dora was a serious challenge. She was able to have friends bring her various drugs, and on one occasion, her boyfriend was arrested for introducing Methedrine into the hospital. Dora was not considered schizophrenic or in need of hospitalization. However, outpatient care was considered warranted and will be continued although her prognosis is guarded.

Religion.   Undoubtedly representing additional rebellion against her father, Dora professes to be a practicing Buddhist. She describes at length nine stages of life and rather proudly reported attainment of the eighth stage. She purports existence in the form of a cat during the seventh stage, but is unable to describe any previous stages. With amusement, Dora related discussing her religious beliefs with her father. It infuriated him.

Diagnostic Procedure Findings.   Dora seems expansive and somewhat hypomanic on the tests. She fears depression but perceives it as inevitable with her mood swings. She seems to try hard to avoid thoughts of the future. A simple, happy existence with a minimum of pain and suffering seems her goal.

Impressions.   This 18-year-old woman has rebelled against her strict, prudish, unyielding father in every form available. In doing so, she has become thoroughly aligned with the drug subculture, resulting in drug usage, sexual promiscuity, mobility, and antisocial behavior. Her native ability permits her to rationalize her behavior through pseudo-intellectualization. There is no evidence of motivation for behavior change. While her present existence is obviously self-destructive, Dora does present some strengths: returning from California in time to appear in court, maintaining appointments at Fort Logan before the instant offense, and displaying a native ability. The aspect of cause-effect looms from the gross inconsistency between parental figures.

Psychiatric Evaluation.   Dora appears not to have recovered from her Methedrine psychosis. She is confused about time and somewhat about place. Her speech is rapid and distorted. She complained that she couldn't keep up with her mind. Her affect was at times silly and inappropriate. Her relationships appear superficial and self-serving.

(signed)   E. W. Brown, M.D.

Corrective Recommendations.   Coerced drug rehabilitation would seem to be the means of achieving the immediate goal of allowing the defendant to withdraw from the effects of drug usage. Probation supervision would also be useful, providing the defendant with an opportunity to correct her behavior if she so chooses. A penalty and probation supervision is recommended. It is expected that the defendant will be very difficult to supervise.

Respectfully submitted,
D. R. Gomez
By: A. O. Smith and W. D. Jones
E. W. Brown, M.D.

Summary of Probation Services

The court sentenced Ms. Alias to one year in county jail. The sentence was suspended on condition that she reenroll in a residential drug treatment program at Conway House and successfully complete the program. A one-year period of probation was imposed in order to monitor and enforce the program.

Susan Koch, M.S.W., probation officer, met with Ms. Alias at Conway House to review the conditions of probation and to set the probation program in motion. She found Dora to be coherent and pleasant.

Ms. Koch explained to Dora that the continuation of her probation was contingent on remaining drug free and completing the ten-month treatment program. She further explained that any detection of drugs in Dora's system would result in her being returned to court for imposition of the jail sentence. This was framed as a decision that Dora must make. By her actions, she could remain free or become incarcerated. Dora expressed her wish to be free but indicated she couldn't do it without help.

When asked what she meant by help, Dora explained that she needed people around her who were "clean." Ms. Koch explained that she, the court, and the probation office would do everything to provide this help but the help would require that Dora make some important choices.

Contracting

The first choice Dora was given was the degree to which she wanted to use the services of the probation office. She was asked whether she wanted to participate in counseling or chose to simply be "checked up on." Dora was confused about what kind of counseling Ms. Koch would provide, wondering if she was a "shrink." Ms. Koch assured her that she was not a shrink but would be available for listening and talking about any problems Dora wished to discuss. Dora said she knew she would need to be checked on and she would be willing to talk to Ms. Koch about problems as well. Ms. Koch explained that reports on Dora's progress would be made to the court and that she would write these reports with honesty and integrity and that, in the final analysis, Dora's behavior would determine what was said.

Before leaving, Ms. Koch asked Dora to complete a written assignment before their next conference. The assignment was for Dora to state her goals for the following year. Dora seemed surprised at this, noting she hadn't done anything like that before. Ms. Koch gave her encouragement and said she was confident Dora could manage the assignment.

Ms. Koch visited Dora one week later at Conway House. Dora was asked whether she had completed her assignment. She proudly presented a sheet of paper with three goals: to be independent, to get a job, and to complete school.

Deciding What to Do and Doing It

Dora was commended for completing her assignment. Ms. Koch negotiated a behavioral contract with Dora, in which Dora would go for an interview at the alternative high school. This was easy enough for Dora because a representative of the high school visited Conway House weekly. She was also asked to formulate a list of possible jobs that she felt qualified to perform.

Ten days later, Dora advised Ms. Koch that she could be admitted to the alternative high school in the fall. (Ms. Koch later confirmed this fact.) Dora also submitted the list of jobs: waitress, bagger at a supermarket, and a worker at McDonald's, although she expressed some reservations about working in a fast-food restaurant because the pay was only minimum wage. Dora was urged to submit applications to supermarkets and restaurants and share the results with Ms. Koch in 30 days.

The Conway House staff were very pleased with Dora's progress during her first 30 days there. She cooperated with all urine-testing procedures, participated actively at in-house meetings, and had put on some badly needed weight.

Dora called Ms. Koch in early August saying she had been offered a bagger's job at a Safeway store eight blocks from Conway House. She was certain her hours could be arranged to accommodate attendance at school in September.

Dora enrolled in school in September. She was assigned to a volunteer tutor from the alternative high school, who also agreed to provide Ms. Koch with regular reports on Dora's progress. Dora made good progress throughout her probation period. At the time of her discharge from supervision, she had completed the Conway House program, receiving a "Certificate of Completion," and had rented an apartment with one of her co-workers at Safeway. Dora confided in Ms. Koch that although she was fearful of going to jail, she realized that she needed something to stop her behavior and she saw probation, her school, and her volunteer tutor as vital in helping her stay away from drugs. She had decided to visit her parents only on Sundays and then only for an hour or two at a time.

◆

This example shows the social worker in a setting where clients (probationers) are involved in a coercive program of directed change. In spite of this, the worker applies the principles of empowerment by joining with the client in goal setting and providing appropriate opportunities for the client to make choices. The worker recognizes the client's competencies and supports prosocial behaviors. The worker demonstrates her comfort with authority and authority actions while maintaining her client's dignity.

SUMMARY

Social work practice is a reflection of community values and purpose. One of the purposes of the community is social control. As social workers carry out this purpose, there is a resulting demand for the protector or guardian role.

Although a subject of controversy within the profession, the role of guardian is nevertheless well institutionalized in practice. Occupying this role requires workers to examine their bases of power: coercive, reward, expert, connection, referent, informational, and legitimate. Applications of power result in authority actions, which are screened through social work values and ethics. To carry out authority actions, the social worker must be authoritative rather than authoritarian, recognize and communicate to affected parties the limits of his or her power, be sensitive to the negative impact on the clients, and join with and attempt to improve those who bear the brunt of the actions.

STUDY QUESTIONS

1. Explain the difference between the terms *social control* and *socialization*. What would be an example of each?
2. Define and give examples of coercive, reward, expert, connection, referent, informational, and legitimate power.
3. Define and give examples of institutional, positional, and expert authority.
4. Review each of the 25 authority actions listed in this chapter. Which of these actions would you have the most trouble carrying out? Why? Which of these actions would you have the least trouble carrying out? Why?
5. Differentiate between the concepts of *authoritativeness* and *authoritarianism*. Provide an example of each.

REFERENCES

Carkhuff, R. (1983). *The art of helping*. Amherst, MA: Human Resource Development Press.

Chess, W., & Norlin, J. (1988). *Human behavior and the social environment*. Boston: Allyn and Bacon.

Compton, B. R., & Galaway, B. (1989). *Social work processes* (4th ed.). Pacific Grove, CA: Brooks/Cole.

Feld, A. (1987). Self-perceptions of power: Do social work and business students differ? *Social Work, 32*(3), pp. 225–226.

Freedberg, S. (1989). Self-determination: Historical perspectives and effects on current practice. *Social Work, 34*(1), pp. 33–39.

Gothard, S. (1987). Power in the court: The social worker as an expert witness. *Social Work, 34*(1), pp. 65–67.

Hutchinson, E. D. (1987). Use of authority in direct social work practice with mandated clients. *Social Service Review, 61*(4).

Murdach, A. (1980). Bargaining and persuasion with nonvoluntary clients. *Social Work, 25*(6), pp. 458–461.

National Association of Social Workers. (1980, January). *NASW NEWS* 25(1), pp. 24–25.

National Association of Social Workers. (1981, September). *NASW standards for the classification of social work practice.* (Policy Statement 4, p. 18). Silver Spring, MD: National Association of Social Workers.

Palmer, S. (1983). Authority: An essential part of practice. *Social Work, 28*(2), pp. 120–127.

Index

Abbot, Edith, 38
Abbott, Grace, 38
Abortion, as social issue, 41–42, 48
Abramovitz, M., 2
Absolutist school, deviance and,
    78–79, 95
Aburdene, P., 2
Action planning, 59
Action research
    case study of, 155–158
    compared with other types of
        research, 153–154
    decision making and, 154
    evaluation process and, 152–158,
        181, 185
Action system, 128, 217
Activism, deviance and, 91
Addams, Jane, 38
Adultery as deviant behavior, 77
Advancement phase, of empowerment
    process, 110–111
Advocate role. See also Case ad-
        vocacy; Cause advocacy
    case management and, 249
    case studies of, 140–142, 179–180
    conflict and, 209, 216
    defined, 166, 207
    demonstrating need through, 221
    dilemmas of, 209–211
    empowerment and, 207, 217
    framework for, 217–222
    mediator role and, 254–255
    networking and, 216
    optimism and, 216–217
    organizational support and, 221–222
    pluralistic nature of, 218–220, 222
    politics and, 213–217
    social policy and, 212–213
    social reform and, 212
    in social work practice, 25–26, 133

Advocate role (continued)
    three levels of, 208–209
    values and, 221
AFDC, 103, 115, 176
Affirmative action
    as positive visibility, 94
    as redistributive justice, 208
African Americans, oppression and,
    87
Agenda setting
    for social problem solving, 216
    in social work practice, 65–66
Agent. See Change agent
Aid to Families with Dependent
    Children (AFDC), 103, 115, 176
AIDS
    homosexuality and, 38
    increase of concern about, 57
Akers, R. J., 83
Albee, G., 63, 94, 108
Albert, R., 212
Alcoholics Anonymous (AA), 50, 109
Alienation
    deviance and, 88
    in postindustrial era, 2
    powerlessness and, 103
    rehabilitation programs and, 49
    school dropout problem and, 9
Alinsky, Saul, 48
Alzheimer's disease, 282
Ambiguity, tolerance for, 216
Amendment Two, homosexual rights
    and, 75–76, 78
American Association of Retired Per-
    sons, 91
American Psychiatric Association, 90
Amish, deviance of, 80
Analysis
    of data from evaluation process, 149
    of problems, 55–59

Exploration
case-study example of, 182–183
in social work practice, 8, 172–174
Expressed need, defined, 228

Facilitator, enabler role as, 188–190
Family
case history of conflict resolution
in, 266–267, 268–269, 270, 271,
272–273
conflict resolution in, 258, 262–263,
267
dysfunctional, 199
fragmentation, 195, 198
as mediating structure, 103
school dropouts and, 9–11
as support system, 240–241
Federal Bureau of Investigation (FBI),
231
Federation of Domestic Violence
Agencies, 141
Feedback in communications process,
70
Feld, A., 284
Felt need, defined, 228
Field, S., 135
Field survey approach to community
needs assessments, 232
Fiene, J. I., 241
Findlay, P. C., 13
Fischer, J., 135
Fisher, R., 265, 272
Food stamps, stigma of, 85
Ford Foundation, 54
Ford, J., 207
Forensic social workers, role of, 283
Formative evaluations, 151
Forums for community needs assess-
ment, 230–231
Fragmentation in groups and families,
195–196, 198
Freedburg, S., 282
Friendly visiting programs, 102
Friere, Paulo, 109

Galaway, B., 85, 125, 152, 169, 188,
254, 274–275, 281
Galper, J., 51

Gangs, alienation and, 88
GAS. See Goal attainment scaling
Gays. See Homosexuals
Generalists, social workers as, 2–3
Generality, degree of, 65–66
Gentry, M. E., 168, 189, 258, 260
Getting to Yes (Fisher, Ury, and Pat-
ton), 265
Gilbert, N., 210
Gilliland, B. E., 88
Gilmartin, K., 215, 235
Gitterman, A., 254
Global warming, 39
Goal attainment scaling (GAS)
case management and, 242
case study of, 159–162
evaluation process and, 158–162,
181
Goals
alternative solutions to, 199–200
of change agents, 129–130
personal values versus professional,
138
Goal setting
advocacy and, 212
case management and, 241–242
case-study example of, 183–184
conferee role and, 176–179
evaluation process and, 149, 151
Goldberg, G., 213
Goldstein, A. P., 45
Goode, E., 77, 81
Goods and services, broker role and,
227
Goodwin, D. K., 82
Gordon, D. M., 42
Gordon, M., 213
Gothard, S., 287
Gould, K. H., 256
Government, political ideologies and,
43–44
Grant writing, 233
Green, A., 44
Grinnell, R. M., 150, 159
Group leadership
enabler role and, 189–190, 191–193,
195–196, 203–204
mediating role of, 203–204

TO THE OWNER OF THIS BOOK:

We hope that you have found *The Integration of Social Work Practice* useful. So that this book can be improved in a future edition, would you take the time to complete this sheet and return it? Thank you.

School and address: _____

Department: _____

Instructor's name: _____

1. What I like most about this book is _____

_____

2. What I like least about this book is _____

_____

3. My general reaction to this book is _____

_____

4. The name of the course in which I used this book is _____

_____

5. Were all of the chapters of the book assigned for you to read? _____

   If not, which ones weren't? _____

_____

6. In the space below, or on a separate sheet of paper, please write specific suggestions for improving this book and anything else you'd care to share about your experience in using the book.

_____

_____

_____

_____

_____

_____

Optional:

Your name: _____ Date: _____

May Brooks/Cole quote you either in promotion for *The Integration of Social Work Practice* or in future publishing ventures?

Yes: _____ No: _____

Sincerely,

Ruth J. Parsons
James D. Jorgensen
Santos H. Hernández

FOLD HERE

NO POSTAGE
NECESSARY
IF MAILED
IN THE
UNITED STATES

BUSINESS REPLY MAIL
FIRST CLASS   PERMIT NO. 358   PACIFIC GROVE, CA

POSTAGE WILL BE PAID BY ADDRESSEE

ATT: _____ *Drs. Parsons, Jorgensen, and Hernández* _____

Brooks/Cole Publishing Company
511 Forest Lodge Road
Pacific Grove, California 93950-9968

FOLD HERE

Brooks/Cole is dedicated to publishing quality publications for education in the human services fields. If you are interested in learning more about our publications, please fill in your name and address and request our latest catalogue.

Name: _____

Street Address: _____

City, State, and Zip: _____

FOLD HERE

NO POSTAGE
NECESSARY
IF MAILED
IN THE
UNITED STATES

BUSINESS REPLY MAIL
FIRST CLASS   PERMIT NO. 358   PACIFIC GROVE, CA

POSTAGE WILL BE PAID BY ADDRESSEE

ATT: *Human Services Catalogue*

Brooks/Cole Publishing Company
511 Forest Lodge Road
Pacific Grove, California 93950-9968

FOLD HERE